MW01067613

RUNS
IN THE
FAMILY

RUNS
IN THE
FAMILY

AN
INCREDIBLE
TRUE STORY

OF FOOTBALL,
FATHERHOOD,
AND BELONGING

SARAH SPAIN
AND DELAND McCULLOUGH

SIMON ELEMENT

New York   Amsterdam/Antwerp   London
Toronto   Sydney/Melbourne   New Delhi

**SIMON
ELEMENT**

An Imprint of Simon & Schuster, LLC
1230 Avenue of the Americas
New York, NY 10020

First Simon Element hardcover edition June 2025

SIMON ELEMENT is a trademark of Simon & Schuster, LLC

For information about special discounts for bulk purchases, please contact Simon & Schuster Special Sales at 1-866-506-1949 or business@simonandschuster.com.

The Simon & Schuster Speakers Bureau can bring authors to your live event. For more information or to book an event, contact the Simon & Schuster Speakers Bureau at 1-866-248-3049 or visit our website at www.simonspeakers.com.

Interior design by Silverglass

Manufactured in the United States of America

10 9 8 7 6 5 4 3 2 1

Library of Congress Cataloging-in-Publication Data has been applied for.

ISBN 978-1-6680-3628-0
ISBN 978-1-6680-3630-3 (ebook)

Some names have been changed to protect privacy.

To my family: This is a testament to the grace and mercy that have carried us through every challenge. Faith, forgiveness, and love have shaped our journey, reminding us that no setback is greater than God's grace and mercy. I dedicate this to my family and friends, embracing the scars that tell our stories—because when we learn from them, they become beauty marks. May our faults and successes serve as lessons in growth, self-awareness, and resilience.

—Deland McCullough

To my parents, who have always given me unconditional love and support, and who taught me to be curious and kind.

—Sarah Spain

CONTENTS

MAN IS NOTHING ELSE BUT WHAT HE MAKES OF HIMSELF.
[IT IS A MATTER OF CHOICE, NOT CHANCE.]

—JEAN-PAUL SARTRE

PROLOGUE

Mark Twain famously said, "The truth is stranger than fiction, because fiction is obliged to stick to possibilities." What to make, then, of the strangest of truths? The stories that defy possibility. How do we reconcile the uneasy feeling that something more than just coincidence must be at play?

We start by giving these stories meaning, and thus power. We search them for messages and lessons to be learned. We seek out the source of their authorship.

Sometimes we call it magic. Or fate.

Sometimes we call it destiny. Or God.

No matter what we call it, these stories make us look up at the stars and wonder. There are few stories that will make you wonder more than the true, strange story of Deland McCullough.

NOVEMBER 12, 2017

It was a warm November evening in Southern California, the sun's heat lingering in the air hours after it had set. Forty-four-year-old Deland McCullough got home from work to find his wife in the kitchen holding a thin envelope from the Pennsylvania Department of Health.

"It's here," she said, handing it to him gently.

Deland took a deep breath. He couldn't believe his entire identity could fit in a simple white envelope. He wedged a finger into the back, carefully ripped open the side, and pulled out the letter, half-expecting it to be written on gold leaf or in calligraphy. It wasn't. It was just a single typed page, in black and white, but it was everything.

"This is it," he said quietly, almost in disbelief. "It's my birth certificate."

The sheet of paper contained just forty-two words and eight numbers. Forty-two words and eight numbers that would change his life forever.

NONCERTIFIED COPY OF ORIGINAL BIRTH RECORD

DATE OF BIRTH: DECEMBER 01, 1972   STATE FILE NUMBER: 150296–1972

DATE ISSUED: NOVEMBER 7, 2017   DATE FILED: DECEMBER 14, 1972

NAME GIVEN AT BIRTH: JON KENNETH BRIGGS   SEX: MALE

PLACE OF BIRTH: ALLEGHENY COUNTY

PARENT: CAROL DENISE BRIGGS

AGE: 16

PARENT: INFORMATION NOT RECORDED

"My name is Jon Kenneth Briggs," Deland said. "Baby Jon."

"My mother's name is Carol," he said as he read, almost whispering. "She was sixteen."

"It doesn't list a father."

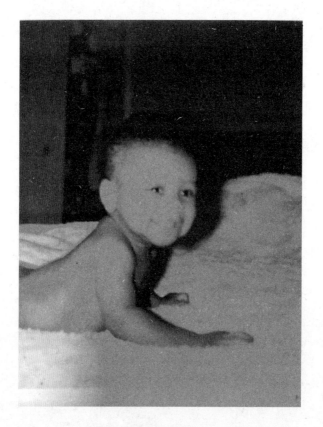

Baby Deland

CHAPTER 1

Deland knew this was a real bad fight. He'd never seen his stepfather so angry. And he'd definitely never seen him with a gun. As usual, his mother didn't seem to have any interest in calming things down. Deland was too young to understand what their fights were about, but he knew that his ma, Adelle, liked pushing people's buttons and escalating things. Setting fires just when things seemed to be calming down. She loved hard and would do anything for her kids, but she could be rough around the edges. Friends and family called her Ma Barker—shoot first, ask questions later. Sometimes literally.

It seemed like John and Adelle were always doing something or other to make each other mad. Deland didn't like their yelling, but he could deal with it if it meant John would stick around. They had a good life. They were off food stamps, their furniture was paid for, and he didn't have to wear those hand-me-downs the kids at school ragged on. They had settled into a routine that felt like family, and Deland worried that if his mom and John didn't get through this, John would leave. Like the last guy.

Deland kept his eyes fixed on the gun as John rocked back and forth in the driver's seat of their 1976 Ford Gran Torino, red with the white stripe, just like on *Starsky & Hutch*. They were parked in the garage, but the car was still running. The house was *right there*. Deland was only seven, so what did he know, but he wondered why they couldn't at least get out of the car and talk about this inside. Or, even better, talk about this later when tempers had cooled. Deland pressed his body up against the leather of the back seat and wondered if he could somehow press hard enough to melt through the seat crack, slide out the trunk, and run away. He looked over at his brother Damon, four years older than him and the toughest person he knew. But Damon suddenly looked very small.

"Go get my gun off the side of the house," Adelle said. She was talking to Damon but she never took her eyes off John.

Deland held his breath as he watched Damon disappear inside, down the breezeway and back, reemerging holding Adelle's silver pistol with the green grip. It felt like time stood still as he watched his mother and stepfather trade threats, guns waving back and forth, but the exchange didn't actually last more than a few seconds. Neither John nor Adelle really wanted that mess. Eventually they all got out of the car and went inside, John and Adelle bickering as they went, the two boys racing off to their room. Deland didn't remember ever seeing John's gun again, but the fighting certainly continued.

And Deland's worries were well-founded—within a year, John was gone. When he left, the good life left too.

Adelle had met John Comer at the bowling alley, a favorite haunt for them both. You could find them playing in a league at one of several local lanes almost every night of the week. Adelle was a tiny woman with brown skin, bright eyes, and high cheekbones. She looked sweet but she was a firecracker.

Never short on suitors, she was popular for her intelligence, her outgoing personality, and for toeing the line between churchgoing mom and flirtatious rule-breaker. She'd had a wheezing sort of cackle ever since she was a girl, like her breath ran out every time she laughed. It always made her seem older than she was, like she'd seen some stuff. John didn't have a particularly electric personality, but he was steady and kind. He was medium-height and well built, with tawny skin. Damon always said he looked like Bootsy Collins's older brother Catfish from Parliament-Funkadelic.

After they married in 1978, John moved into Adelle's house at 46 Allerton Court, on the east side of Youngstown, Ohio. John took on the responsibility of helping raise Deland and Damon, and sometimes his children from his first marriage, Dee Dee and Lil' John, would come over to play. It wasn't until years later that they all realized Adelle and John's first wife had been best friends as kids. Youngstown could be like that—sometimes it felt so small, like everybody knew your business, and sometimes it felt like there might as well have been an ocean between you and someone living right across town.

John was Adelle's second husband, a hopeful second chance. It started off well, with a honeymoon in Niagara Falls they enjoyed so much they took the boys back in the fall. They all visited the Guinness World Records Museum, wore out the waterslide in the motel pool, and donned ponchos to ride under the falls on the famous *Maid of the Mist* boat. The good times didn't last long, though. The marriage soon devolved into constant bickering and not enough good there to fight for. Deland liked John enough to hope they'd work things out. There was just something about John's voice when he and Adelle would argue; inasmuch as a little boy can pity a grown man, Deland pitied him. Deland thought John was just a guy doing his best. And he knew firsthand how overbearing Adelle could be when she was arguing her side of a fight.

Damon was a different story. Never much liked John. Never forgave him for forgetting him at the football field one day when he drove a bunch of the boys home after a game. By then John had accidentally backed the Gran Torino into the fire hydrant at the bottom of the driveway, so he had moved on to a brand-new dove-gray Dodge Diplomat with burgundy leather interior. Not that Damon got to enjoy the leather that day—he had to get a ride home from Coach Hightower in his van. Damon was a self-proclaimed mama's boy who always took Adelle's side, so he was never gonna let John off the hook for that, or for any grief he caused either one of them. He knew Adelle had a temper sometimes, and the last thing he wanted was someone else who boiled over when things went sideways. And John could boil over.

One time the four of them went to see an air show at the Youngstown airport. Organizers anticipated a far smaller crowd than the one that arrived that day, and the open field set up for viewing was already full even as a line of cars sat in bumper-to-bumper traffic on the highway waiting to get in. Adelle, John, and the boys were in that line of cars. The longer they sat there without moving, the angrier John got. Eventually it became clear that they were going to miss the whole show. He put the car in park, got out, opened the trunk, and started throwing the folding chairs they'd brought into a ditch on the side of the highway, putting a little more muscle into each chair until he sent the last one flying all the way onto the berm past the ditch. He screamed a few unintelligible words and then announced that he was walking home. Adelle yelled at him to come back but he ignored her and kept walking. She got in the driver's seat and drove the boys home in silence.

One time after another big blowup, John's brother Richard was over at the house while John was out. Adelle started venting. "He's got that quick fuse," she told him. "And he's selfish. He just can't seem to put me and the boys first." Richard had heard this plenty. "Our mother raised John to be a king," he said. "He's always had his way and he's always *gonna* have to have his way. And because of that he don't know how to put anyone else first. He don't even know how to love anybody else." That line stuck in Adelle's head for weeks.

Damon got so frustrated with John and Adelle's fighting that at one point he called across town to Grandma Maretta, Adelle's mom. "This ain't even worth saving, Grandma," he told her. "Can you just come over and end it for them? I don't wanna hear it no more." He was only eleven but he thought he had it all figured out. Little did Damon know things could get a whole lot worse than a bunch of hollering.

John was a good gift-giver; Damon had to give him that. In fact, John was responsible for the boys' best and most memorable Christmas. It was December 25, 1979: Eleven-year-old Damon got his first ten-speed with disc brakes and seven-year-old Deland got the first BMX bike of any kid in Lincoln Knolls, their neighborhood just south of McElvey Lake and north of Roosevelt Park. It was a 1979 Mongoose Supergoose, silver with red padding and a red seat. John got the boys a pinball machine that year too.

It was also the Christmas when the boys learned the truth about Santa Claus. Ever since they could remember, Deland and Damon had a tradition they called their Christmas morning hug. They would meet between their beds for a hug and to say "I love you" before going down for presents, buzzing with excitement and squeezing each other with anticipation over the goodies they'd find under the tree. That particular year, John and Adelle had bought so many toys they weren't done putting them all together by the time the Christmas hug was over and Damon and Deland came racing down the stairs. The boys got quite a shock, but it only hurt for a minute—who cares about Santa when you've got a brand-new BMX?

John was an especially generous stand-in for Santa because he had a great gig over at General Electric. It was one of the best jobs you could have those days in Youngstown, where jobs were suddenly very hard to come by. So hard to come by, in fact, that even little boys caught up in toy trucks and football knew there weren't many men in town making good money anymore. Two years earlier everything had changed in northeast Ohio's Mahoning Valley. September 19, 1977: Black Monday. Youngstown Sheet & Tube announced the closure of a large portion of its steel plant. More than five thousand people lost their jobs that day, and that was just the beginning.

On the occasion of the fortieth anniversary of Black Monday, former Youngstown Sheet & Tube salesman Lou DeSimone told *Belt* magazine about the day everything changed for the thriving steel town.

I knew immediately it was going to be bad. A rule of thumb was that for every steel mill job there is, there are approximately four other jobs in the community, anything from telephone operators to dry cleaners to bartenders. It wasn't just the 5,000 people who lost their jobs, you had another 20,000 that were going to lose their jobs through the next year. I knew that was going to happen, and I knew it was going to be devastating. You take 25,000 jobs out of here, people are going to leave.

Changes in the steel manufacturing process and competition from international manufacturers had been threatening Youngstown's steel industry for decades, and as large conglomerates bought out local owners in the mid-1970s, they discovered outdated mills that would need expensive upgrades to meet new U.S. pollution regulations. Without a vested interest in the community, it was easier to shutter the mills and do business elsewhere. So they did, one by one. And suddenly a city of people that could tell time by the sound of the steam whistle saw Youngstown become the face of deindustrialization.

"The open hearths tapped out and shut down," former Brier Hill Mill worker Gerald Dickey told *Belt* of the shock of the Black Monday news. "Then they shut down the blooming mill. The guys cleaned out their lockers because they weren't coming back, and as they crossed the bridge to leave the mill, a lot of them just threw their bags right into the river. The mills were finished."

The mills had quite literally lit up the sky in Youngstown and when the industry buckled, the city went dark. Within five years, fifty thousand jobs were lost. At the peak of the steel industry Youngstown boasted a population of nearly one hundred seventy thousand and had some of the highest homeownership rates in the United States. By 1990 the city's population had dropped below ninety-six thousand and Youngstown had the coldest housing market in the country. What happened to Youngstown was so dark, so sudden, so painfully American that Bruce Springsteen even wrote a song about it. "Youngstown" begins by telling the story of the steel city making the cannonballs to help the Union defeat the Confederacy and later manufacturing the tanks and bombs to arm America in foreign wars. But when the soldiers return home and the mills are closed, the workers view the damage done by the corporate owners on par with the devastation of war.

Well my daddy come on the Ohio Works when he come home
from World War Two
Now the yard's just scrap and rubble, he said, "Them big boys did
what Hitler couldn't do."

The steel industry was the most powerful force in Youngstown, but a close second was an unusually ingrained Mafia presence. Youngstown was in a good spot, sitting at the halfway point between Chicago and New York City on Interstate 80, about sixty miles southeast of Cleveland and sixty miles northwest of Pittsburgh. Beginning in the 1930s, mob-run casinos, brothels, and bars thrived, supported by the dollars of successful steelworkers and folks whose businesses and shops were propped up by a thriving economy. Youngstown was too small to have its own mob family but did big enough business to draw interest from warring families in Pittsburgh and Cleveland. In the 1950s, Mafia hits, car bombings, and "disappearances" were common around town, but limited to the shady figures involved in organized crime. When Charlie "Cadillac" Cavallaro and his eleven-year-old son were killed by a car bomb in late 1962, things shifted. The people of Youngstown were enraged that an innocent kid had been caught up in mob dealings. More importantly, the incident caught the eye of the feds and Youngstown started to get an unfortunate national reputation.

The March 9, 1963, edition of the *Saturday Evening Post* ran a story about Youngstown with the headline "Crimetown, U.S.A.: Youngstown Has Had 75 Bombings, 11 Killings in a Decade, and No One Seems to Care." Noted crime journalist John Kobler authored the piece, writing, "The Youngstown area exemplifies the truism that rackets cannot survive without two basic conditions—the sanction of police and politicians, and an apathetic public. Here those conditions have combined to produce a breakdown of the democratic process. Buffoons and incompetents succeed to important civic posts. Officials hobnob openly with criminals. Arrests of racketeers are rare, convictions rarer still and tough sentences almost unheard-of."

The "Crimetown, U.S.A." nickname stuck, and seemed even more fitting when the plants closed and the city fell into depression. As the steelworkers who had frequented the Mafia-owned gaming halls and establishments all began to move away, organized crime got more desperate and more violent. But who was left to fight it? Without the steel mills, it felt like the mob was the only company still hiring. David Grann detailed the resulting collapse of Youngstown's middle class in a piece for the *New Republic* titled "Crimetown USA: The City That Fell in Love with the Mob."

If prosperity had brought the mob to the valley a half-century earlier, depression cemented its rule. The professional classes that did so much to break the culture of the Mafia in Chicago and Buffalo and New York in the 1970s and '80s practically ceased to exist in Youngstown. Much of the valley's middle class either left or stopped being middle-class. And so Youngstown experienced a version of what sociologists have described in the inner city. The city lost its civic backbone—its doctors and lawyers and accountants. The few upstanding civic leaders who remained were marginalized or cowed. Hierarchies of status and success and moral value became inverted. The result was a generation of . . . kids who worshiped the dons the way other children worshiped Mickey Mantle or Joe DiMaggio.

The mob's control of the city's top officials in the late 1980s and early '90s was almost unprecedented. Grann writes:

[Youngstown was] a place where the Mafia still controlled a chief of police, the outgoing prosecutor, the sheriff, the county engineer, members of the local police force, a city law director, several defense attorneys, politicians, judges, and a former assistant U.S. attorney; a place whose residents had grown so used to a culture of corruption that they viewed it casually, even proudly; a place, in a sliver of America, where a malignant way of life was left largely untouched for almost 100 years.

It was this Youngstown, a half-century deep in the clutches of the mob and newly adjusting to economic collapse, that was home to Damon and Deland during their formative years.

They weren't old enough at the time to understand the long-term effects Black Monday would have on their hometown, but they saw and felt the change over the years. In their own neighborhood, stores closed down and city-funded holiday displays and events disappeared. They overheard plenty of talk about the lack of good jobs and saw plenty of salacious news stories about the drugs, city corruption, "disappearances," and violence. In fact, the details of the biggest, most shocking stories were nearly impossible to miss. Like the story of John Magda. Just twelve days after the boys' memorable 1979 Christmas, the body of the forty-two-year-old Pittsburgh Mafia associate was found in a garbage dump in nearby Struthers, Ohio, wrapped head to toe in duct tape. They learned on the news that he had first been immobilized by a stun gun, then wrapped up in the tape like a mummy and left to suffocate to death.

That's what you get for talking.

Crime of all kinds was omnipresent in East Youngstown, where the boys lived. Petty theft, drug deals, murders—everybody in the neighborhood was either caught up in something or trying to keep their kids from getting caught up in something. After decades of prosperity, Youngstown suddenly wasn't a place that made good headlines anymore. But America would always turn its attention back to the Mahoning Valley when there was another incident like the one that killed Cadillac Cavallaro and his son. In fact, car bombs rigged to explode when the ignition turned on came to be known across the country as "Youngstown tune-ups."

If you were a poor kid growing up in "Crimetown, U.S.A." in the early 1980s, you knew the odds were stacked against you. Life would be tough and, most likely, life would be small. Stay outta the muck and you'll feel safe enough most of the time, but don't go looking for big money or big opportunity. Temper your dreams, learn to accept your circumstances, and keep quiet about other people's business. Matter of fact, best to keep quiet about your own business too. Try not to make things even harder for your family by chasing trouble, complaining about what you don't have, or asking for more than just enough.

Damon and Deland

CHAPTER 2

One day not long after John and Adelle divorced, Damon gathered his mother and brother together and gave them a speech that reflected a maturity well beyond his twelve years. "With the steel jobs gone there's no good cats out there," he said. "Everybody's taken. Stop having your happiness depend on these bums, Ma. It's just going to be us three. It ain't about no man no more."

He tucked his shoulders back and stood up as tall as he could—not much more than five feet at the time. Even as a kid Damon was a dead ringer for Adelle—same compact body, same big toothy smile, same wheezing laugh. "We got this," he said. "It's always going to be about us. And no matter who else come through here, this part of life is over. We controlling our own destiny. And I got you. I got both y'alls' backs."

Young as he was, Damon's wisdom came from experience. John wasn't the first guy he had seen leave; he'd watched his own father go just a few years earlier. He was six and Deland was just two when A.C. McCullough walked out. Now that was the marriage worth saving, Damon thought—even Grandma Maretta agreed. (She told Adelle as much for years after.) Back when Adelle and A.C. were together, 46 Allerton Court had been the party capital of the neighborhood, full of friends and family and music—always the best music.

A.C. was a popular radio deejay at WHOT, Youngstown's home for rock and roll, and he got promotional records from the hottest bands around before they were available to buy. Marvin Gaye, Booker T. & the M.G.'s, Stevie Wonder, Sly & the Family Stone. They had the best sound system, the nicest house on the block—right at the end of the cul-de-sac—dozens of friends, and, most importantly, a young couple in love who served as enthusiastic hosts. On any given weekend Damon might be running around the cookout out back or dancing along to Curtis Mayfield's "Super Fly" in the basement with extended family. It seemed like the house was always full of a couple dozen aunts, uncles, cousins, and those close enough to be called cousins.

Damon's first memory was of moving into that white ranch house on Allerton Court in 1971. Adelle and A.C. hadn't planned on leaving their old apartment at Eastway Terrace, but after they lost their baby Alex to an intestinal birth defect just twenty-eight days after he was born, Adelle refused to go back. Damon remembered her bringing home a little white plastic dove from the funeral, packing everything into the back of the car, and setting off for a fresh start. He didn't know that A.C. never once visited Alex in the hospital, or that Adelle had to force A.C. to go to his own son's funeral. There was a lot Damon didn't know about A.C. back then.

Since she was a teen, Adelle had been writing down baby names and dreaming of having up to a dozen kids. She felt as though God's purpose for her was to be a mother, to raise and care for children. After Alex passed, she and A.C. were advised not to try for any more kids, so they started serving as temporary foster parents. For a few months those kids helped heal her heart. Then, in January 1973, she got a call from their social worker about a month-old baby boy at a Methodist orphanage in Pennsylvania, the only Black baby up for adoption in the nearby counties. They didn't have a lot of money at the time, but they were deemed financially responsible enough to take in a child. They had good savings and Adelle had a background in accounting, so their books were tight as the lid on a honey jar.

A.C. and Adelle, twenty-five and twenty-three at the time, went to Pittsburgh to meet the baby. When a staffer from the adoption agency lifted the little boy out of his bassinet and put him in Adelle's arms, he woke up and looked right into her eyes. She felt an instant connection—

mother and son. They had been calling him Jon at the orphanage, but they said she was welcome to name him. Adelle stared into his big, dark eyes and decided on Deland, a name she had read meant "dark eye."

Damon was there when Adelle and A.C. officially adopted baby Jon that March and renamed him Deland Scott McCullough. About four years old at the time, Damon wanted to look his best when he met his little brother, so he picked and patted his Michael Jackson–inspired Afro and straightened the lapel of his suit before peering into the green and white bassinet. When he saw Deland, he broke into a big smile imagining all the things he could teach him. When it came time to close the case, Damon sat on the judge's lap and got to hit the gavel on the desk to bring Deland home. He wasn't sure why this baby didn't start in his mama's belly, but he didn't care. He was getting a new brother—and he was positively giddy about it.

The McCulloughs were still recovering from the loss of Alex, but they were happy to be a family of four again. Adelle loved having a baby in the house. She doted on little Deland, staring into his eyes and talking to him all day. Early on she took him to the doctor with a concern that he never seemed to stop eating. "He eats huge!" she said, shaking her head. "They gave me a baby with worms or something!" Compared to baby Damon, it felt like Deland was already eating like a teenager. "He just likes to eat," the doctor said, laughing. "He's just fine."

Damon was a happy kid. He organized his comics and lined up his model cars, waiting for the day Deland would be old enough to play with him. In the meantime, any time he could be around A.C. was a good time. It was A.C. who bought Damon his first bike, a little red Schwinn with the big high handlebars and a curved black seat, and taught him how to ride it in the driveway. Damon would go watch A.C. and his WHOT coworkers play in a local baseball tournament run by Youngstown construction millionaire and pioneer of the suburban shopping center Edward DeBartolo Sr. He'd hang out in the basement while A.C. and his brothers practiced boxing, spinning their gloves over and over on the taut cowhide of the Sugar Ray Leonard speed bag they'd bought over at Hills department store in the plaza. Later Damon and Deland would use those same gloves for boxing matches with the neighbors in their garage, the perfect size for a makeshift ring. They would re-create fight scenes from·Rocky or playact as Joe Frazier and Muhammad Ali in The Thrilla in Manila.

A.C.'s job gave him access to tickets for local concerts, so there would be stacks for Parliament-Funkadelic or the Monkees on the table in the basement. Plus, Adelle's family was full of musicians—piano, guitar, xylophone, the spoons, you name it—so they knew all the local musicians and even some of the touring bands coming through town. Between A.C.'s job and Adelle's family, that meant trips to a lot of concerts at Idora Park, affectionately known as "Youngstown's Million-Dollar Playground," and Damon got to tag along. At five or six he wasn't yet tall enough to ride the Wild Cat, a three-thousand-foot wooden roller coaster that ranked as one of the top ten coasters in the world, but he could go backstage with Adelle to watch the shows in the big open-air ballroom. All of Youngstown's young, hip folks would gather, showing off their new paisley shirts and bell bottoms from McElvey's department store. On the best nights the bands would keep the party going by heading back to Allerton Court to have a home-cooked dinner and party with A.C., Adelle, and the rest of the crew.

Damon loved being in the mix, whether he was giving a high five to Smokey Robinson or touching the basement ceiling with a lift from Tiny Tim.

Another highlight for Damon and Deland was the time A.C. got them on the famous television show Romper Room. The show had both a syndicated national version and its own local franchises, with the Youngstown franchise hosted by Miss Anne Bowman and taped at the local WKBN-TV Studios. The show's mascot, Mr. Do Bee, was a giant bumblebee that taught the kids manners by telling them things like "Do be a good student for your teacher" or "Don't be a chair tipper." After the show all the kids in attendance "graduated" from the Romper Room School, receiving a diploma confirming that each boy and girl had been a "Good Do Bee." Damon and Deland treasured those certificates with Mr. Do Bee on them for years. Adelle cared more about the message they learned there—who and what to be and, more importantly, who and what not to be.

She would have to rely on that second bit more and more as she raised her boys through difficult times.

With all the music, parties, and people, Damon thought Allerton Court must be the best and happiest house in Youngstown. Whatever time and attention he got from A.C. felt like more than enough, but Adelle knew that A.C. was changing. He had been ever since he lost his job at Commercial Shearing and got hooked up with the folks at the radio station in June 1970. A.C. had some experience working for the Armed Forces Network when he was in the Army, so WHOT started him out working weekends. He was the first Black disc jockey the station had—though Adelle thought they were only willing to hire him because he sounded white. It didn't take long for A.C. to get some afternoon opportunities and eventually his own show during the coveted morning drive.

The radio station became his whole world. He loved being a local celebrity, and boy did he love the attention from the young women of Youngstown.

Adelle heard the stories of the prostitutes who got called to the radio station at all hours of the night. A.C. told her not to come to the concerts he emceed, but sometimes she would drive over to the venue only to find him flanked by little white girls who barely looked eighteen years old. One night she sat him down and told him, "At least don't bring the philandering home or do that mess in front of the children," but one day Damon came home crying after A.C. was hugging and kissing on a girl at a local basketball game. That day Adelle told A.C. he wasn't allowed to take Damon anywhere without her. He didn't respect their home and didn't respect her. She couldn't believe she had to parent her husband as much as her sons.

Over time the lies hurt Adelle less than keeping quiet about them.

Everybody acted like A.C. walked on water, and she knew she couldn't say anything different. Adelle was raised by an old-school woman who taught her that wives should just grin and bear it. What happened in your home wasn't meant for other people to know. *Maretta doesn't wanna hear no moanin' about my marriage,* she would tell herself anytime she was tempted to complain. Adelle knew Maretta was fooled by A.C.'s charm, impressed by his radio job, and, frankly, a little jealous that A.C. had gotten Adelle that nice house on the cul-de-sac when she was still waiting for a big house of her own.

So Adelle tried to keep A.C.'s behavior quiet and keep up the image of a perfect family as best she could. She understood you just didn't talk about that sort of thing.

Plus, Adelle could remember when she was still charmed by A.C.

Heck, she fell for him back at East High even though he'd already had a baby by another girl. "That girl was stuck on stupid," she would later tell people about her high school self. But it was too late now. She was going to keep this family together. She wanted her sons to grow up in a steady, two-parent household.

More importantly, she wanted to keep Deland from being doubly scarred—having never met his biological father and then losing the only father he did know to divorce. Not that Deland knew A.C. wasn't his birth daddy yet. Adelle was still trying to figure out how and when she wanted to drop that bombshell.

For all her attempts at patience, Adelle's temper could get the best of her when A.C. would act up. One time when Damon was only about five years old he remembered A.C. trying to climb through the window after Adelle locked him out for some foolishness. Damon awoke to yelling and went down to the kitchen to see A.C. trying to back his way in—his butt and legs dangling over the sink—with Adelle standing in wait, that silver pistol with the green grip in her hand. That time she didn't use the gun, but another night she got so mad at A.C. she shot through the wall of the house. Just to make a point.

Things really started to unravel when Adelle's father, William "Sonny" Van Cobb, had a stroke. Damon was six and Deland was almost two, so friends and family helped out at the house while Adelle went to visit her dad in Columbus. As Sonny's health continued to decline, Adelle and her cousin decided to bring him back to Youngstown, where he could live in the house at Allerton Court. A.C. refused, demanding that they put him in an assisted living facility, but Adelle told A.C. *he* would sooner end up in a nursing home than her daddy would.

Adelle finally gave up on A.C. when she felt he had lost his way with God.

Like many others in the late 1960s and early '70s, Adelle had been dabbling in transcendental meditation. Celebrities like the Beatles and the Beach Boys were raving about the teachings of the Maharishi Mahesh Yogi, who did a series of world tours and presentations teaching people the simple power and profundity of *japa*, mentally repeating a mantra. A devout Christian, Adelle saw the practice as a way to better pursue inner peace and be still in God's presence. The way A.C. and the guys were doing it at the radio station worried her, though. She believed that if you didn't have the right intention while your spirit was out there opened up, any entity could attach to you. Even demonic ones. She would hear A.C. chanting on the phone with his work friends and swear they must've crossed over to the satanic side.

One day when they were fighting about it, A.C. told Adelle, "I don't need God, wife, or children." No amount of protestation from Grandma Maretta could convince Adelle that this man was worth fighting for. He had to be dragged to his own son's funeral, couldn't keep his hands off other women, barely showed any interest in Damon and Deland, and now he was saying he didn't need God? It was time to go. And when he went, in March 1975, taking all the money with him, Maretta said to Adelle, "Well, child, what did *you* do wrong?"

After they separated and A.C. moved out, Adelle had to explain to the boys why he wasn't living at Allerton Court any longer. Never one to sugarcoat things, she told them straight up that A.C. didn't want to be a husband or a father anymore. The way Adelle had learned it, God was the real head of the household anyway. "I'm gonna tell you something," she said to the boys. "I cannot be your mother and your father. I'm your mother. You have a Heavenly Father. That's number one. And He will never, ever leave you and will always be there for you. So y'all focus on that."

A.C. tried every way he could to avoid paying Adelle child support and alimony, including trying to get custody of the boys. He sent the health department to Allerton Court, telling the judge overseeing their divorce that she was an unfit mother who had the kids around roaches and rats. He went along with a few visitations early on—took them out to lunch or for a drive—but one day things changed. Damon and Deland were standing at the door ready and waiting when A.C.'s red Mustang pulled into the driveway. Before they could even take a step toward the car, A.C. had put it in reverse and driven away, leaving the boys wondering what they had done wrong. Later A.C. told the judge that Adelle wouldn't let them out of the house that day. She wasn't following their custody rules, he said, so he shouldn't have to pay child support. It was all a stunt to avoid paying his share. A stunt he put the boys right in the middle of.

Visits were all but nonexistent after that. A few weeks before Christmas the next year, A.C. called out of the blue and told the boys he'd take them out shopping. They were thrilled. Deland, who was all of five years old, wasn't even excited about the toys, he just loved the idea of going out shopping with his dad. He and Damon were dressed and ready more than an hour early, perched on the couch so they'd be able to see his car pull in. When A.C. picked them up he told them plans had changed a bit. He drove to the local fitness center and sat them down just outside the glass of the racquetball court. They sat there for more than an hour watching him play with a couple of friends and then he dropped them back at the house empty-handed. Damon wrote him a letter sharing how disappointed he was that A.C. would spend their rare bit of time together with his friends instead. A.C. accused Adelle of putting him up to it.

The divorce took two and a half years to finalize, and A.C. spent the whole time fighting his court-ordered payments, so Adelle and the boys had to get by on food stamps. Well, food stamps and the money she made selling marijuana.

Adelle's half brother Ben had made friends with a Mafia-affiliated drug dealer in nearby Campbell who fronted her the first couple of pounds to sell. Eventually she got into a rhythm, selling only to family members or friends. Her cousins would come to the house for every sale to keep her safe from attempted robberies, and if anybody brought a stranger with them to pick up the goods, they weren't gettin' any goods that day. Adelle sold weed for two years to buy food and clothes for the kids and finish the layaway payments to keep their beds, couches, and other furniture. She got quite a reputation around town with both dealers and buyers for her sharp tongue and tough attitude. Small but mighty. Not to be messed with. Determined to provide for her boys and even more determined to not get caught.

Times were tough without A.C.'s income, but Adelle worked hard to bring joy to her boys and surround them with family. Grandma Maretta and her second husband, Hubert, would come over often and hold court in the living room with Sonny, talking about all the latest goings-on in East Youngstown.

Sonny would take the boys to the bowling alley where Adelle worked the fryer some nights, serving them plates of chicken wings in between their games.

The parties continued at Allerton Court, with or without A.C. and Smokey Robinson. In 1976, when the United States celebrated its bicentennial—the two-hundred-year anniversary of the adoption of the Declaration of Independence—Adelle threw the biggest Fourth of July party East Youngstown had ever seen. There was the usual—all kinds of barbecue and apple pie, drinks flowing, and games in the yard—but she took it up a notch with the fireworks that year. She went to Pennsylvania to get the good stuff that was illegal in Ohio. You'd have thought she was trying to compete with the big Macy's fireworks display down at Hills.

Deland and his best friend, Tony, who also lived in Lincoln Knolls, sprinted back and forth down the big side yard with sparklers in hand and did tank races on the sloped driveway, lighting the ends of the red, white, and blue tanks and cheering for the sparks and smoke and the crackle of faux gunfire.

Later they'd make way for the adults, who shot the big fireworks from two giant tree stumps in the yard. Damon remembered looking up that night and seeing nearly a dozen people who had climbed up on the roof of their house to get the best view of the show, darkened silhouettes illuminated against the sky every time a firework exploded above them.

When Adelle met John Comer she stopped dealing and settled back into a comfortable routine, welcoming the help she desperately needed and the love she craved. It felt like she and the boys had gotten through the worst of it, but she knew she was keeping some very big secrets from them that she wasn't yet ready to share.

Adelle

CHAPTER 3

ADELLE

Adelle Marie Van Cobb was born in Youngstown on December 6, 1948, to William "Sonny" Van Cobb and Maretta Dorothea Walls. Sonny already had two teenage sons, Billy and Ben, and he and Maretta had three children of their own, Adelle, Tamara, and Gregory. When Adelle was six years old her parents divorced, and a few years later Maretta remarried. She and her second husband, Hubert Dois Clardy, bore two more children—Maurice and Hubert Jr., whom everybody affectionately called "Yub." That's seven kids total, if you're keeping count.

Maretta worked at General Electric, and it was her claim to fame that she once got to meet future president Ronald Reagan, who made appearances at GE facilities around the country as part of his contract hosting the television series *General Electric Theater*. Maretta famously didn't cook or keep house; she was a beauty queen and Sonny was more than happy to treat her like royalty. Sonny was in politics, working for the mayor's office in Campbell when Adelle was born and later running for mayor, though he didn't win. He was also a businessman, running a club on Wilson Avenue that was a front for the Mafia. Sonny had a good relationship with the Italians and the Greeks, kept his business associates happy, and was successful enough to buy two homes, one for Maretta and the kids they shared and, right across the street, another house for his ex-wife Rachel and their two boys, Billy and Ben. Adelle spent a lot of time at both houses and felt as though she grew up blessed with two mothers.

When Maretta married her second husband, Hubert, Adelle got another father too. Maretta, Hubert, Adelle, Tamara, Gregory, Maurice, and Hubert Jr. all lived in Maretta's mother Edna Armstead's house, a big old house at 950 Rigby Street. Rigby had nine bedrooms on three floors and most days at least fifteen people lived there, plus a few dogs. Everybody called Edna "Mawn" and she was the matriarch of not just the family, but the neighborhood. She had her union card from working in the steel mill, but worked just as hard at building a big extended family of East Siders. If you joined the family—by blood, by marriage, by someone taking you in—you were part of Mawn's clan and welcome at 950 Rigby forever. In fact, Sonny moved to Columbus to work for Senator Charles Carney and when he'd come back to Campbell he'd stay at Rigby, sleeping a few doors down from Maretta and Hubert. No jealousy, no drama. Once family, always family.

Adelle was put in charge of keeping her four younger siblings in line. Tamara, Maurice, and Yub all listened to her most of the time, but she and Gregory fought like cats and dogs. He was the funniest person in the family and usually stayed in line, but didn't take to being bossed around. Adelle wasn't much for rules either. When she got to East High School and started running around with the boys, Maretta said she was too wild to be trusted. Adelle was allowed only as far as the front porch without supervision, right up until she left for college. Of course that didn't keep her from starting up a relationship with Alexander "A.C." McCullough, who was a year ahead of her at East High. Tall and confident, popular and always smiling, A.C. already had a son with another East High classmate but Adelle was too head over heels to care. Maretta thought all her rules would keep her wild child safe, but Adelle wanted to be able to make decisions for herself.

A.C. left for the Army, and soon after Adelle was thrilled to get some independence too, going to study business and accounting at Central State University, an HBCU in Wilberforce, Ohio. She was only seventeen when she left—turning eighteen at school that December—and was enrolled in a work-study program. In her second year at CSU, the Black Campus Movement arrived in Wilberforce. Beginning in 1965, African American students at nearly a thousand colleges and universities had begun organizing and demanding a more diverse education, with more Black professors and Black history courses. On November 2, 1967, a few months into Adelle's sophomore year, a Central State sociology student named Michael Warren spoke at a rally at nearby Wilberforce College, looking to drum up support for CSU's Black Student Union, Unity for Unity. When Wilberforce president Rembert Stokes arrived and met chants of "Uncle Tom," he shouted back, "If you students want to call me an Uncle Tom, then I'm an Uncle Tom." Warren fired back, "When the revolution comes, I will kill you." When informed of the threat, CSU's president expelled Warren and walked him off the Central State campus with a warning of arrest if he returned.

Warren did return, on November 13, and when the local sheriff was called he arrived to find fifty students blockading the building in which Warren lived and several hundred more students looking on. They refused to let the sheriff through to make the arrest. Roughly three hundred National Guardsmen were called to the scene, where they joined local forces in facing a growing number of Central State students who threw rocks, bottles, and a few Molotov cocktails at the officers, shouting "Black Power." Adelle called Sonny from a pay phone in the hallway of her dorm, crying, and followed his instructions to hide under the bed until the riot ended. Within a few hours the forces withdrew, taking with them nearly one hundred arrested student activists, including Warren.

That April an already tense campus broke open with grief after the assassination of Martin Luther King Jr., who had been given an honorary degree at CSU a decade earlier. Adelle joined students by the hundreds who gathered for a memorial in the Central State gymnasium, then linked up with students from Wilberforce College to march down US Route 42. An estimated 1,500 marched peacefully and mostly silently, occasionally chanting "Long live Dr. King, down with racism, up with equality" or singing "We Shall Overcome." They marched to Xenia, Ohio, a suburb of Dayton, before turning back to return to campus and continue demanding meaningful change in education.

Adelle never graduated from Central State. She got pregnant with Damon, and by the fall of 1968 she was living back in Youngstown, starting a life with A.C. Damon arrived before they got married, earning Adelle plenty of judgment from the particularly pious folks in the neighborhood.

Over the years Adelle and the boys spent a lot of time over at 950 Rigby, attending Bible study or playing in the big yard while Hubert mowed the lawn and Maretta made dinner. Damon and Deland learned a lot about faith and commitment from their grandparents; they saw what a married couple who stays together looks like. Adelle was named after Sonny's mama, Adele, who founded Shiloh Baptist Church over on Bright Avenue in Campbell. The church where both Damon and Deland were baptized. Where Maretta was the first female minister and Hubert was a deacon. In addition to being the spiritual center of the family, Hubert worked hard over at the Republic Steel mill, setting an example of discipline and dedication for Damon and Deland. In addition to her work at General Electric, Maretta also hosted a weekly "Spiritual Moment" on local television.

Maretta and Hubert instilled in Adelle a faith she wanted to lean into but from which she often strayed. Nine-fifty Rigby was the place for spiritual practice, for your godly self, while Adelle and A.C.'s house represented the other side of the coin for folks in the neighborhood. Allerton Court was the place where people were people—flawed human beings. The place where the parties happened and folks did the things they'd ask forgiveness for come Sunday. At Allerton Court you could be yourself, comfort yourself, or lose yourself during tough times. Rigby was where you went the next day to get yourself right.

Adelle learned that her wild side—the one her Christian brethren had condemned—was forgiven when her house was full of booze, music, and dancing. Everybody loved a free drink. If being the life of the party was the answer, she'd be that. She didn't need to be perfect, or holy, or fake. And she didn't need to let anyone get close enough to judge her; she could hold court telling stories and pouring drinks. If anybody wanted to pass judgment on her choices, they could go tell someone else about it. And she wasn't gonna bother anyone with the shit A.C. was putting her through; she'd just shove it all down and put on a smile. Everybody'd better watch themselves, though: that smile could flip in an instant.

Adelle didn't find out until her early twenties that some of her family members had wild sides of their own. In fact, some of the branches on her family tree bent in a different direction than she'd been told. Notably, a close relative was raised to believe that the man who fathered her siblings was also her father. When the girl turned eighteen and was told otherwise she was surprised, but not upset. The elders of the family had always made the message clear: family was as much about who raised and cared for you as it was about DNA. The way Adelle saw it, a baby was a blessing no matter how it came to you—or by whom. Family was what you made it. She grew up with two mothers, two fathers, six siblings, and an endless collection of aunts, uncles, and cousins. There were no step-anythings or half-anythings or baby mommas or baby daddies. No qualifiers needed. Just family.

When in doubt, Adelle's parents told her, trust in God and that He's got a plan. In fact, when baby Alex died Maretta told Adelle just that. "Jesus got you," Maretta said. "Trust his plan and get over it." The way Adelle heard it, whatever suffering you're dealing with, you gotta figure out how to put it behind you. *We just don't talk about that sort of thing.* Adelle didn't know if any words could have helped her heal in that moment, but "get over it" definitely didn't. "Let go and let God" might have felt like a solution for generations of family before her, but it didn't feel like comfort when she looked at the empty bassinet in the corner.

Adelle was deeply affected by the language and responses modeled in her family system. A family system is the group of people someone grows up with and even those who came before they were born—the folks who established the patterns and behaviors that continue to get passed down through the generations. The language and messaging of that family system is the family's emotional DNA. Family patterns expert Judy Wilkins-Smith describes emotional DNA as "the blueprint for the system we and our ancestors have created. This blueprint is a set of patterns and outcomes based on past events and decisions. As our lives unfold, we repeat versions of these patterns that may have been created generations ago. . . . Following patterns is often our way of belonging in the system. It is deeply unconscious, yet faithfully and blindly repeated."

"For example, 'I will never speak my mind again, it's too dangerous' can become a pattern of withdrawal and a repeated behavior of not sharing thoughts or feelings," Wilkins-Smith continues. "On the other hand, positive patterns can emerge from events in our past and our ancestors' lives. In this case, you may see a pattern like, 'In our family we all become successful doctors.' Simply put, events and decisions about them create imprints that become blueprints for the way systems act and react."

For most people, this everyday messaging is so organic, so ingrained, they don't even notice that a particular way of thinking is a choice, not an actuality. If a parent always responds to bad luck or misfortune by saying "it doesn't matter how hard you work, the system is built to keep you down," their child might internalize the idea that they're incapable of having an impact on their own life's direction. But if a parent repeats a phrase like "hard work pays off," the child might feel in control of what happens next. Repeated commentary about money–"there's never enough" or "we always find a way"—might influence how a child views personal finance for the rest of their life, creating an ingrained response to money regardless of hardship or abundance. Wilkins-Smith writes:

> When a significant event occurs we make immediate decisions, we tell ourselves things about what has happened. We might say "I will never" or "I will always." This creates a pattern of the way things are in this system until we choose to do things differently. When

we do this mindfully, we break limiting cycles and the language, actions, thoughts, and feelings all change to align with the new way of
thinking and being. . . . New insights and perspectives lead to new
emotions and new thoughts, which in turn lead to new language,
new choices and new actions that result in new outcomes. . . . Once
you learn to see patterns and understand what they mean to your
system you can begin to choose what you wish to repeat, grow, and
do differently in your life. You'll find that even one simple word or
small repetitive action can be an important part of unlocking and
rewiring this system.

Members of a family system might have reacted to plans falling apart
by saying "this always happens to us," but later generations can choose
to change their response to "how can I make the best of this?" A grand-
parent might have reacted to losing efforts by saying "in this family we
only celebrate winners," but later generations can choose to change their
response to "what matters is that you tried your hardest and did your
best." Repeating those new phrases can actually change the way one's
brain naturally reacts and responds to situations.

"When you put these concepts into action, you begin to lay down
different neural pathways," writes Wilkins-Smith. "So you're changing
the way you think. You may even be able to activate or deactivate the
physical genes that you carry."

Gene activation and deactivation is at the heart of epigenetics, an emerg-
ing area of scientific research into how your behaviors and environments
can cause changes in how your genes are expressed. Epigenetic changes
don't alter your DNA, but they do change how your body and brain react
to and read a DNA sequence, effectively highlighting, dulling, or silencing
genes or gene segments. Sort of like an on-off switch with a dimmer. A
particular gene might be active, inactive, or just partially expressed, de-
pending on how it interacts with the chromosomal packaging around it.
Epigenetic differences are one reason a pair of identical twins who share

the exact same DNA might differ in meaningful ways—everything from differences in susceptibility to disease to one being adventurous while the other is timid. Identical twins have the most similar epigenetic profiles when they're young, but those profiles diverge exponentially over time as environmental factors accumulate and enact change.

From the University of Utah's Genetic Science Learning Center:

Some mother rats spend a lot of time licking, grooming, and nursing their pups. Others seem to ignore their pups. Highly nurtured rat pups tend to grow up to be calm adults, while rat pups who receive little nurturing tend to grow up to be anxious. It turns out that the difference between a calm and an anxious rat is not genetic, it's epigenetic. The nurturing behavior of a mother rat during the first week of life shapes her pups' epigenomes.

From Harvard University's Center on the Developing Child:

During development, the DNA that makes up our genes accumulates chemical marks that determine how much or little of the genes is expressed. This collection of chemical marks is known as the epigenome. The different experiences children have rearrange those chemical marks. . . . This means the old idea that genes are "set in stone" has been disproven. Nature vs. Nurture is no longer a debate. It's nearly always both.

Adverse fetal and early childhood experiences can—and do— lead to physical and chemical changes in the brain that can last a lifetime. Injurious experiences, such as malnutrition, exposure to chemical toxins or drugs, and toxic stress before birth or in early childhood are not "forgotten," but rather are built into the architecture of the developing brain through the epigenome. The "biological memories" associated with these epigenetic changes can affect

multiple organ systems and increase the risk not only for poor physical and mental health outcomes but also for impairments in future
learning capacity and behavior.

The epigenome can be affected by positive experiences, such as
supportive relationships and opportunities for learning, or negative
influences, such as environmental toxins or stressful life circumstances, which leave a unique epigenetic "signature" on the genes.
Recent research demonstrates that there may be ways to reverse
certain negative changes and restore healthy functioning. But the
very best strategy is to support responsive relationships and reduce
stress to build strong brains from the beginning.

Whether we're aware of it or not, the messages and responses acquired via
emotional DNA and the epigenetic changes that result from things like stress,
nutrition, and parenting style work together to uniquely form and shape us all.
We are all the product of both our genetic makeup and our influences.

Of course, Adelle's struggles with her family messaging weren't based
on the latest research or any understanding of epigenetics; she was just
following her instincts and listening to her heart. She was looking lovingly
at her two boys and wondering what they would learn and inherit from
her. Only one carried her DNA, but both were certain to carry the lessons she passed on. Certain to carry the language and ideas of the family
system they were born and adopted into. And Adelle knew Deland would
also carry the DNA and emotional DNA of generations before him in his
biological family system. She didn't understand the science behind it but
she believed the truth of it with her whole heart. It kept her both drawn to
her family system and tempted to pull away.

It was Mawn who helped Adelle see, for the first time, how things
might be better if she rejected some of the patterns established by her
elders. Weeks after Alex's death, Mawn finally pulled Adelle aside to offer
more than prayer. She shared that she had lost two of her own children

in their infancy. She spoke openly, honestly, and from the heart about the pain she had suffered. She held Adelle, they cried together, and finally, Adelle started to feel like herself again. *Is honesty the way to healing?* thought Adelle. *Is it possible that talking about the pain makes it hurt less?* It both scared and thrilled Adelle to think about doing things differently.

She didn't want to step out of line or remove herself and the boys from the family system, even though she knew it wasn't always healthy for them. She wanted so badly to belong and to carry on messages of faith and inclusion. She wanted to carry the pieces of God that helped her navigate disappointment, disorder, and tragedy, while leaving behind the pieces that felt restrictive, repressive, or unhelpful. It felt like she was in a state of constant push-and-pull between what she'd learned and her desire to create a new way. She questioned what she'd been taught, but couldn't let go of the messages with which she'd been raised.

As the oldest girl, everyone assumed Adelle would be the next family matriarch, following in the footsteps of Mawn and Maretta. But first there was the divorce with A.C., and then the divorce with John Comer. The partying. The drama. That smile that could flip on you. Adelle wouldn't fake piety for praise, so she was often seen as disrespectful or even heretical. And so, despite her strong convictions, she was rarely looked to for guidance. Uncle Yub was a pastor and a respected man in the community, so he took up the mantle and became a beacon to the family. Adelle was hurt, but insisted on being true to herself. In the absence of extended family seeking counsel, she focused on counseling Damon and Deland. She clung to those boys. They were her everything.

Deland, Adelle, and Damon

CHAPTER 4

"**B**reaker. This is Nighthawk."

"Breaker ten-two. This is Wildflower."

"Watch out. Smokey's at your back door."

"Big ten-four. Keep your eyes and ears open and your black stack smoking."

"Keep the shiny side up and the greasy side down. Threes and eights."

For all the jobs Adelle worked over the years, from switchboard operator to waitress, social worker to short-order cook, she never did try her hand at truck driving, despite her fascination with the lifestyle. She joined the CB radio craze of the 1970s and '80s and loved talking to the drivers coming through town.

Citizens band radio had been around since the 1950s but when the equipment became more affordable for everyday folks, they joined truckers on CB stations, learning their special jargon, full of code words and acronyms. They hopped on to share information about traffic, gas prices, police officers (smokeys), and rest areas (nap traps), or just to chat up strangers on the road. They were emulating language and behaviors they saw in pop culture, like the hit show *Dukes of Hazzard*, the movie *Smokey and the Bandit*, and the chart-topping novelty tune "Convoy" by C. W. McCall.

Each user had his or her own CB handle; Adelle's was Wildflower. She always saw herself as the girl from the 1972 Skylark song of the same name. The lyrics describe a young girl who was dealt a tough hand and bore the weight of all her fears and sadness on her shoulders. A girl who carried sorrow no one else could understand and paid for the debts of others. "Let her dream for she's a child . . . she's a free and gentle flower growing wild."

Underneath the hard exterior, the rebellious streak, and the stubborn approach to damn near everything, Adelle was fragile. She wanted help and didn't know how to ask for it. Wanted to rebel against the restrictions of her youth but also sought the salvation and security of a life given to Jesus. She wanted to know her boys would grow up okay, care about God and family, and have a life bigger and better than hers. She wanted to raise them without feeling like she had to raise the men she was with too. Wanted to keep her house, keep the lights on, and go bowling or out to a nice dinner every once in a while.

After A.C. and John left, she told herself she had everything under control. No sense feeling sorry for herself or dwelling in the darkness. If she just put stuff out of her mind it would eventually fade away. "Pity parties," she would always say, "I don't give 'em and I don't attend 'em." Though years later when the boys were grown, she'd admit to one stretch of hopelessness. It was shortly after John left, their marriage undone by his jealousy and what she perceived as an unwillingness to put the boys first. One incident in particular had been the final straw. Adelle had a hutch in the kitchen where she kept family photos—pictures of the early years and the boys with A.C. One day she went to grab something out of the cabinet and couldn't find the photo albums. John admitted that he'd taken them all out of the hutch and burned them. He didn't want her to have any memories of or connection to A.C., even if it meant keeping the boys from having those pieces of their history. Adelle was as hot as you can imagine that day, but it quickly changed to hurt. The boys had lost something that she wouldn't ever be able to replace.

For a handful of days Adelle refused to sleep in the bed she'd shared with John. She stayed in the third bedroom and ate M&Ms all day, fighting to find a good reason to get out of bed. She felt a deep depression all the way in her bones. She'd been fighting so long to protect the image of a happy family, but her body was hanging on to every wound. Every scar from baby Alex passing away. Every bit of pain from A.C.'s cheating. Every tear she'd cried about John leaving. Every fear she had about who and what her kids might become. *Don't let 'em see you worry*, she thought. *I have to be strong.* Eventually she pulled herself out of bed and got back to life, never telling anyone how she was suffering, never giving herself the time or energy to truly heal. Of course, the boys were watching, and while Adelle thought she was teaching them toughness, what they learned was how to bury your pain. How to suffer in silence. They learned that you just don't talk about that sort of thing.

Adelle had signed up for the journey of parenthood with A.C., but now it was on her and her alone to raise two young Black boys in a city full of wrong paths and dangerous decisions. She kept them busy with sports and activities, telling anyone who would listen, "These boys don't have time to find trouble!" Sporting events were a favorite escape, so she'd save up to take them to at least one Browns, Indians, and Cavaliers game a season. They got into heated matches of backgammon, Yahtzee, and Uno on the floor in the living room and she taught them how to play tennis at nearby Roosevelt Park on hot summer days.

Adelle took them to the library at least twice a week and told them that books were the gateway to the world. She enrolled them in classes at the local playhouse, where Deland designed and built sets and Damon and his friend John wrote and performed an original play.

Damon was also a talented musician and Adelle managed the family gospel group he was in, the Chosen Generation. They would wear tuxedos for performances and Damon would sing with his whole body, swaying as he soloed on songs like "Jesus the Savior of Men."

Adelle talked to the boys about being a good member of one's household and community, teaching them how to cook and clean, budget their finances, and save enough allowance to tithe at church. She budgeted too, saving up to buy the boys one big gift every few years—a Huffy bike for Deland one year, a telescope for Damon so he could look at the stars and what he called "the holes in the moon."

"I want you to go somewhere where I have to take a plane to see you," Adelle would say to the boys about their future. She'd list off cities they might move to, jobs they might get. She wanted Damon and Deland to imagine big opportunities for themselves outside the limitations of Youngstown. She didn't want to worry them with talk of the realities of life, so she carried the weight of financial struggles, infidelity, and violence all on her own. She wished she could provide them with more of the comforts some of their friends had, but she knew she could make a lesson out of their struggles.

"Ma, can we stop buying shoes at Picway?" Damon would ask, kicking up his legs to show off his scuffed-up old sneakers. "Can we just once get Adidas?" In the late 1970s the new Adidas Shooting Stars were everything. "You show me in the Bible where God tells me to buy you Adidas, and you'll have a pair of Adidas," Adelle said. "Otherwise get a job, buy your own shoes."

Blessings were in God's Time. Struggles were in God's Plan.

Adelle had no problem delivering sermons. If it was time to give tough love about drugs, the importance of school, or staying out of trouble with the law she could talk for a whole dinner, seemingly never stopping to take a breath. But Lord did she want to skip past the conversations she didn't know how to have. If she couldn't bulldoze her way through it, she wasn't going to do it. When it came to the tough stuff, her emotional DNA ran deep. "God's got you" was an easy answer to every difficult problem, the thing to say when life seemed unfair or too difficult to face head-on. If you don't talk about your hardships, the pain will go away. Take what you learn from tough times and keep it moving. Talking to others about your struggles is burdensome and acknowledging your trauma is a "pity party." Head down, press ahead. God will handle it.

These were the lessons Adelle applied to handling Deland's adoption. She'd been called on to show this little boy love, and God would help lead her through it. She and A.C. never spoke to any counselors or therapists about Deland's adoption. They hadn't read any books or sought out any advice about how this new little boy might be different from their first. Surely if they just gave him a home and taught him manners, hard work, and faith, the rest would figure itself out. It wasn't a secret that he was adopted, they just didn't ever talk about it. When Damon was about eight or nine, some neighbor boys who liked to cause trouble told him they heard a rumor that Deland was adopted, expecting a big reaction. "And?" said Damon. "Even if he is, he's still my little brother. What's your point?"

Damon wasn't really sure he understood what it meant to be adopted but he didn't like the way those boys said it. *Adopted.* Spit it out like it was something nasty. Damon didn't want to disrupt the close relationship he had with Deland by bringing it up. And more than that? He didn't care. Deland was his brother; the details didn't matter.

Adelle didn't think it was a big deal either, and at the time many experts agreed. Many believed the best practice was to treat an adopted child just like a biological child, limiting any conversations or behaviors that would "other" them. In the early twentieth century, disclosure had been the norm when it came to original birth records and abortion-related court documents, but by 1945 most states had adopted a policy of secrecy and confidentiality. When Deland was adopted in the early 1970s, closed adoptions were standard; it was rare for an adopted child to know anything about his or her birth parents. In some cases adoptive parents even wrote out explicit instructions in case of their deaths to prevent adoptees from having access to any documents with information about their birth parents, family members, city of birth, or otherwise.

In order for an adoptive family to be accepted as a child's "real" family, some believed it was necessary to reject or sometimes even fully erase the existence of the birth family. This was easiest when an adoptee looked like the rest of his or her adoptive family, so "matching" became the prevailing philosophy when placing children. "Matching" a child with a couple that looked like biological parents was believed to protect the adoptive parents from the stigmas of infertility and the child from the stigmas of adoption.

Ellen Herman writes about matching on the University of Oregon's Adoption History Project site:

During much of the twentieth century, matching was the philoso-phy that governed non-relative adoption. Its goal was to make fam-ilies socially that would "match" families made naturally. Matching required that adoptive parents be married heterosexual couples who looked, felt, and behaved as if they had, by themselves, con-ceived other people's children. What this meant in practice was that physical resemblance, intellectual similarity, and racial and religious continuity between parents and children were preferred goals in adoptive families. Matching was the technique that could inject naturalness and "realness" into a family form stigmatized as artificial and less real than the "real thing." Matching stood for safety and security. Difference spelled trouble.

Under the matching paradigm, one family was substituted for another so carefully, systematically, and completely that the old family was replaced, rendered invisible and unnecessary.

Matching confronted the central problem of modern adoption. It attempted to create kinship without blood in the face of an en-during equivalence between blood and belonging. The results were paradoxical. Matching reinforced the notion that blood was thicker than water, the very ideology that made adoption inferior, while seeking to equalize and dignify it. . . .

Matching was an optimistic, arrogant, and historically novel objective that suggested that a social operation could and should approximate nature by copying it.

For decades the push and pull of seeking "normalcy" versus accept-ing and embracing difference led much of the decision-making around adoption, confidentiality, and the sharing of information. Throughout the twentieth century, even during the closed adoption era, many experts urged adoptive parents to tell adoptees about their status so they could learn the truth from loving parents instead of nosy neighbors or gossiping relatives. Parents were encouraged to emphasize to adoptees that they were "chosen" to offset any negative connotations associated with their surrender and the adoption process. Some adoptive parents still preferred secrecy despite research that had long shown that adoptees who met their birth parents or were given information about their birth family had better relationships with their adoptive parents, established a better sense of identity, and better healed from feelings of abandonment. Those parents worried about the societal stigma around "illegitimacy" and many harbored fear or insecurity about how "real" their role was in the child's life.

Feelings of rejection, loss, or being "othered" are normal but painful for adoptees, and are so deeply rooted in the body they often show up even in those who are never told about their adoption status. Some adopted children feel like there's an invisible barrier between themselves and their adoptive parents; some feel like they've lost something, though they can't place what it is. Others feel like they're constantly being doubted and need to prove that they're worthy and they belong. Being removed from the care of a birth mother is a type of trauma, no matter how loving and supportive an adoptive family is. As hard as it may be, adoptees are better off facing that trauma than being prevented from knowing about it. In his book *The Body Keeps the Score*, noted psychiatrist and author Bessel van der Kolk shared the powerful words of one of his professors, prominent American psychoanalytic psychiatrist Elvin Semrad. "The greatest sources of our suffering are the lies we tell ourselves," Semrad would tell his students. He urged them to help their patients "acknowledge, experience, and bear" the realities of life because they wouldn't be able to heal without "knowing what they know and feeling how they feel."

Adelle, like many adoptive parents of her time, worried it would be confusing or painful for Deland to talk about his "situation." There weren't any other families in town with adopted children—at least none that were open about having gone through the process—so she couldn't reach out to anyone for advice. She and A.C. were also a relative rarity at the time, legally adopting a Black child as opposed to the far more common practice of Black children being informally adopted by a family member or friend.

From the Adoption History Project:

> For a good part of the twentieth century, African-American birth parents and children were simply denied adoption services by agencies because of their religion, race, or both. . . . Discriminated against and reluctant to establish racially exclusive organizations when integration was synonymous with equality, African Americans relied instead on traditions of informal adoption to take care of their own.

By the time Deland was old enough to understand what adoption was, A.C. was long gone and Adelle still didn't have a plan to tell him. Maybe she wouldn't ever tell him. If he found out one day, so be it. All that mattered was that she would be there for him no matter what happened. She would be there with an ear, a hug, a prayer, or a lesson. She was his mother. Always would be. No difference if she gave birth to him or chose him. In fact, sometimes friends and family would laugh when Adelle would accidentally say, "When I had Deland . . . " It felt like second nature to talk about him as her biological child.

Years passed and Adelle had herself so convinced the whole matter was inconsequential, she didn't even think about Deland's adoption anymore. So it was that one day when Deland was about seven years old, sitting on the carpet playing with Hot Wheels at a family friend's house, he heard Adelle say, "Pittsburgh is actually where we went to pick up Deland when we adopted him."

He slowly turned his head toward his mother on the couch. "I'm adopted?"

"Yes, baby," she said. And she went back to talking to her friends. Conversation over. No more questions.

In the car on the ride home, Damon fumed. Why did his mom have to go and tell Deland? They were thicker than thieves, brothers in every way but blood.

What if Deland felt differently about him now? What if he pulled away, or shut down?

"We're a family!" Damon finally shouted at Adelle—in her retelling of the story she'd swear she saw actual steam coming out of his ears. "Blood or no blood! Everybody's woven into the blood of Christ. We got relatives that ain't even related by blood that are still relatives. Everybody's still family."

He turned around and looked at Deland, sitting quiet and wide-eyed in the back seat. "You're my brother," he said gently. "It's not even . . ." He looked for the right words. "There's no separation or anything. This changes nothing."

Deland sort of understood what it meant to be adopted, but he didn't think it was something to be upset about until he saw Damon so angry. *Maybe this did change everything*, he thought. If Adelle and A.C. weren't his parents, then what else might not be true? His mind started racing. What were his birth parents like? Did they want to meet him? Did he want to meet them? Why didn't they want him? Was it the same reason A.C. didn't want him? Would Adelle leave him too?

Who was he? Who did he belong to?

"Everybody's born for a reason, okay?" Adelle said, catching and holding his eyes in the rearview mirror. "The first baby that was adopted was Jesus, 'cause Joseph was not his father, okay? How you gonna complain about getting adopted? Jesus was adopted."

There was a long pause.

"Picks-burgh," he said slowly. "Are my parents there now?"

"Enough," Adelle said, definitively. A door slam in a word.

Deland went silent. Damon started sobbing in the front seat. He couldn't keep it in.

There's something else, Adelle wanted to say. A tiny voice inside her screamed, *Just get it over with. Say it all. Get it out!* She couldn't. Damon was already so upset. She just wanted to move on.

That part is done, she told herself. *Deland knows. Now let's forget about it and be a family.*

When Deland got to school the next day, the excitement of having a big secret drowned out the reality of Damon's sobering response. Deland carried the news of his adoption with him like the best kind of secret—a surprise party, a love note passed in class, a bouquet of flowers tucked behind your back. At first it felt powerful to know something that no one else knew, but as the day went on he just couldn't keep it in. This was big news and there was no telling how excited his classmates might be. Unfortunately, they were six- and seven-year-olds. Some of them had even grown up learning there was no meaner taunt from a sibling or a friend than "I heard you're adopted." There was no tenderness or warmth from them. There definitely wasn't any excitement. After telling a couple of friends and getting more mockery than anything else, Deland decided to tuck the secret back inside. No one else needed to know.

When he got home, he was overcome by emotion. He didn't know whether he was sad, angry, scared, or all of them at once. The only solution he could think of was destruction. He took a pair of scissors and cut three big gashes into the arm of the burgundy faux-velvet couch Adelle had just finished two years of layaway payments on. When she got home he had to admit what he'd done.

"Before I kill you, you wanna tell me why you did this?" Adelle said, her voice rising.

"Do you love me less, Ma?" Deland replied quietly, terrified of the answer. "Because I'm not yours? Do you love me less than Damon?"

"Oh, baby," Adelle said, all the anger gone in an instant. "I just love you differently. One of you because you were in my belly and the other because I chose you."

For a few weeks after that, whenever Deland was somewhere with a lot of people—the mall, a baseball game, Idora Park—he'd scan the faces in the crowd, looking for himself. He longed to see someone who resembled him. It was unsettling to check the mirror every day and see only himself and no one else. He was anxious about looking, though. It felt like looking was akin to asking, and he'd gotten the message about that loud and clear on that car ride.

A few times over the next couple years Adelle, totally out of the blue, would ask Deland if he wanted to try to find his birth parents. She promised she wouldn't be mad, and though he believed her, deep down some part of him was already convinced it wasn't okay to look. "It's fine," he'd say. "I don't need to know." And he meant it. *There are enough problems*, Deland thought. It felt like every day he saw somebody in Youngstown going through something serious. He didn't need to go looking for trouble.

After he shrugged off her offers a couple of times, Adelle stopped asking. Adelle and Deland didn't talk about his adoption again. Not for another thirty years.

Deland

CHAPTER 5

After John left, Adelle and the boys were back to three, and this time she knew she needed to find a real job. She couldn't go back to dealing—too risky—and since neither A.C. nor John had wanted her to work full-time while they were married, she had been out of the employment game for years. She and the boys went through stretches with no phone, heat, or hot water at Allerton Court as she struggled to pay bills on time. The boys knew times were tough, but things never felt desperate—they could always get help from neighbors in Lincoln Knolls and go to the soup kitchen or to family nearby to get a good meal when Adelle couldn't buy groceries. After months of just getting by, leaning on family and friends, she finally found a gig at the Department of Job and Family Services in Cleveland, an hour and fifteen minutes by car each way.

When she first started at the welfare office she would stay overnight in Cleveland for the week, crashing with Christina Doon, an old classmate from East High. Then for a stretch she rented a room in Cleveland and stayed over a few nights a week to go to graduate school classes for court stenography. Eventually she got into a groove, leaving on Monday and returning every Wednesday night to be with the boys. While she was gone Deland and Damon, nine and thirteen, would hang out with Adelle's half brother, Billy, who had come up from Atlanta to live at Allerton Court.

Billy was sixteen years older than Adelle, funny as all get-out, and a bit of an eccentric character. He taught the boys a lot, including the fundamentals of baseball and how to oil up their gloves. He had thick sideburns and a goatee with flecks of gray in the corners of his chin.

He had big strong hands, kind eyes, and a kind heart. He loved the Yankees, Elvis Presley, ballads, and big women.

He expressed his gratitude often by telling anyone who would listen how much he loved his family. He collected obituaries to learn about people and liked to tell Damon and Deland the truths he saw in the hearts of the people in Youngstown—both good and bad.

Damon and Deland spent a lot of time those days playing catch with Billy, organizing neighborhood football games along the side of the house, or playing with their all-time favorite toy, their NFL Electric Football Game. The boys would comb through the newspaper box scores and stories to find their favorite football players' names, cut them out, and glue them onto the tiny plastic men on the board. Damon was a huge Tony Dorsett fan, so his side of the board was the Cowboys, while Deland was into the Steelers, who were riding high after a handful of recent Super Bowl wins. Football was everything to them. Billy always got a laugh out of Deland loving his football so much he'd take it to bed with him.

Billy joined teachers, coaches, neighbors, and other family members as surrogate fathers for Damon and Deland, all of them working to keep Adelle's boys in line when she wasn't around. A favorite associate pastor used to take the boys fishing, while the dads in the neighborhood would teach them how to work the grill during beach days at West Branch State Park. They needed men to talk to them about girls, their bodies, and everything else that makes the preteen and teen years so delightfully and painfully awkward. Damon was a father figure for Deland as well. He showed his younger brother how to navigate school and sports, and approached life with a sort of cool confidence that Deland aspired to but wasn't sure he'd ever manage to achieve.

Adelle desperately wanted to find a partner for herself and give her kids a steady male role model, but after A.C. left and things ended with John, she doubted herself and her choices. The men she was drawn to and the things she wanted for herself as a woman weren't what would serve her boys. Too often she couldn't make her intentions match her outcomes. After seeing men come and go, she worried the boys wouldn't know what it was to be a stand-up guy. Her daddy used to tell her, "If a man has his hand out to you, it should have everything you need and want in it." She wanted Damon and Deland to grow up knowing a real man can provide for his wife, provide for his kids, and stick around. The men she'd given her hand to hadn't done that.

After A.C. left, Adelle tried for years to get him to spend time with the boys. When he rejected her requests she never talked bad about him, just let the boys figure out for themselves what kind of man he was.

"God gives you an example of what to be and what not to be," she'd always tell her sons. "You make the choice." She wanted them to hear it, but she also needed to remind herself: *You make the choice.*

Meanwhile, they could all see that A.C. was living large just across town.

He was omnipresent on the radio and active all over town emceeing concerts and attending sporting events. Deland was so young when A.C. left, most of his memories of him came later, when they would randomly cross paths around town or he'd spot A.C. across a parking lot at a local football game. And of course, from the radio, where A.C.'s smooth baritone announced the day's weather, introduced Youngstown to a new Top 40 song, or promoted his upcoming appearances at the Metroplex, Idora Park, or various fairs in the Youngstown area. He was even the man kids tuned in to on cold winter mornings hoping to hear those two magic words: "Snow day!"

A.C.'s voice was a constant in Deland's life, even if A.C. the man never was. Like pairing the narration of one film with the visuals of another. Deland tried to shrug it off, but the older he got and the longer he lived wearing that man's last name, the more confused he was that A.C. had so much to say to everyone else and nothing to say to him.

Deland never forgave A.C. for giving up on him and Damon. Biological or adopted, they were his sons. He had wanted them. He had chosen them. If it was that easy to leave a chosen child, how meaningful was their connection? A.C. stirred up feelings deep down that Deland couldn't name and didn't yet understand. Feelings about his birth parents abandoning him. If the people who were supposed to love him most kept leaving, why would anyone stay? This deep feeling of loss and rejection didn't manifest as a tangible anger or sadness so much as a void. A sort of vacuum that stole energy.

That hollow feeling was likely due to the separation from his birth mother—a void felt more in his body than his mind. His body knew her voice, her smell, her heartbeat; knew the body they had shared. Then it was all gone. A disrupted connection. An imprinted loss. He couldn't explain it with words. Just a deep, primal wound that closed and scarred over but never disappeared.

Deland's shyness and anxiety may have been the result of that separation as well, especially if his early days and weeks were spent without the close care of a mother. In the first weeks of life the development of an infant's brain is very experience-dependent—especially the limbic system, which processes and regulates emotion and memory and becomes wired for attachment to others. Attachment theory, developed by psychiatrist and psychoanalyst John Bowlby and expanded by developmental psychologist Mary Ainsworth, explains how the relationship between a primary caregiver and a child provides a safe base from which to explore the world. Biologically the infant seeks connection for survival; psychologically they seek connection for a feeling of security. The attachment style that results from that first bond can impact a person's relationships with other people for the rest of their life. Secure attachments are formed when a caregiver is sensitive and responsive during stressful situations or moments of need; anxious-ambivalent attachments occur when caregiving is inconsistent; anxious-avoidant and dismissive-avoidant attachment forms when an infant's needs are rarely met; and disorganized or disoriented attachment is often the result of trauma, neglect, or abuse, or occurs because the caregiver was dealing with unresolved trauma themselves.

Was Deland regularly tended to and cuddled as an infant? By either his birth mother, another family member, or nurses? Chronic stress, a lack of attentive care, or the sudden disappearance of the comforting sounds and smells of a mother's body after nine months of gestation can affect development, impact stress hormones, and contribute to both mood—things like anxiety and depression—and future behavior, including self-regulation and impulse control. Deland didn't know anything about early childhood development, but he knew how he felt—that hollowness, that sensation of having suffered a loss. And he knew that he wasn't going to be able to forgive A.C.'s decision to leave. Abandonment of any kind triggered deeply rooted feelings within him.

Damon was more forgiving of A.C.—of just about everything, really. He let things roll right off him and kept moving. For as close as they were growing up, the boys were as different as could be. Damon was outspoken, well liked, and easygoing. He excelled in sports and the classroom and got along with everyone. Deland had trouble concentrating in class and barely spoke when he was young. He was so shy around everyone except his brother that one time Grandma Maretta asked Damon, "Does your brother even talk?" Another time Aunt Juanita pulled Deland aside on her patio and gently asked why he didn't talk much. When he just smiled and shrugged, she turned her head toward Adelle and a grateful Deland slipped away. He couldn't put a name to it; he just felt safest when he kept everyone at a distance.

While Deland's shyness was a concern to family, it was a source of frustration to teachers and staff at his private, Catholic school, most of whom misread his diffidence as disrespect. At Holy Trinity he often found himself in hot water with the nuns for looking down at his desk and not participating. Once when he was trudging down the hall, moving at his typical speed of molasses slowed by quicksand, tiny, mild-mannered Sister Mary Margaret got so frustrated with him that she punched him in the back and shouted for him to move faster. Nowadays teachers or counselors might try to find out what was going on at home or try to root out the causes of his timidity, but back then the reaction to him not fitting in was to punish or presume some sort of deficiency. Sometimes both.

Punishment was usually detention. At first Deland told the nuns they couldn't possibly keep him after school because he had no ride home—Adelle was going back and forth to Cleveland at the time so if he didn't take the bus, he was stuck. Little did he know just how angry Sister Marjorie was about his actions—or, more accurately, inaction. She was so determined to show him consequences for his poor attitude that on several occasions she stuck around until after detention and drove him all the way back to the house on Allerton Court. Some days he was held late because of his lack of participation or unresponsiveness, others because he'd been intimidating other kids until they gave them their snacks. He never threatened anyone; he'd just firmly suggest that they hand over their Oreos until the cookies were his. When he wanted a special treat like that, he didn't want to trouble Adelle for it, especially since she sometimes didn't have it to give.

One day after yet another Oreos detention, Sister Marjorie told Deland to wait in the front lobby of the school for a moment while she gathered her things to leave. As he turned the corner to the lobby and looked down the hall, he saw something even scarier than an angry nun: his mother. This was clearly a strategic, coordinated, and timed attack. It was four o'clock in the afternoon on a Tuesday—Adelle didn't have any reason to be back in Youngstown other than to cuss him out. The nuns had gotten so fed up they'd called Grandma Maretta, who had called Adelle at work. Adelle was none too pleased about having to leave early to drive all the way home from Cleveland and deal with yet another complaint about Deland's bad behavior. She was especially mad because that job in Cleveland was the reason she could pay the deeply discounted tuition Holy Trinity had worked out for her. Twenty-five dollars a month for Damon, thirty-five total when Deland started going there too. It was the first bill she paid every month, even if it meant not paying others. If she had to rob Peter to pay Paul, so be it. The boys' education was the most important thing.

Adelle put the fear of God in Deland that day, threatening him with all sorts of punishments. Most of her threats were empty, though. In the end, Deland just got a tongue-lashing and had to promise not to do it again. She'd scared him, that was enough. Her anger had already softened by that night when she told him, "You know, when you turn eighteen, legally I don't have to feed you anymore!" There was a smirk on her face as she walked away.

In the spring of 1985, two MJs were dominating sports and entertainment across the globe. Michael Jackson had cowritten the song of the year, "We Are the World," which was sung by a who's who of the country's top musicians and benefited famine relief in Africa. Deland's fifth-grade class rehearsed and performed it at a school assembly. Meanwhile, Michael Jordan was about to earn Rookie of the Year honors in the NBA, thrilling fans in his debut season with the Chicago Bulls. His new Air Jordan sneakers were a hit, and that Christmas was the first of many that saw a pair of Jordans on Damon's and Deland's wish lists. The boys would mimic his famous wagging tongue as they played basketball, practicing driving the lane, taking off, and wondering if they too could fly.

The closest Deland felt to flying was always when he was playing sports with Damon or his classmates. The rest of the day he felt as if he were lugging around a backpack full of giant textbooks, so heavy his shoulders pressed forward and down, curving his body toward the ground and away from the world in front of him. But when he was out on the court moving his body, the backpack disappeared. He was free. He could fly.

School didn't come easy to Deland like it did for Damon. Even when he did focus and work hard, it didn't show up in excellent grades or academic awards. Sometimes he felt like it wasn't worth trying if the results weren't going to change. That fifth-grade year the whole class had to take a nationally normed aptitude test—the Iowa Assessments—to gauge achievement and growth across learning standards. Deland struggled with a few questions early on, got frustrated, and just scrapped it. Deciding to be a wise-ass, he marked random ovals and completed the test in ten minutes, then stared at the wall for the next two hours while everyone else kept working. When the results came back and his scores indicated he tested at a first-grade level, he was surprised to find he was deeply ashamed. The shame turned into embarrassment when his classmates all started to discuss their scores. *You make the choice*, he heard Adelle's voice echoing in his head. Before his mother, the nuns, or anyone else could take him to task for it, he realized he wanted to be better for himself.

He paid more attention in class and his grades improved, but sometimes things would still set him off unexpectedly. Like the time his face got hot when his science teacher talked about genetics and DNA, or when he acted out on purpose to get sent to the principal while the class did an exercise on family trees. He could even feel himself tensing up when the teacher talked about American history and slavery. All those families separated, all those generations of African Americans left unable to find their roots. He didn't even know who his parents were, forget about where his grandparents, great-grandparents, and beyond came from. What was his lineage? West African? Caribbean? Even if Deland could have figured out how to verbalize the turmoil going on inside of him, he wouldn't have bothered anybody with it. Besides, who would he even talk to about this stuff? He didn't know anyone else who was adopted.

And so he kept quiet. Being stoic and detached in the face of difficult circumstances had become Deland's default. He understood you just didn't talk about that sort of thing.

Damon had never given Adelle any trouble—he was a star in sports and seen as a child genius in the classroom—so Adelle was at her wits' end about Deland's combination of muteness and misbehavior. As she struggled to motivate Deland academically, she was faced with another challenge. Around the same time he was tanking his Iowa Test, Deland decided to dabble in shoplifting. He so coveted the Ranger action figure from the G.I. Joe collection he tried to steal one from the local Hills department store. Took it out of the packaging in the aisle and shoved it in his pocket. He made it all the way across the street to the movie theater and probably would have gotten away with it if not for his next-door neighbor Pooh getting caught. The Hills security guard spotted Deland across the street and walked him back over, insisting he empty his pockets. He was embarrassed, frightened, and a little bit confused about why he had tried to steal the toy in the first place. He knew it was wrong. He'd been told plenty of times it was wrong. But he hated the feeling of wanting and not getting. The feeling of having needs not met. He was plagued by anxiety about what his family didn't have and fearful of losing the things they did. He felt out of control.

The manager at Hills couldn't call Deland's house because their phone had been disconnected again, so Pooh's dad got the call and tracked down Adelle, then both parents showed up together. Deland had seen Adelle get mad plenty of times but the reaction from Pooh's dad put some real fear in him. He'd never seen a man be so angry and so disappointed all at once. The might of his deep voice, the size of his towering body leaning over them in anger. *The power of a man*, Deland thought. He decided he didn't ever want to get in trouble like that again. Of course, he wouldn't be able to resolve the issue that moved him to steal until he identified it. And that wouldn't happen until after he'd run afoul of the law a few more times.

Deland didn't want to be difficult, it was just his way of coping. He struggled to find his words with most everyone other than Damon and he never knew what to expect from the unpredictable adults around him. The easy solution was to try to block everybody out, keep his thoughts inside, and try his best to disappear into the background. Of course, the result of holding everything in was that sometimes the dam burst, and those moments led to bad decisions like the one he'd made at Hills. He just didn't feel secure enough to open up and talk about what was on his mind. While Damon had a sort of confidence and strength that came naturally, Deland's shyness was paralyzing. He never could shake the feeling of being doubted, of feeling like he had to prove himself and his worthiness. He internalized every rejection and every slight, determined to one day prove his doubters wrong. He didn't know if somewhere deep down his feelings were the result of being rejected by his birth parents, or if every young Black boy in Youngstown felt like the world didn't believe in him.

Years later Damon would describe their differences using the brothers' basketball idols of old. Deland was like Michael Jordan, he said—always a chip on his shoulder, always something to prove. Damon likened himself to Magic Johnson—just happy to be there, a big smile on his face damn near all the time. They might be living in the same place and experiencing the same things, but they were seeing life through vastly different lenses. As adults they would reminisce about growing up in Youngstown and it felt like the same footage edited by directors of different genres. Like Damon was living *Friday* and Deland was living *Boyz in the Hood*.

Deland's struggles manifested in new ways as he got older, especially when Billy moved out and Adelle started dating a new man named Frank. Things were never worse for Deland, Damon, and Adelle than when Frank was around.

Tony and Deland

CHAPTER 6

Frank Doon was an East Side guy, brother to Adelle's old high school friend Christina. They reconnected when Frank's best friend Gregory started dating Adelle's sister Tamara. Deland was in fifth grade, about eleven years old, when Frank started coming around. Damon was fifteen. A US Army vet, Frank worked as a laborer, doing plumbing, electrical, and carpentry work. He loved playing basketball and teaching Deland and Damon tricks like the old missing-thumb gag. He was dark-skinned and stoic-looking, and the boys thought Frank had the vibes of West African royalty. Or maybe a saxophonist in an R&B band. Sometimes he got a menacing look about him, though, so they were cautious around him almost immediately. Damon's friends referred to Frank as "cockstrong"—a guy who doesn't look all that built, but you don't wanna scrap with him because he's too self-assured to lose.

Adelle, Frank, Tamara, and Gregory had a whole lot of fun together and Adelle fell hard and fast for Frank. They'd hang out in the breezeway or patio at Allerton Court playing George Clinton's latest album or O'Bryan's "Soul Train's a Comin'" on their new JVC double-cassette boom box, dancing and singing along. Frank would sweet-talk Adelle and throw his big arms around her, squeezing her and making her feel safe. He'd talk to the boys about sports and crack jokes. They thought he was a pretty cool guy, but it was clear from the jump that he had a bit of an edge to him. In fact, when Frank and Adelle started seeing each other he was on trial for assaulting a police officer. He and Gregory had already been on probation for robbing a junkyard when they decided to throw a big party on the South Side of Youngstown. When the police came to break it up they fought a couple of the officers and landed in jail.

Despite red flags big and bold enough to stop a NASCAR race, Adelle was smitten. Clouded by infatuation, she couldn't look past what drew her in to see the reasons she might want to pull back. She was determined to stay loyal to her new boyfriend, even after his sentencing: two to fifteen years at the Ohio State Reformatory in Mansfield—the same prison where they later filmed *The Shawshank Redemption*. The original architect for the building, Levi T. Scofield, had built the structure to look like a castle, believing the combination of Victorian Gothic, Richardsonian Romanesque, and Queen Anne architecture would help the inmates experience a rebirth and find their spiritual centers.

For all the beauty of the facility—now operating as a tourist stop for ghost tours and visits to the re-created set of Andy Dufresne's fictional incarceration and escape—the experience of the inmates at Mansfield was far from idyllic. In 1990, just six years after Frank's stint ended, the reformatory was closed by federal order. Inmates had filed a class-action complaint years earlier alleging overcrowding, deteriorating facilities, roach and rat infestations, and other unsanitary and unconstitutional conditions.

Adelle regularly visited Frank at Mansfield and on a few occasions she brought the boys with her. Damon was fascinated by the place. Everything was huge—from the front doors to the visitor's room, a wide-open circle with inmate cells spiraling above it on the higher floors. There were curtains pulled in front of the cells and he imagined the men behind them—who they were and what they'd done to get there. Years later Damon remembered having to cross a moat to get into the prison, but that was just childhood fantasy—an understandable response to Mansfield's castle-like exterior. Deland hated going to Mansfield. He was spooked by everything—from the sight of the inmates to the loud clicking of doors locking when you passed through them. More than anything, Deland wondered why he was there. Frank wasn't his father. He wasn't even a guy who'd been around all that long. Every time they went to Mansfield he wished Adelle had dropped him off at Grandma Maretta's instead. Damon told him the visits were in service to Frank and a kindness to their mother. "Ma really loves him," he'd say. "It ain't anything to go."

Adelle was both honoring Frank's request to see the boys and trying to teach them a lesson. She wanted them to see what would happen if they got on the wrong side of the law. She knew she wasn't giving them the best example in Frank and tried to quiet some of her guilty feelings by telling herself these trips to Mansfield would scare them straight. There weren't any good men left in Youngstown, right? So she'd fix this one, make him the man the boys needed and put that old adage to work: *God gives you an example of what to be and what not to be—you make the choice.* At the time, stealing candy or toys from the store was the most she had to worry about with the boys, but she hoped the lesson would stick as they got older and more vulnerable to the pull of Youngstown's darkest corners. Damon didn't need much scaring straight, but he got a taste of it all the same. One time when they visited, Frank was nursing a wound in his side. He said one of the automatic cell doors closed on him and the lock jabbed him in the side, but Damon remembered Adelle saying he was stabbed. He never did find out which one it was.

Whatever happened inside Mansfield, Frank came out after eighteen months with more of his edge and less of his cool. The boys could see immediately that he was a different guy. Frank moved right into the house at Allerton Court and things started going sideways quickly. Adelle's relationships had always been contentious, but this one often got physical. Usually the boys had already gone to bed before trouble started up, but they weren't spared the soundtrack to Frank and Adelle's toxicity. They quickly came to learn the sound of someone being smacked or a wall being punched.

The boys were terrified of Frank's behavior and confused by Adelle's insistence on poking and prodding him until she got a reaction. They didn't know how much Adelle wanted them to have a man in the house. They didn't understand the complexities of intimate partner violence and abusive relationships. They just wanted a little peace in the house. They felt like Frank could never get on proper footing after Mansfield because Adelle kept piling on him about this or that and what he did or didn't do. She seemed to believe in him more than he believed in himself, but she couldn't find a way to constructively build him up and motivate him. Damon and Deland knew there was no excuse for Frank's behavior, but they understood how he could get frustrated. It felt like every time he put one fire out, she'd set another.

Seven months after Frank arrived, the family had to move. A.C. was a veteran, so he and Adelle had purchased the home on Allerton Court with a V.A. loan. When they divorced, the V.A. inspector let her stay there for a few years while he very slowly began the process of foreclosure. When she married John, also a veteran, she moved the mortgage to his name. After their divorce she managed to stay for another couple years before the inspector finally forced her out in 1986. Frank had served in the Army too, but this time they didn't have the money to avoid foreclosure.

When it was time to pack up and go, Damon and Deland didn't ask why. They understood you just don't talk about that sort of thing.

So they left behind the house on the cul-de-sac, the neighbors who had become family, and their memories of parties, fireworks, and football in the big side yard. They moved about fifteen minutes south to a house at 31 Montgomery. It was nestled between Jerusalem Baptist Church, a couple hundred feet to the south, and St. Nicholas Byzantine Catholic Church, a couple hundred feet to the west, but despite the geographic prayer circle, 31 Montgomery felt cursed. It would become the site of some of Frank's most notorious outbursts.

Deland loved escaping the house whenever he could to work his paper route, taking the long way home on his bike to avoid witnessing potential drama. He loved having money to buy things and felt good about being able to help Adelle. The rides were also a respite from the constant stress at home. He felt like he was on high alert all the time; every conversation was rife with potential danger, every comment might be the thing that set someone off. When he rode his bike, legs pumping, wind in his face, he got precious moments of freedom from worry.

At night he would beg Damon to let him tag along with the older guys when they went out because the worst times were at home alone with Frank and Adelle—no Damon to calm things down or check Frank's temper. Sometimes one or two of the uncles would come over and try to give Frank a talking-to, but the boys knew that as soon as they left, Frank and Adelle would start back up again. After the worst of their fights Frank would threaten to leave for good. Adelle would tell Damon and Deland to comfort him. "Tell Frank you want him to come back," she'd say. "Tell him you miss him and need him back home."

The idea of comforting Frank made Deland feel sick. Damon could see some good in Frank and wanted to show him grace, but even he wasn't willing to go that far—they didn't need Frank and they sure as hell didn't miss him when he was gone.

Damon knew it was ultimately up to his mother just how many chances Frank would get, but sometimes he couldn't help but intervene. One spring night he walked into the house and heard yelling in the bedroom. Frank had Adelle pinned down on the bed and was holding her by the wrists. Damon knew he'd only get one shot at him, because if it came down to fisticuffs Frank had him by too many inches and pounds. Damon grabbed a broom and swung on him. Frank turned and tried to block it, taking the brunt of the broom and Damon's strength on the wrist. The thin skin stretched across bone burst and the blood came quickly.

Damon turned and ran. He jumped down four stairs to the landing halfway down the staircase, pivoted, leapt down the second set of stairs, then ran straight out the front door. He held the 100-meter record at Campbell Memorial so he knew he could get out of there fast. He also knew he was finished if he faced off against Frank in close quarters. If they were gonna square up he needed a bigger ring: the whole damn front yard and plenty of escape routes through backyards or streets. When he got outside he decided he didn't even want to chance it. He kept running and stayed away a few hours before coming home.

While Damon's approach was to occasionally challenge Frank, Deland's only response was to disappear, either into himself or the safety of a friend's house. When he wasn't on his bike he was hanging at Tony's. Deland could get a good meal or play pool, video games, and Ping-Pong—Tony even had a full basketball court out back. Tony's mom and dad had divorced when he was young, but she had a good job at Delphi Packard Electric, a subsidiary of General Motors, so they had financial stability. She was one of the lucky ones who worked somewhere that thrived even after the steel mills closed.

The abuse that had precipitated the split between Tony's parents didn't disappear altogether after the divorce, unfortunately. Tony's dad had built a house down the street to be closer to his sons, a positive for Tony and his brothers most of the time. Unfortunately, sometimes he would drink too much and come back to Tony's house to start things up again. From a young age Tony and Deland found in each other someone who understood the anxiety and tension that come with living in a constant state of unpredictability and violence. After witnessing his dad's behavior for years, Tony was turned off by alcohol and didn't drink at all through high school. Deland didn't either. He'd seen the way Adelle and others acted when they had too much to drink or got into other substances. It was tough enough to read how someone might act when they were sober; things were even more unpredictable when booze and drugs were involved. He didn't want any part of it.

Deland and Tony bonded quite a bit over their shared desire to stay on the straight and narrow, avoid getting caught up in anything criminal, and focus on finding success as adults. They took pride in having a solid moral compass that they managed to maintain even as so many other young men in Youngstown were chasing trouble.

There was always a part of Deland that wondered if trouble had gotten to his birth mom. Maybe that's why she gave him up. Was she on drugs? In jail? What was he predestined to become if he got himself tied up in that stuff? What secrets and truths were hidden in his body? In his genes? It was hard to know where he was going if he didn't know where he came from. Like writing a story that starts in the middle.

Deland didn't want to risk discovering a side of himself he didn't yet know. And more than anything, he understood there was enough worry in his house without him bringing more into it. For months, Frank's increasingly volatile behavior had kept everyone in constant fear of another major outburst. Deland felt like he should be able to do something about it, but he was still so small. So small and so scared. At night he would lie in bed listening to Frank and Adelle fight and quietly pray to God to let the argument end without incident.

"God, if you're listening," he'd whisper, squeezing his eyes shut, "don't let nothing crazy happen. Don't let nobody get hurt. Please God, I just want us to get through the night."

Sometimes he would stare up at the big crack in the ceiling above his head, tracing it with his eyes to where it met the wall. He'd run his eyes back and forth until it got blurry, until there were two cracks running alongside each other. Sometimes he would put a pillow over his face to erase the crack and try to drown out the noise. Other times he'd listen in and wonder why they continued to fight about such stupid things. He knew he didn't fully understand their conversations, but he understood enough to know they'd be better off putting themselves to bed. He'd try to sleep but he couldn't stop his heart from racing. If one or the other of them said the wrong thing, this would go on for another hour.

When he got a little older, Deland's prayers changed. He'd pray to be given the tools to find success. He'd pray to have the opportunity to do something better than what he felt was lined up for him in Youngstown. He wasn't sure where or doing what, but he prayed to get out.

In the first fifteen months after getting out of Mansfield, Frank struggled to find and keep jobs. He would call Adelle long-distance for no good reason while she was at work in Cleveland, racking up phone bills and acting erratically.

Adelle vented about his behavior to a coworker who said it sounded like he was abusing drugs. She suggested Adelle search the house. The very next time Frank was out she picked apart every room until she found a plate and crack-cocaine paraphernalia in the rafters of the basement ceiling. She also found tickets from the pawnshop hidden in the pockets of clothes tucked away in the closet. Receipts showed that he'd pawned her expensive sewing machine and the tools she'd bought him to try to get carpentry work.

Adelle confronted Frank immediately and he broke down, admitting he needed help. She set him up with classes at a nearby halfway house but allowed him to keep living at Montgomery. She saw how his presence affected her boys, but she desperately wanted to make things work. She could still see the disappointment on Deland's face when John moved out. She could still hear the sound of her mother's voice after A.C. left: *Well, child, what did you do wrong?* This one had to stick. She loved Frank and believed there was good in him. She could fix him and make him the man they all needed; it would just take some time.

A few months after Adelle first called out Frank's crack use, the money from Deland's paper route went missing. She knew exactly who had taken it.

Deland's system had been to collect the money from subscribers and keep it under his mattress until it was time to deliver payment to the local newspaper, the *Vindicator*. This time when he went to gather the money it was gone. Adelle told Deland to get in the car and she drove them nearly thirty minutes away from the house to give herself plenty of time to cool off and get in the right headspace before Frank got home. Stealing from her son? She was worried she might kill him.

Another night she stood on the side of Route 46 for hours waiting for Frank to pick her up. She was part of a car-pool group, six girls taking turns driving the seventy-five miles to and from Cleveland every day so they could get back to their families at night. On the days she wasn't in charge of driving she would leave Frank the car so he could go looking for work. On this night she'd been dropped off after work at the usual meeting spot on Route 46, but Frank was nowhere to be found. It got later and later, darker and darker. Finally, he pulled up. No excuse, no apology. That night she took away his car privileges. Told him he could never use her car again.

She couldn't believe she was once again having to raise a grown man.

When things got tough, she would try to focus on the good times they had together and the positive qualities she saw in him. Before they'd moved into the Montgomery house, Adelle had encouraged Frank to use his carpentry skills to fix it up, hoping to instill in him more confidence and a sense of self-respect. Instead of looking around town for trouble, he could be put to work with her at the house. The hardwood floors at Montgomery were a dark black, so the two of them sanded them all down and redid them in a lighter stain. They did the attic and the hallway floors, redid the bathroom, and stripped years of paint layers off the banister and repainted it.

Adelle wanted to keep him busy and remind him he had value and something to add. The work he did was really good. He was talented. She tried to remember those moments and cling to those shared experiences when he let her down.

In the meantime, Deland had started solving his problems at school the same way Frank and Adelle handled them at home. While he remained shy and introverted, he would occasionally use his deep voice and commanding presence to get what he wanted, earning a reputation as sort of a de facto classroom enforcer. Unlike his minor misbehavior as a youngster, this wasn't about demanding snacks, it was about disciplining disruptive kids who kept the class from going out to recess. If someone acted out or interrupted the day's lessons, their teacher would cancel or delay recess, ruining Deland's day. Playing football and running around outside was the only time of the day he felt free. That feeling of the big backpack full of books dissipated, his head picked up, and his shyness slipped away for a while.

Deland didn't know it, but every time he rode his bike, played a pickup game with friends, or ran around the track, he was regulating his nervous system's stress response. Being in a constant state of stress kept his body hovering over the gas pedal all day, pumping adrenaline, waiting and watching for signs of danger. When he ran around, he relieved the tension in his muscles and took deep, gulping breaths, letting his body know it was okay to put on the brakes and relax; he wasn't in danger.

Deland wouldn't have been able to explain it, but he knew it felt like healing.

If he couldn't put words to why those moments of play mattered so much to him, he definitely couldn't express his frustration to the kids who got in the way of them, so he used his powers of intimidation. Soon he realized that if he could get classmates to see him as a tough guy, he could also keep them from making fun of the holes in the sides of his pants or his too-small T-shirts. Deland couldn't stand being the butt of anyone's jokes or made to feel less-than. He made sure kids knew he wouldn't abide being ridiculed.

Deland didn't want to be like Adelle and Frank, but he brought so much pent-up anger with him to Holy Trinity. He was angry that he couldn't stand up to Frank. Angry that when things got heated he folded himself up instead of fighting back. Though Damon was short in stature, he was strong and capable. Sure of himself and brave, he was willing to challenge Frank despite their differences in size and age. It absolutely wrecked Deland that he couldn't defend his mother the same way. He knew it wasn't his fault that Frank acted the way he did, but just because something isn't your fault doesn't mean it's not your responsibility. He wished he could be responsible for protecting her.

Adelle was worried and frustrated by Deland's behavior at school and at home. He wouldn't talk to anyone but Damon, so she took him with her to the local YWCA to meet with a therapist. Not only did she want him to get over his hatred for Frank but she also hoped to address the shyness, the outbursts, and the complaints from teachers. When they got to the therapist's office, Deland was quiet and Adelle was defensive. She wasn't yet ready to do the work required to help herself or her son. She didn't want to talk about Frank's abuse, nor did she want to get introspective about her own role in the volatility at home. Deep inside, Adelle knew there was something to be gained by finally being honest, but she'd kept herself closed up for so long she couldn't find the courage. Adelle was suffering, but all her life she'd been taught to hold it in. To suffer in silence. Nobody told her silence makes you sick.

Adelle and Deland only went to one or two more sessions at the YWCA. Adelle never mentioned to the therapist that Deland was adopted.

In sixth grade, Deland's class was scheduled to take a field trip to Niagara Falls. Adelle was struggling to scrape together the money needed, so she suggested going over to A.C.'s house to see if he would chip in. Deland didn't want to, but he never said no to his mom or his brother, so when Damon offered to take him over there, he begrudgingly accepted. When they arrived at the house, A.C.'s new wife greeted them kindly and ushered them in, offering a drink and a snack. She introduced their daughter to the boys and even said, "These are your brothers." Deland couldn't believe it—she was treating them like they meant something! For as long as he could remember, A.C. had pretended they didn't exist.

A.C. came out of the kitchen a few minutes later, and after a little bit of small talk, Deland screwed up the courage to ask for the money. Not a lot, just a little to help get him there.

"Nah," said A.C.

Nothing more. Just "nah." And with his next breath A.C. was asking Damon to come check out some computers he'd found and was trying to fix up, a pair of Commodore 64s. Deland sat on the couch and waited to go home.

Deland wasn't mad that day. He was used to A.C. being a nothing in his life. In fact, by that point he and Damon were more embarrassed by the situation than anything else. As far as their classmates knew—and as far as the paperwork and their last name said—A.C. was their father, but he was nowhere to be found. As Deland sat on the couch, he felt his cheeks get pink and hot. Embarrassed, not mad. He'd have to expect something from A.C. to be mad. Expect nothing from others and you'll never be disappointed.

By seventh grade, Deland's eye had turned to girls. Whitney Houston was on the radio singing about wanting to dance with somebody, and boy, did Deland hear that. He had found a powerful reason to work on his shyness. He also realized being the angry guy at school wasn't getting him the kind of attention he wanted. He worked on his confidence, tried to breathe through his frustrations, and committed to controlling his behavior. He started to find a little bit of swagger on the football field, the basketball court, and the track. He didn't yet stand out from the rest of the kids as any kind of special athlete, but just being part of a team and learning how to push himself gave him self-assuredness and something to look forward to at school.

Unfortunately, come winter of that year, Deland's Frank troubles showed up at Holy Trinity. Unbeknownst to Deland, Frank had signed up to be the assistant coach for his basketball team. No matter what had gone down at the house, Deland would have to sit silently in the front seat of Frank's beat-up Chrysler all the way home from practice or to a game. Deland's closest friends, Tony and Brian, knew what was going on and they could always tell Frank had started something again when Deland walked into the gym with a look in his eyes like he wanted to light the whole building on fire.

"This guy's a fucking menace," he would mutter as he dropped his bag. "I don't wanna be here." Hours after watching Frank kick down a door or pull his mom by the hair, he'd have to treat him like an authority figure and give him respect.

As a coach, Frank was volatile, just like at home, but in different ways. The boys were too young to understand the effects various sub-stances might have on adults, but they knew some days Frank was drunk or high. Just not altogether there. "Man, that guy is on *something*," they'd say to each other. On those days Frank was extra tough on Deland. All the other kids could see it, but no one could do anything about it. The head coach knew Frank's relationship with Adelle and took a hands-off approach to coaching Deland. Some days Deland wanted to swing on

Frank but was too afraid, so instead he would act out in practice, goofing off to avoid treating Frank with respect. The winter dragged on. Deland's safe space in school was no longer safe.

That January of 1986, Deland sat with his classmates and watched in horror as NASA's space shuttle *Challenger* exploded live on television just seventy-three seconds into its flight, killing all seven crew members on board. Media attention for the launch had been especially high because of enthusiasm for the journey of schoolteacher Christa McAuliffe, who had beaten out more than eleven thousand other applicants to be part of President Ronald Reagan's new Teacher in Space Project. Teachers across the United States had spent the year leading up to the launch incorporating NASA-developed lesson plans into their classrooms, and McAuliffe's planned in-flight lessons were scheduled to be broadcast from space to nearly every public television station across the country. Deland and the rest of the students at Holy Trinity were among the estimated 2.5 million kids watching that day at school as the *Challenger* exploded.

There was disbelief, grief, and even anger. Teachers and students alike cried as they watched the coverage of the disaster. Deland couldn't tell if he was horrified or comforted by the fact that the rest of the world felt as out of control as he did.

Frank coached Deland's basketball team his eighth-grade season as well, and Deland found it harder by the day to concentrate in practice. He finally said something to Adelle, mumbling, "I don't want to play basketball anymore if Frank's coaching." She went to one of the practices to see for herself, standing behind a bleacher so Frank and the kids couldn't see her. It was clear that Frank was laying into Deland for every mistake while letting the other boys slide.

Whatever she had going on with Frank was her problem; she didn't ever want him to take it out on her kids. She told Frank after practice that it was time to step aside. She was willing to deal with whatever the fallout might be if it meant giving Deland back a precious safe space.

Just a few months later, Adelle broke things off with Frank. Between the abuse, the drugs, and Deland's complaints, she decided it was time to give up on this particular reclamation project. *Not everyone can be saved*, she thought. *At least not by me.* This time Damon and Deland thought it would actually stick. Frank was out of the house for a few weeks and Adelle even started going on a few dates with a new guy—somebody Damon would later describe as a "low-budget Dolomite." Adelle thought he dressed so fly, but Damon saw the guy as utterly swagless. Tiny— looked like he weighed about ninety pounds—with a perm so dry it looked like the ends of his Afro might snap off.

Damon just called him Dry Perm, but his name was Greg Price and he worked at the mortuary over in New Castle, Pennsylvania. One night Damon was in the kitchen with Adelle and Dry Perm when they heard a car pull into the driveway, the unmistakable sound of rattling and hissing getting louder as it neared the garage: Frank's Chrysler with the busted muffler. Damon knew things were about to get bad. "Tell him to go out the back door," he said to his mom, nodding at Dry Perm. But Adelle pretended she couldn't see what was coming. She kept on washing dishes and didn't say a thing.

Frank skipped knocking and came straight through the front door. When Adelle protested, Dry Perm foolishly tried to play man of the house, charging at Frank. He was immediately thrown back onto the dining room table. They wrestled on the table until it collapsed under them, Damon screaming for Adelle to do something. After a bit of a struggle, Frank jumped up and ran out of the house, hustling to his car and peeling away. It took a minute for Damon to realize that Dry Perm had a knife in his back. He saw the broken-off handle on the dining room floor next to the busted table, then saw the point of it lodged between Dry Perm's shoulders. It was one of Adelle's paring knives from the kitchen; Dry Perm had grabbed it when he charged Frank, but with all the adrenaline pumping through him, he didn't even realize he'd been stabbed.

Damon winced as he pulled the knife out of Dry Perm's back. "My man," he said. "You need to go to the hospital."

Damon thought maybe Adelle secretly enjoyed the idea of men fighting over her, but in truth Adelle hadn't stepped in because she saw an easy way to avoid having a conversation with Dry Perm about ending things. Adelle had found out Dry Perm was addicted to embalming fluid—had been stealing it from the mortuary—and she was more than happy to be done with that mess. No vulnerable one-on-one chat or emotional back-and-forth required if Frank could just take care of things and scare him off.

Frank had come to the house because he'd secretly been trying to win Adelle back. He had been calling her at work and showering her with affection, and his sweet behavior reminded her of when they first met. Despite the dustup with Dry Perm, she was beginning to wonder if she'd made the right decision giving up on Frank. His kindness made her believe, once again, that he could change. As is common in abusive relationships, Adelle had become conditioned to seek out the moments of positivity that broke up the times of conflict—a pattern called intermittent reinforcement. Adelle knew their relationship was toxic, but somehow it felt safer going back to the flawed man she knew than it did to go looking for new love. She was afraid to find out if she could be loved well and loved fully for who she was.

"Emotionally, we crave what we know," writes Dr. Mariel Buqué in her book, *Break the Cycle: A Guide to Healing Intergenerational Trauma.* "We crave the familiar: familiar people, familiar patterns, familiar behaviors. Even when the familiar is something that hurts us, we gravitate toward it. We repeat it. That's why many of us stay in dysfunction. We stay tied to family bonds that, albeit hurtful, can feel comforting because they are predictable and keep us from facing uncertainty."

As renowned author and psychotherapist Virginia Satir famously put it, "People prefer the certainty of misery to the misery of uncertainty."

Family systems and emotional DNA can tell us not only to keep quiet about traumatic situations but to stay in them too. People can even begin to associate trauma with love, or abuse with connection. Canadian neuropsychologist Donald Hebb coined the phrase "neurons that fire together, wire together." If an experience is repeated over and over, the brain learns to make a shortcut, grouping neurons together into a network and triggering them all at the same time when the experience happens again. In tragic instances where feelings of love are accompanied by abuse, eventually the brain fires feelings of connection and care right alongside feelings of fear and anger. Children who grew up in a volatile household or who established insecure attachments to loved ones might recognize and feel comfortable in destabilized relationships. They may even seek out relationships later in life that feature the highs and lows of intermittent reinforcement.

When Frank showed up that night, Adelle saw a way out of her new relationship and a way back into the one that felt most familiar. And so it was that Frank moved back in. He took the sweatshirt Dry Perm left at the house into the backyard and lit it on fire. Damon and Deland never saw Dry Perm again.

Damon and Deland

CHAPTER 7

In the summer of 1987, Deland was getting ready to start classes as a freshman at Campbell Memorial High School when the family moved again. Turned out their house on Montgomery Avenue wasn't technically in the Campbell school district—just the backyard was. In order to avoid Deland being removed from the school, they moved two blocks over to an old two-bedroom, one-bathroom house built halfway up a sloping hill—26 Morley Avenue. If you placed a marble in the middle of the street outside their house it would roll down Morley less than a quarter of a mile to Youngstown Pipe & Steel, one of the few factories that hadn't completely closed up shop in the years after Black Monday.

As Deland settled into yet another new house, Damon was preparing to leave. An excellent student and a standout football player, Damon had been recruited by football coaches across the country, including several Ivy League universities, but a financial and academic opportunity had set him on another path. He earned a scholarship through a program started by Cleveland's first Black mayor, Carl Stokes, and was accepted into a prestigious cooperative education program with the Central Intelligence Agency at Northeastern University in Boston. The program combined classroom study with real-life professional experience, allowing Damon to be paid a salary for his CIA work while also getting a free college education.

For most of its nearly hundred-year history, Northeastern had been a local commuter school with a predominantly white, male student population, but it began diversifying in the 1960s, recruiting more women,

people of color, and foreign students, and expanding in size and enrollment. By the time Damon applied it was one of the largest private universities in the country. He would be studying with classmates from all
over the world and living in the heart of Boston, about a ten-minute
walk from Fenway Park. Adelle was so proud she was practically floating
for the whole week after he got accepted. No matter what they'd been
through, her boy had made it. She took great pride in how tough she was
on her sons and how hard she'd worked to get them a good education.
She'd miss Damon, but this was what she'd always hoped for—he'd be
so far away she'd have to take a plane to see him.

Damon wasn't just far away geographically; his new life felt like a
whole different world. He started getting briefings from the CIA in the
weeks before he left for Northeastern and got right to work when he got
to Boston. He worried about Adelle and Deland—especially when one
or the other would call him in distress—but he was more than ready to
move on from Youngstown.

Meanwhile, Deland was a high school freshman but just 115 pounds
soaking wet. He still felt like a little boy at home, where Frank and Adelle's
fighting escalated without Damon around to mediate.

If he could have, Deland would have stayed up in his bedroom all day
every day to avoid interacting with Frank, but 26 Morley was a uniquely
designed house, built straight up and down on a long, narrow lot. The
only bathroom was in the basement, so any time Deland wanted to use
the toilet, take a shower, or brush his teeth, he'd have to run the risk of
passing Frank on the stairs or in the kitchen, or accidentally waking him
up after he passed out on the couch watching TV. Deland wasn't afraid of
what Frank would do to him; he just couldn't stand the sight of him. Frank
never got physical with the boys. As is the case with so many situations of
intimate-partner violence, the abuse wasn't about anger or a temper that
Frank couldn't control, it was about power. Power over Adelle.

One night as another argument raged, Adelle yelled at Deland to come
downstairs from his room. "Come on!" she said, pushing Deland toward

the front door. "Get in the car!" she yelled as she pushed him toward the driver's side and ran toward the passenger side.

"I ain't never drove!" fifteen-year-old Deland yelled as he tried to start the car. "Faster!" she said, as he backed down the narrow gravel driveway, trying to avoid the mailbox and the fire hydrant. He never did learn why she couldn't drive that night, or why they needed to get out of there so fast. Years later he could almost chuckle about that being the first time he ever drove a car, but only because he didn't wreck it or hurt anybody.

Another night, Deland had already been kept awake for hours by the sound of Adelle and Frank fighting when he heard their back-and-forth get more and more hysterical. Suddenly he heard Adelle calling for him to come downstairs. It must have been three o'clock in the morning.

It's late. I've got school tomorrow, Deland thought, but he knew it was pointless. He'd never had any say-so with his mom. He went down to the living room and Adelle pulled him next to her so they were both facing Frank.

"You won't do that in front of my son," Adelle said, defiantly. "You won't do that while he's here."

But Frank would. And Frank did.

Deland knew the noise a fist could make hitting a person, but actually seeing it up close was enough to shock even a boy who had gotten all too used to violence. He was stunned stiff. Frozen. Frank shoved Adelle down to the ground and punched her. Was it once? Several times? Deland already couldn't remember. The only thing he knew for sure, the only thing he'd never be able to forget, was that he had done nothing. Couldn't move his legs, couldn't move his arms, couldn't even feel that he had legs and arms.

Adelle crawled over and stood up behind him, using him as a shield. He wanted to raise up his fists or yell something. Yell *anything*. He didn't, though. He didn't do or say anything. He just bowed his head, looked at the carpet, and prayed it would end.

Deland was ashamed, once again, by his own inaction. By the fear that kept him from stopping Frank. Ashamed of himself as he went back upstairs and tried to force his way back to sleep. Ashamed of himself the next morning as he avoided making eye contact while passing Frank on the stairs. He decided right then and there that even if he wasn't strong enough to fight back, he'd at least be strong enough to never repeat what he'd just seen in his own relationships. He'd spent enough hours listening to them argue about nothing, accomplish nothing, solve nothing. And now they had put a kid in the middle of that shit. He wasn't gonna be like that. Never ever.

Meantime, Adelle was still thinking she could fix Frank. Save him. Damon was convinced it was the result of her upbringing, coming from a family of devout Christians. While Adelle's attendance at Shiloh Baptist had lapsed as the boys got older, she was still deeply spiritual.

"Everybody is a reclamation project," Damon would tell Deland whenever Adelle would welcome Frank back into the house. "It's the savior complex Christians have. I'm gonna save you, 'cause if I don't save you I'm failing in my Christian spirit."

Adelle could see a light in Frank and she was convinced that if she gave him love, it would get bigger and brighter, drowning out all that darkness. Unfortunately, her faith in God and in all the people God created kept her from giving up on Frank sooner. Not until after he'd stolen some of her light.

Deland had passed Damon in height a few years earlier, but he was still quite skinny and hadn't found any confidence at home. He would soon find it in football. Despite its bruising, unforgiving nature, there was a peacefulness to football that felt healing to him. A chance to control what happened to him and around him. An opportunity to replay moments of inaction at home with a different ending. On the field, he always hit back.

Years later he would learn about a therapeutic intervention called family constellation therapy, in which individuals role-play family interactions with a neutral group to practice confrontations or address past trauma in a safe environment. He didn't know it as a kid, but what happened on the football field mirrored some elements of that therapy. On the football field Deland had a feeling of power and confidence that he could never muster around Frank. He stood up for himself and his teammates. He wanted more of that.

Football was also a meritocracy. Deland could prove himself worthy with statistics. Who could doubt him if the numbers told a story of his greatness, right there in black and white? Who could question him when they watched with their own eyes as he streaked across the field, leaving the other team's players in his wake? On the football field, Deland was in charge.

Sophomore year he looked around at all the bigger, stronger, faster guys on the team and a light went off in his head: if he was gonna be somebody, he needed to outwork everybody. *I'm going to be the hardest worker on the team,* he repeated to himself over and over until it was true. He created new family messaging, a new strand of emotional DNA. In Deland's mind, he came from a long line of hard workers. His birth mom and dad, his grandparents, everyone who came before him, they were all the hardest-working people in every room. Who could tell him different? It was decided. *You make the choice,* he heard in his head.

Deland's work ethic became legendary—not just with his coach, Ed Rozum, but with his teammates too. Whether it was drills, wind sprints, lifting sessions, or scrimmages, he was going full speed, giving 100 percent. In the beginning some guys gave him sideways glances or groaned at how his effort made clear that they were loafing. Even his close friends like Steve didn't get it at first.

You're in a small town; why set the bar so high? they thought. *It's not as though you're gonna get recognized, like in a big conference.* Steve couldn't figure out why Deland saw something bigger for himself than the other guys in Youngstown. While everyone else looked around and believed their circumstances defined their opportunities, Deland was determined to do more. All his life he'd felt doubted and overlooked; he became obsessed with the idea of earning respect and attention.

For a few years now a local Youngstown guy had been making head-lines in the *Vindicator* for starring in a big-time TV show. The guy was named Ed O'Neill. He went to nearby Ursuline High and played football at Youngstown State. Now he was on a new network called Fox every Sun-day night starring as Al Bundy in *Married . . . with Children*. Football had gotten O'Neill out of Youngstown and all the way to Hollywood. Football was gonna take Deland somewhere too, he decided. He was gonna make it happen. He was gonna be almost militant in his approach to football.

After a while Steve started to see Deland's point of view as noble. Al-most radical. He figured the militant approach must have been something Deland learned from Adelle. No denying she was tough. And maybe a lit-tle bit of influence from one of Deland's favorite rap groups, Public Enemy. If Deland had to tell himself he was public enemy number 1 and that ev-eryone doubted him, so be it. It made him work.

It didn't take long for the rest of the team to join Steve and give Deland respect instead of eye rolls. They realized he truly believed he was gonna be something. That was rare in Youngstown. They started to believe he'd be something too. Starting then and continuing for years after, people around Campbell Memorial would talk about what a beast Deland was in practice.

As he got more confident, Deland also got more frustrated by the family's financial issues. He knew Adelle was doing her best, but he was out of luck if he wanted to take a girl out to the movies or buy a pair of football cleats, the new colored Levi's or a Starter jacket. Those Run-D.M.C. guys had it right:

P-p-p-prices go up, don't let your pocket go down,
When you got short money you're stuck on the ground

Like in most high schools, kids who didn't have the right clothes or the latest styles were likely to be made fun of. Deland was acutely aware of not having the resources he needed to fit in and avoid ridicule. And just like when he was a kid, he failed to self-regulate in the face of need and want. The summer before his sophomore year, he stole a pair of Levi's jeans from Family Dollar. Then a pair of Bugle Boy pants from the mall. He was nervous and embarrassed but escaped undetected both times, faring better than in his failed G.I. Joe caper. He didn't want to take the stuff but he was getting taller and stronger and had a heightened awareness of how he was being perceived at school. He just couldn't stand how it felt to be mocked. The need to quiet that feeling was stronger than the guilt of doing something he knew was wrong.

He dreaded asking Adelle for anything when money was extra tight, so he decided it was time to get a real job, not just a paper route or odd jobs around the neighborhood. After his sophomore football season ended, his friend helped him get hired at the Kentucky Fried Chicken on McCartney in East Youngstown. A few weeks later he helped Tony get a job there too. Most nights they'd ride there together in Tony's car. After a few weeks Deland figured out a side hustle, selling leftover chicken after hours to friends or even bringing it to school the next day to sell at a discounted price. Health codes wouldn't let the restaurant keep it, so instead of throwing it out he'd sneak it into a bag and make some extra cash. Deland put in the same effort at KFC as he did on the football field, working as many hours as he could.

Just like the paper route, it felt good to make his own money and get out of the house, but it wasn't long before Deland saw a bunch of his high school friends really living large and started to question if his KFC gig was enough. His friend Steve dressed really nicely, was wearing gold chains to school, and was always riding around town in his flashy drop-top truck or his brand-new, universally coveted Honda Elite 80 scooter. Steve was the guy Deland wanted to be. Charismatic, good athlete, parents who were still married, and a connected family around town. Deland knew Steve got most of his nice clothes and jewelry from selling weed, and he wanted in.

Unfortunately, Adelle had made such a name for herself when she was selling, local guys didn't want anything to do with Deland. He couldn't believe it, but Campbell's toughest weed dealers were terrified of five-foot-two Adelle. On multiple occasions over his sophomore and junior years, Deland went to the store at the Campbell projects and tried to get in the mix, but he'd always hear some variation of "Man, I ain't *tryin'* to hear your mother's mouth."

Some might call it fear. Adelle would call it respect.

Both Steve and Brian were hustlers, but they were surprisingly good examples for Deland when it came to their generosity and friendship. Brian had a job at the country club and sold weed on the side, making enough money to treat Deland to meals at the mall or give him some cash whenever he'd see him out. And when Deland and Tony weren't working the same shift, Steve would pick up Deland from KFC and drive him home or take him out. A lot of Deland's friends believed that he was on a different path than them. Something bigger. They did their best to keep him out of trouble and get him where he was going, wherever that was.

Though he was frustrated at the time, Deland would later see all those thwarted opportunities to make money as not just a coincidence but the work of something bigger than him. A higher power. He wasn't sure he believed in guardian angels, but he couldn't deny how many people had stepped into his life and pulled him out of the way of danger or pushed him into a good opportunity. He managed to stay on the straight and narrow while friends like Steve later landed in jail. For Deland, every guardian angel—even Steve himself—was there to set him straight. Every dodged bullet, literal and figurative, was a blessing.

Deland, Adelle, and Damon

CHAPTER 8

Frank was still living at the house on Morley in December 1988 when Adelle made up her mind she was done with him again. A few days earlier, Adelle's half brother Ben, an insurance salesman, had gone to a house on a sales call. During their small talk the older couple that lived there told him excitedly about their daughter getting married . . . to a man named Frank Doon. Not only was Frank sneaking around with a coworker when he went to work nights as a maintenance technician at the post office, he was actually going to marry her.

And in just a few weeks! Adelle was heartbroken.

On January 7, 1989, Frank and Laura Dorsey were married, but Frank was still stuck on Adelle. He showed up at the Morley house one night soon after the wedding, and to this day Adelle doesn't know what his plan was—be married and have her too?—but she was determined not to let him in. He continued to try to court Adelle for years, including one time putting a bunch of his clothes back in the closet and settling in while Adelle was at work. She called the police on him. If he wasn't happy at home, that was his problem. She didn't throw pity parties for herself, and she sure wasn't gonna attend his.

Deland found more peace at home and at school now that Frank was finally out of the house, but he still relied on Damon for advice, calling him often at college. They never had a working phone at the house on Morley, so every time Deland wanted to make a call he'd walk to a pay phone at a gas station across Wilson Avenue, the main drag a few streets away.

Damon would be at his fraternity house and get a call: "Damon, telephone. It's your brother."

"Man, you'll never believe what Ma did," Deland would start in.

An hour after he'd hung up the phone: "Damon, phone. It's your mother."

"I'mma kill your brother," Adelle would say, calling from work to launch into her latest complaint.

Damon came home to visit when he could, avoiding the drama at Morley whenever possible and spending a lot of time with Adelle's youngest brother, Yub, a close confidant and mentor for him. Now that Damon was working for the CIA he tried to keep a low profile when he came back to Youngstown. There were too many bad people doing too many bad things, and he didn't want to end up in the wrong place at the wrong time. He'd gotten out and he wanted to stay out.

During one visit back during his sophomore year of college, Damon was driving to Uncle Yub's and saw cars lined up and down the block at the funeral home. Yub told him it was the service for Freddie Harris, the fantastic singer, keyboard player, and regular organist for the New Bethel Baptist Church, a sort of local genius when it came to music. Freddie played with the Sensational Six out of Memphis on albums like *I've Been Singing So Long,* and his own band, Freddie Harris and the N.G.'s, released the gospel albums *I Believe in Miracles* and *Reach Out and Touch.* When acts came to town a lot of them would have Freddie play with them, including funk band the Ohio Players, famous for their hit songs "Fire" and "Love Rollercoaster."

Damon had taken some piano lessons from Freddie as a kid and remembered Adelle telling him that she and Freddie had dated back in the day. Freddie popped by every once in a while over the years and lent Adelle his car for a while one summer. In fact, just before Damon left for college, Freddie had invited him to get a drink at the local VFW to impart all sorts of wisdom about going off into the world and becoming a man. Damon went by the house on Morley later that day and asked his mom if she'd heard about Freddie passing.

"Freddie Harris?" Adelle said, distraught. She hadn't heard.

"We just spoke . . ." she said softly, trailing off. She paused, then looked up at him. "You know Freddie was your real father."

For years Adelle hadn't been sure she'd ever tell Damon about his dad.

She'd wanted to say something, felt burned up inside about holding it in, but he was young and she felt it was easier to let him keep believing A.C. was his biological dad. A.C. was on the birth certificate, after all.

Adelle and Freddie had recently reconnected and decided Damon was old enough to be told the truth, but now they wouldn't get the chance. Freddie had been found dead in his apartment—the newspapers said it was natural causes due to his asthma. He and Adelle never got to tell Damon, and here he was, learning too late.

Adelle always felt her lies about Freddie and A.C. were in service of a greater good. Her family had always said a baby was a blessing, no matter how it came to you. Besides, it was an easier story to tell. The truth was stickier: She had been in college at Central State when she slipped and hit her head on the stairs in the cafeteria and passed out. At the hospital she heard the nurse tell the doctor they couldn't do X-rays because she was pregnant. She'd been seeing Freddie whenever she visited back home, and when she called to tell him they were pregnant he sheepishly admitted that he was married. Adelle was furious. She told him she was immediately going to find his wife and tell her. Freddie talked her into meeting with both him and his wife, Bootsy, at the Buckeye Elks Lodge, and the three of them decided together that they wouldn't tell anyone that Freddie was the father.

By the time she was seven months pregnant, Adelle realized she had to drop out of school, and even worse, she realized it was time to tell her mother. She was shocked to hear Maretta suggest they arrange for an abortion. "Seven months, Ma!" she said. Maretta realized she was speaking out of fear and anger. Maretta had tried so hard to protect Adelle, but her wild child had gone and gotten herself in a mess all the same. Maretta was also embarrassed about the public optics of a young daughter pregnant out of wedlock. What would everyone at church say? Many young women of the time were sent away to a maternity home for single mothers or a Catholic adoption center, kept away from school and the community to hide their pregnancies. Maretta let her stay in Youngstown but suggested she stay home and avoid church and other social gatherings to limit the number of people who might learn (and gossip) about her pregnancy. She also recommended Adelle be honest about the baby with her high school sweetheart A.C. Adelle and A.C. had been communicating via letters while he served in Germany. He didn't know she'd been seeing Freddie until she revealed the pregnancy.

Damon was born on November 3, 1968. When A.C. got home less than a month later, they sat on the porch and talked through what they would do next.

A.C. wanted to be with her, wanted to marry her, and said he'd be willing to put his name on Damon's birth certificate so he wouldn't have a blank space where a father should be. An attorney said that since Damon was still so young, they could tell the courts A.C. was the father. And so it was that Damon's birth certificate read Damon Charles McCullough.

Having a child out of wedlock earned Adelle plenty of criticism from those in her inner circle. No one knew Freddie was the father, but they knew Adelle got pregnant before A.C. returned home from overseas and they knew she had the baby before she got married. *Everybody's a Christian until you actually need some unconditional love*, Adelle thought. *Then all you get is judgment.* The idea of giving grace is certainly easier than the reality of it. Adelle realized the people in her support system weren't going to be the loving Christians they claimed to be, so she'd just have to rely on herself. And after A.C. and John left, she only got more independent. If she was gonna get let down, it was gonna be by herself, not anyone else. Expect nothing from others and you'll never be disappointed. But she also wasn't gonna let folks fake being high-and-mighty—she would expose them as hypocrites any chance she got.

It would have been healthier for Adelle to forgive them and their judgments, or at the very least find a way to move on, but she couldn't get past the pain folks had caused by turning their backs on her. *If they're gonna be phony and pretend to be good, I won't even pretend. I'm just gonna be me*, she decided. She was doing the best she could and they vilified her? Well, if they wanted a villain, she could be one.

Of course, Adelle didn't tell Damon all that. Didn't tell him Freddie was married or the agreement they'd made with Bootsy either. Adelle just told Damon she'd needed to hide the pregnancy because it was out of wedlock and that when she started dating A.C. they had added him to the birth certificate. Also told him that his middle name, Charles, came from his dad, Freddie Charles Harris. Another name he'd carried for a man who wasn't there.

Damon went quiet for a while. He remembered the times he'd spent with Freddie and the bond they'd formed over music. How Freddie had taken a particular interest in Damon singing and performing with the Chosen Generation. How Freddie hadn't wanted to claim him but had wanted to be in his life. He thought about how talented and successful his dad was and wondered what kind of relationship they might have had if he'd known years earlier, while Freddie was still alive. He immediately pushed those thoughts away. He'd never had a father who was present, so why ask questions about the one who just passed? Adelle wouldn't have wanted to answer them, anyway. Damon knew she just didn't talk about that sort of thing.

By the time Damon had driven the nearly ten hours back to Northeastern he finally let himself feel the impact of what he'd just learned. He bought a bottle of Captain Morgan rum, and when he got to his room he sat down to pour himself an alcoholic drink for the very first time. As he sipped on his rum and Coke, he sorted through his feelings. He laughed through tears at the way he'd grown up thinking he saw himself in A.C. How he always used to say he and A.C. had the same smile. What a joke! It would be funny if it weren't so humiliating. His face got hot thinking about how Adelle had known it wasn't true every time he said it but hadn't said anything. He was embarrassed for a moment, but it passed. He couldn't stay mad. He knew Adelle had always done what she thought was best for him. And he knew how hurt Adelle had been by A.C.'s decision to abandon them. A.C. had chosen to start a life with Adelle and a child that wasn't his own—eventually two children that weren't his own!—only to change his mind, changing all their lives forever. Adelle had been through a lot. He didn't want to add to that by being angry.

As he continued to pour through his memories he realized he was happy to be Freddie's son, proud to be Freddie's son. And he saw his childhood differently now. It still hurt that A.C. had signed his birth certificate and claimed him only to abandon him, but it hurt less knowing he wasn't his blood. Damon wasn't mad at Freddie or A.C. or anyone else; in fact, he felt like maybe it was just his turn to get some sort of tough news. Felt like everyone around him in Youngstown had *something*, this was his. Deland was adopted and, in a way, so was he. Turned out they both had birth fathers who didn't choose them or want them and they both had an "adoptive" father who claimed to want them but left. Damon decided he'd have to be okay with that.

Freddie was the man with whom he shared DNA, and A.C. was the man with whom he shared a last name. Neither had been a father to him. And he was grown now anyway, so it didn't much matter anymore. Feeling sorry for the years he lost with Freddie would be playing the victim. No pity parties, just keep it moving. *I had a beautiful childhood*, Damon thought. *I had a lot of support. So many others got it so much worse. Who cares about my "real" father? Or any father? What's a father anyway?* He would push through the pain and embrace the lesson: unlike his two missing fathers, he would be present for his own kids one day.

He started to think about a time years earlier—he was about ten, Deland was six. They'd spent a few days talking about this new guy Adelle had gotten serious with, John Comer. How he didn't seem all that. How he'd better not try to act like he was their dad. Sitting next to each other in church at Shiloh Baptist, the boys listened as the pastor asked if anyone desired to come up and be baptized, to give themselves to Jesus Christ. Without speaking, Damon and Deland looked at each other and locked eyes. They would do it. Adelle always told them they had a Heavenly Father, the only father that mattered. In that moment they wanted to profess their faith in that father. In that moment they felt connected by a force bigger than themselves. Bigger than the church building in which they stood. Bigger than any connection they could have felt with a human father, if they'd ever had one.

Deland didn't learn the truth about Damon and Freddie Harris for another dozen years, and only because Damon mentioned it to him in passing at a family function. He made an offhand remark about how he was basically adopted too, since A.C. wasn't his real dad. Deland was shocked. Why didn't Damon confide in him right when he found out? Why didn't he remember Adelle mourning Freddie's death? It stung for a minute, but then it made sense. Deland had always confided in and relied on Damon for support, but Damon had handled problems privately and independently. For most of Deland's childhood it felt like things affected him more deeply and more painfully than they did Damon. In a way he wasn't surprised that Damon had found a way to shrug off even the most shocking of news. Plus, neither A.C. nor Freddie had been there for Damon anyway, so what was the difference? What was a father, really? He and Damon had never needed one.

While Freddie died before he got the chance to tell Damon the truth, A.C. chose never to tell him. Damon never told A.C. he knew either. The two carried the secret separately despite staying in touch with the occasional phone call all the way up until A.C.'s death in 2023 at seventy-six years old—still the voice of WHOT. A.C.'s obituary mentioned his life partner, Amy, and their three children, plus Alex, the infant son with Adelle who preceded him in death. Neither Damon nor Deland was mentioned.

Deland and Sherman in the University of Miami locker room

CHAPTER 9

Adelle and Deland moved again at the end of the summer of 1990, just before his senior year at Memorial High. She told Deland she'd fallen behind on the rent at Morley and he didn't ask any questions, just packed up and got ready to go. The place they moved into was the roughest spot yet, 270 Jackson Street.

Adelle always called the rows of housing units built into the hillside on Jackson the "Sheet & Tube Quarters," but everyone else just knew them as an extension of the Campbell projects. Deland didn't mince words about the new place when he called Damon at school: "It's a dump, but it's home."

The buildings dated back to 1917, when Youngstown Sheet & Tube built employee housing in response to a workers strike that had culminated in a deadly riot on January 7, 1916. Steel manufacturers were thriving as the industry continued to grow, but steelworker wages hadn't gone up. Workers couldn't keep up with the cost of living and struggled to find living quarters in a busy market, so they demanded the factory provide affordable housing.

The Sheet & Tube Quarters, aka "Blackburn Plat" in Campbell, was one of four housing developments built by Youngstown Sheet & Tube and was specifically designed to house immigrant and African American workers. The April 11, 1918, issue of the *Engineering News-Record*, a weekly magazine for the construction industry, featured an article about the innovative new building style reflected in the project, remarking that "precast slabs, poured in a yard and erected by a traveler, are being used for the first time in this country to construct dwelling houses."

The Society of Architectural Historians noted not only the architectural novelty of the building units, but also how the project made workers even more beholden to their employer.

"Socially, the project reflects the early-twentieth-century corporate paternalism as industrialists attempted to quell worker unrest by providing improved living conditions," writes Rebecca M. Rogers. "While workers at the Campbell Works might have appreciated these improvements, which included indoor plumbing and electricity, company-owned rental housing bound them even more securely to Youngstown Sheet and Tube, which was now both employer and landlord."

Youngstown Sheet & Tube sold the houses in the 1940s, and over the years they became more and more dilapidated. Per a request from the Campbell Historical Society, they were declared a national historic site in 1982, even as families continued to live in them. Squatters, vandals, criminals, and abandoned units were common during Adelle and Deland's tenure there, but the folks who lived there full-time worked to fix up their homes as best they could. Deland remembered seeing inside his neighbor's unit once and marveling at the nice wood furniture and decor. Those same neighbors—a skinny old white man and a middle-aged Black woman who always seemed to be bickering—let Adelle and Deland run a big orange extension cord out the window and into their kitchen when Adelle couldn't afford to pay the electric bill.

Deland was never more aware of their financial struggles than at the Jackson house. When power came from the neighbors, the gas and hot water at their house wasn't turned on. In the mornings Adelle would wake up early and start heating Tupperware containers full of water in the microwave, walking them upstairs to the bathtub to get Deland enough bathwater to wash up for school. Deland's friends never said anything to him about the place, but he was embarrassed all the same when they'd pick him up for school or to go out on the weekends. Not only did he never have friends stay the night, he never even let anyone inside the house. He felt judged and embarrassed, and his embarrassment would mix with guilt whenever he thought about Adelle going up and down the stairs with those bowls of water. She was doing her best and Deland loved her for that.

The worst days were the days before a big rivalry game. The Campbell Memorial cheerleaders would go to the houses of all the football players and decorate their mailboxes and trees with streamers, then leave a big sign outside the front door: "Go Deland!" or "Beat the Wildcats!" Deland dreaded those days. He'd spent his whole life feeling doubted and disrespected, and where he lived was just another chance for him to feel less-than in the eyes of his classmates. No one ever actually gave him a hard time about it, but he could feel their pity, which was somehow even worse.

Deland and Adelle were borrowing electricity at Jackson but they did finally have a working phone, which would come in handy as Deland started receiving recruiting calls from college football coaches. Deland had been a solid football player in his junior year, starting as a defensive back most games, but senior year things really took off for him. He'd been a backup to a really excellent running back, Damien Dutton, for his whole high school career, and now Damien had graduated and moved on. Damien had been another guardian angel for Deland, picking him up from work, giving him free haircuts, and showing the type of toughness on the football field that Deland admired. Damien should have gone on to play at a big-time college, but everybody—including the college recruiters—had heard the rumors that he was selling weed. Deland knew about the rumors too. What he didn't know until a full year after they'd met was that Damien was his cousin, related through the Van Cobb side of the family. Youngstown could be like that—all sorts of families twisted together like braids, weaving into each other over here, separating and then weaving back together over there.

Deland admired Damien's play, so he never questioned the limited reps he got at the running back position or dreamed of being anything other than a solid backup. He had no idea just how good he could be until he was given the opportunity. When the minutes and carries came his way in his senior year, everything changed. Deland helped Campbell win its second straight Mahoning Valley Conference title and earned AP Division IV First Team honors for the Northeast district.

At one of the home games, one of his teammates said he spotted A.C. sitting on the opposite side of the stands. Deland just shrugged. He'd seen him. His "father" was over there supporting his wife's nephew, who played for archrival Warren JFK. *Yep, that's my "dad" over there cheering for the other team and pretending he don't know me,* he thought. Sometimes he resented seeing **McCULLOUGH** in big block letters on the back of his own jersey. *That name don't deserve the glory I'm gonna bring it,* he thought.

Adelle was a fixture at games on the correct side of the stadium, watching as Deland racked up 1,450 yards that year, leading his team to a 12-1 record. Adelle didn't have a car anymore, so one game when her ride didn't show up she rode Deland's moped to the game. He'd saved up his money working at KFC to buy the moped and be able to get to and from work and school on his own. Adelle hopped right on it, rode it over, and still had the helmet on when Deland spotted her up in the stands, cheering him on. "D-MACK!" she yelled every time he made a big play. "D-MACK!" Another game she stood on the field just past the end zone and yelled to Deland "Run to me! Run here!" the whole game as he made his way down the field, carry by carry. With every win and every score from Campbell's 5'10", 150-pound tailback, more college coaches perked up and more reporters raved about his feats. Deland had found a place to shine at Campbell Memorial Stadium. A second home. One where the lights were always on.

In one particularly memorable regional final game against Warren JFK, Deland had a state playoff-record four touchdowns to lead Campbell to a decisive 33–0 victory. The day after the game Deland was hanging out with Steve and his girlfriend, Anna, who had brought along her niece, Cassie. Anna had graduated high school a few years earlier, while Cassie was a junior at the time, going to high school in Youngstown. Steve started reading aloud from the local newspaper about Deland's big game, hyping him up and hoping to spark some interest from Cassie. It worked. Deland and Cassie started dating that winter and fell hard for each other. She was the first serious girlfriend Deland had, and the first girl he ever said "I love you" to.

Things started off great with Cassie. A Puerto Rican girl with caramel-colored skin and bodacious curves, she was beautiful and she knew it. She was a flirt and had a pretty domineering personality, but Deland was used to that—almost drawn to that—because of Adelle. It felt comfortable to be around a woman who took charge and had a lot to say. Cassie really liked Deland, but she struggled with jealousy. A previous boyfriend had cheated on her and she was constantly checking in on Deland to make sure he wasn't stepping out. Cassie's family moved midway through the school year, and she spent the second semester of her junior year at Campbell Memorial. Being at the same school as Deland helped assuage her worries somewhat, and also made it easier for her to keep an eye on him.

Deland and his friends soon came to learn that Cassie's jealousy wasn't just about the ex-boyfriend. As is often the case, the ones most worried about being cheated on just might be doing the cheating themselves. Tony went to a different high school and didn't see Deland and Cassie together often, but what he did see he didn't like. He told Deland he worried about how Cassie stressed him out and pulled him away from his oldest friends. He warned him about rumors of her flirty behavior with other guys. When Deland told Cassie about Tony's concerns, it only made her more controlling—and less trusting of Tony. Cassie was most comfortable around Anna and Steve, so the three of them and Deland became a nearly inseparable quartet. Tony and some of Deland's other friends took a back seat, spending less and less time with him.

Whenever Deland and Cassie talked about the following year, when he'd be gone and she'd still be in high school, Deland always pictured himself in the Navy. The thought of Deland joining the military instead of going to college infuriated Adelle, but she couldn't afford to pay for college and his grades would never earn him an academic scholarship—

in fact he'd been forced to sit out the track season his junior year because he was academically ineligible. He hadn't seen the field enough in his first few years of football to consider an athletic scholarship a possibility, though he did score well enough on his SATs to qualify. In fact, his score was so surprising that Coach Rozum pulled him out of class when he heard about it, grabbing him by the shoulders and enthusiastically telling him, "Do you know what this means? You're eligible! You can get a football scholarship!" The thought of playing at the next level was thrilling, but didn't seem realistic to Deland.

He had always been seen as a middle-of-the-pack guy on the football team, but over time his tremendous work ethic unlocked a talent that started to earn him some attention. He wasn't getting the recruiting letters and calls that had started for Damon early in his junior season, though, so he still believed the Navy was the most realistic next step. And, more importantly, the best way out of Youngstown. He assured Cassie they'd still be together and see each other as often as they could.

As Deland's fantastic senior season was winding down, recruiting calls started ramping up and he realized he'd have a lot of options outside the military. He had sent handwritten letters to schools like Butler and the University of Indianapolis in the spring of his junior year and hadn't gotten much of a response, but things had changed. One night, Jim Tressel was on the line to talk about his Youngstown State Penguins; the next, Gerry Faust was calling to see if Deland had thought about becoming an Akron Zip. Then the home visits began. If Deland thought it was embarrassing when the cheerleaders decorated the outside of Jackson, having a big-time college coach in the living room was a new level of mortification.

Whether Adelle spoke to them in person or on the phone, she made sure to grill all the coaches about the expectations they had for players in the classroom. She asked them what grade-point average a player would have to dip below in order to lose his scholarship. If they went too low—2.3, 2.1, 1.8—that was that. "You're not going to that college," she'd tell Deland. "Football is not gonna care if anything happens to you. This is a business. You're a commodity to them. Nothing is promised, so you get an education."

Deland wasn't sure where he wanted to play until November, when a visit from the Miami University running backs coach changed everything. Deland was sitting in sixth-period English class when his eyes were drawn out the window to a cherry-apple-red Mercedes, pimped out with gold rims. He caught the attention of a few friends and pointed outside. None of them could take their eyes off the car. A tall man climbed out and disappeared into the school. A few minutes later an administrator came to class with a pink slip calling for Deland to go to the front office. The man from the car was there, his back to the door, and when he turned around to meet Deland's gaze, the moment felt almost cinematic. This man had an energy and presence like no one Deland had ever met in Youngstown. He stretched out a giant hand to shake. "I'm Sherman Smith, the running backs coach for Miami University in Oxford, Ohio."

When Sherman got to talking, Deland understood why he had such an aura about him: he was an NFL star. Tall, broad-shouldered, and charismatic, he had a swagger that Deland soon learned came from years of success in the pros. Turned out Sherman had grown up in Youngstown too and had excelled as a quarterback at North High School before going on to have great success at Miami University. He was drafted to the pros as a wide receiver, but the Seahawks immediately turned him into a running back. He spent eight seasons in Seattle and San Diego, earning the nickname "The Tank," after the Sherman Tank, due to his punishing running style. At 6'4", 225 pounds, he was a big rusher and tough to bring down. He spent a few years coaching at a Seattle high school before getting the call to lead the running back group at his alma mater.

He hoped to convince Deland to follow in his footsteps and play football at Miami.

As for Deland, Sherman had heard he was a thin guy, but powerful. Ran like his hair was on fire. He knew firsthand that Youngstown guys were tough, but he'd heard from Deland's coaches that this kid was something extra special. Work ethic like you'd never seen. Could play multiple positions. Was gonna treat football like a job. When Sherman got to Campbell and talked to Deland, he saw that focus immediately. Yes, sir. No, sir. I'm ready to work, sir. More than anything, this kid wasn't looking for excuses not to make it—he was looking for reasons to succeed. That unparalleled work ethic reminded Sherman of his years playing ball. He was impressed.

Deland was nervous when Sherman came to the house on Jackson to meet Adelle, but there was no need. Sherman took it all in stride. No judgment when he heard they didn't have a car. No mention of the big orange cord snaking out the window. Didn't blink when he asked about Deland's family and learned he was adopted, being raised solo by Adelle. Sherman was a Youngstown guy—he understood. He charmed Deland's mother with his great manners, kindness, and charisma. Adelle noticed immediately that he wasn't just a good football player, he was educated too.

Sherman could see education was important to Adelle. She was a wise lady—and book-smart. He could tell she was focused on giving Deland the structure to succeed in school. He told the story of his own college recruitment, how he'd committed to Kent State because he had a good time there on his recruiting trip, not even thinking or asking about academics. A week later a coach from Miami came to his house and laid out an opportunity that wasn't just about football and a good time. Sherman learned he could go to a great university, be part of a great football program, and leave school capable in more than just sports. He called up Kent State and told them he'd changed his mind, he was going to Miami. Well, he sure sold Adelle with that. She knew he wasn't all about football; he cared about education too. And Sherman really had her when he made it clear that he'd watch out for Deland and be the kind of role model she could trust.

They didn't come across a lot of men like Coach Smith in Youngstown—especially a local boy done good like he did. For the first time in his life, Deland was meeting someone from his hometown who had actually achieved what he could only dream of.

A few days after Sherman's visit, another Youngstown native came to the house with big plans for Deland. Bob Stoops, then the defensive backs coach at Kansas State, was just starting what would become a Hall of Fame career in college coaching. Coach Stoops was one of six children in a football-crazed family, and everyone in Youngstown knew his dad, Ron, from his years of success as the defensive coordinator at Cardinal Mooney High School on the South Side. After playing for his dad, Stoops had gone on to become an all–Big Ten safety at Iowa and saw a lot of promise in Deland's play on the defensive side of the ball. The Kansas State program was bigger and more recognizable than Miami—even a recent string of bad seasons wouldn't keep most guys in Deland's shoes from jumping at the chance to be a Wildcat— but Deland really wanted to try to make it as a running back. He decided to go visit the Miami campus before making his decision.

Because Adelle didn't have a car, Sherman drove back to Youngstown over Christmas break to take Deland and his mom to Oxford for an official recruiting trip. Most of the students were home for the holidays but a few teammates were around to meet recruits, including Deland's host for the weekend, Milt Stegall, a junior wide receiver out of Cincinnati who would go on to play three years in the NFL and fourteen in the Canadian Football League (CFL). Deland met with the head coach of the RedHawks (then known as the Redskins), Randy Walker, a young, hard-nosed guy who was early on in his first opportunity as a head coach. Deland liked him and the rest of the coaches he met. He loved the campus, he loved the facilities, and most of all he loved the idea of getting the hell out of Youngstown—even if he was just escaping to the other end of Ohio.

As they toured the campus, Adelle snapped photos of everything. Deland in front of the Miami University sign. Snap! Deland meeting Coach Walker in his office, giving a firm handshake. Snap! Deland in the RedHawks weight room, looking serious as he stood next to a row of weights. Snap! Deland smiling in front of the bright red lockers in the locker room, standing next to Sherman, nattily clad in tinted glasses and a black jacket over a striped wool sweater. Snap! Snap! Snap!

When they got home and Deland told Adelle he intended to go to Miami, she was beside herself. Deland was going to college! And on a full football scholarship to boot! Deland couldn't believe how far the game had taken him. Something that started out as an escape, a chance at some moments of peace, had given him so much more. Football had motivated Deland. Football had made him believe in himself—and proved to him that others could believe in him too. Football had provided an opportunity Deland never could have dreamed of, and he was about to learn the power of an opportunity.

That is, of course, if he could manage to graduate from high school.

Deland posing before prom

CHAPTER 10

Psychology was hanging over Deland's head. French was hanging over Deland's head. Physics! Oh man, was physics hanging over Deland's head. He was going to have to work hard to earn the required NCAA GPA to enroll at Miami. He'd never been a particularly invested student, so trying to find focus his senior year, one foot out the door, was a big ask, especially with Cassie demanding they spend as much time together as possible during his last few months in Youngstown. And, of course, there was the prom to think about. Everyone was talking about the prom.

Coach Smith was back at school in February on Signing Day and Deland inked his name on the commitment letter to Miami University with a shaking hand. The nerves were equal parts fear about keeping up his grades and excitement over just how real everything felt. It was a big deal to go to college, an even bigger deal to earn a scholarship. Coach Rozum snapped a photo as Adelle looked on, beaming, in her nicest dress and Sherman, sharp in a pair of perfectly creased khakis and a bright red sweater, vigorously shook Deland's hand. As he looked up at Sherman, Deland thought to himself, *I better not mess this up.*

Thankfully for Deland, another one of those guardian angels showed up: Tom Creed, a physics teacher and assistant coach for Campbell's basketball team. Creed could tell that Deland was struggling—not just in physics but at home too. He had always been one to ask students how they were doing and how things were with their family. He understood the plight of a lot of kids in Campbell and cared about more than just what happened inside the four walls of his classroom. Creed knew that a failing grade in physics might be the thing that kept Deland from going to college, and he couldn't live with that. He stayed after school for weeks to give Deland extra help.

"Deland, you can't give up," Creed said one day when Deland struggled with a particularly tough formula. "You're an object in motion headed to a bright future, and I'm not going to be the external force that stops you!" He waited for a laugh or an acknowledgment of his joke. Deland got the reference to Newton's first law but wasn't in the mood for a laugh—not until after he passed the class.

As word got around school that Deland would be going to Miami University, eyes widened. One teacher even said to his face, straight up, "You're never gonna make it at Miami." Deland decided to use that doubt as fuel. Of course he was excited about the football side of things, but he was drawn to the education he could get at Miami too. During the application process he'd learned that the school was one of the eight colleges and universities on the original "Public Ivy" list and was one of a handful of schools sometimes dubbed the "Harvard of the Midwest." That familiar feeling of fear and excitement returned every time he thought about it.

In addition to worrying about his grades, Deland had to make sure he kept up his fitness ahead of his first college football camp. He brought the same beast mentality that had made him the talk of football practices to his senior-year track workouts and meets. Cassie came to a lot of his meets to cheer him on, taking him back to her grandmother's house in Campbell to fill up on good Puerto Rican home cooking after his races. Cassie's family loved Deland, and her cozy house full of aunts, uncles, and cousins was livelier and more colorful than 270 Jackson.

Things were calmer at home than they had been for years, and Deland was often gone—either at work or spending time with Cassie. It felt good not to be anxious every day, but Deland still never felt fully at ease. He knew there was potential for drama to return at any moment. One day that spring he came home to find Frank and his mom in the kitchen talking. He was dumbstruck. Deland hadn't seen this guy in over two years. He thought Adelle was finally done messing around with Frank! This time he refused to stand by and let it happen. Deland demanded that Frank leave immediately. "Get out," he said matter-of-factly, staring directly into Frank's eyes. He was older now and more confident, and the idea that Adele might get back together with Frank was scarier than the thought of what Frank might do to him.

"He's gotta go," said Deland, his heart racing. "Now."

"You heard what my son said," said Adelle. "I've gotta respect my son's wishes."

Frank left, but Deland was heated about him being back in the mix. The next day when Steve picked him up to go to school, he unloaded. "Man, this motherfucker is back." Steve had heard all about Frank over the years and could tell just how much his return was messing with Deland.

"He can be finished today," said Steve. "That ain't nothing but a word. Let me know. This guy could be eliminated."

Deland felt a chill go down his spine. He didn't want Steve to get involved, but he felt better just knowing that he was willing to do anything for him, and that he'd always have his back if Frank came around again. Just like Tony and Brian, Steve was a friend Deland knew he'd be able to count on for life.

Winter and spring of Deland's senior year he spent a lot of time at Anna's apartment. Even though Steve was also a senior in high school, he was making enough money to help Anna with the rent, and stayed there often. Cassie stayed over a lot too and made it a second home, but Deland knew he'd get a whooping from Adelle if he tried to hole up at Anna's permanently. Anna would lend him her car so he could get back over to the house on Jackson and sleep in his own bed. Steve and Anna's place was a spot for Deland to escape school and home and just chill with Cassie. Sometimes he would work on homework or study for an upcoming test; Cassie was an outstanding student, so she would help. Sometimes they'd watch *The Cosby Show* and *A Different World* or listen to the latest albums from A Tribe Called Quest and LL Cool J.

One night when they were sitting on the couch, Deland confided in Cassie that he was adopted. He hadn't spoken to anyone about his adoption in the decade since he'd first shared it with those few friends at school. Their reaction had convinced him to seal the secret back inside, but Cassie made him feel safe enough to open up. He couldn't talk to her like Damon—nobody was Damon—but he could let down his guard more than he had with anyone else. She was sweet about it. He felt safe and understood. But then she asked him something that turned his world upside down.

"Do you want to find your real parents?"

Real. *Real*. The word somehow sounded brand-new coming out of her mouth.

If his birth parents were his real parents, what did that make Adelle? He'd thought about it before, but hearing someone else say it felt different.

Real. If the only family he knew wasn't real, then where did he belong?

Deland shut down the conversation. Told her he didn't know anything about them and he wasn't looking to find anything out. She shrugged her shoulders, gave him a hug, and said she was there to talk about it whenever he needed to. "It is what it is," he said. But he wasn't sure he believed that anymore.

For years he'd thought about what Adelle told him: "I love you because I chose you." It was supposed to make him feel special, but it felt precarious.

Blood is thicker than water. Is birth stronger than choice? He was supposed to feel lucky that he was chosen, that someone wanted him, but that choice was a last resort. A response to loss. His whole life was a response to loss. For everyone. Loss of child for his birth parents. Loss of birth parents for him. Loss of a biological child for Adelle, who had to settle for adoption. He was a backup plan. And if he'd arrived by choice, couldn't he just as easily be rejected by choice? By Adelle or by anyone else. Deland couldn't bear the thought of looking for his birth parents and having them choose, again, not to want him. Yet there was some small part of him that was starting to resent continuing on a path of secrecy. He worried he might never be whole without knowing his beginning.

———————

As the end of the school year neared, all of Deland's friends started making plans for the prom. Single guys plotted who they'd ask, the guys with girlfriends looked into getting bow ties and cummerbunds to match their girl's dress. There were tickets, tuxedos, and corsages to buy, plans to make for pre-prom photos and festivities, and older siblings to nag into getting alcohol for the after-parties. There was a track meet the same day as the prom, and one day after practice a handful of Deland's upper-class teammates told their coach, Brian Danilov, that they would have to miss the meet. Coach Danilov noticed that Deland was quiet.

Deland had been tight with Coach D since freshman year, when he coached him in both basketball and track. Coach D was fresh-faced and blue-eyed with floppy brown hair, young—still in his twenties—and brought boundless energy and enthusiasm to every single practice. He had a sign in his office that read "Champions are made when no one's watching" and would always remind his players to stay in the moment—in this practice, in this game—and just "Win the day."

The previous year, Coach D had led Campbell's JV basketball squad to a perfect 20-0 record and had been promoted to head coach of the varsity team in Deland's senior year. That first year at the helm, Danilov, with Tom Creed on his staff, would lead Campbell to its first district championship in school history.

Within three years they'd go all the way—Division III state champs. After the win Creed had to let the players shave his head, making good on a bet he'd made with them before the season started.

Even though Deland only played basketball his freshman year, he worked with Coach D in track and field every spring and loved to check in with him throughout the year to get inspiration. Danilov seemed to be able to see the potential in everyone and bring out their best. He had non-sensical nicknames for Deland—"Bub" and "Moe"—and had been there to help him deal with the disappointment of sitting out his junior season because of his grades. Danilov was one of the only people that Deland felt seen by. One of the only people Deland knew didn't doubt him.

A few days after the guys told Coach D they were missing the meet, Deland mentioned prepping to be a part of the 4x100 relay and Coach D stopped him. "Moe," he said, "you got prom, don't you?" Deland shook his head. "You got a girlfriend, right?" said Danilov. "You're not going to the prom?" He was incredulous.

"I don't have the money to go to the prom, Coach," said Deland.

"You're going to the prom, Moe," said Coach D.

So Danilov paid for Deland to take Cassie to the prom. Paid for the tickets. Paid for the dinner. Paid for the corsage. Paid for the black tux with the white bow tie that Deland rented to wear. Paid for the white Chevy Corsica that Deland rented to drive them there. Deland had been driving for a couple of years but didn't actually have a license because Adelle told him she wouldn't pay for driver's ed unless he got better grades. Coach D paid for Deland to take his driver's test and get his license so he could rent the car.

A lot of kids who needed that much help just to get to the prom might resent their lot in life. Resent their parents for not having enough or giving enough. Some kids might consider all the things they didn't have. But Deland couldn't help but feel blessed. Touched by some special kind of magic. Magic that must exist if he kept getting support when things looked like they might collapse. Creed and Coach D were another pair of those guardian angels he couldn't explain. He just knew every time he needed it one of those guys showed up and pushed him along. They were pushing him toward something. He knew something was waiting for him out in the world if he kept going. There was a purpose to all these bless-ings. It was up to him to continue to stay worthy of them.

The Chevy Corsica went back the day after prom, so Deland was without wheels again and Adelle hadn't had a car in more than a year. And so it was that on the spring morning Deland was headed to Miami University for Orientation Day, it was Frank who pulled into the driveway in his beat-up Chevy Chevette.

Motherfucking Frank. Deland couldn't believe it. At first he refused to go, but Adelle explained that Frank was the only person she could find willing to take them all the way to Oxford and back. If he wanted to go to orientation, he was getting in the car with her and Frank. That five-hour ride felt like it took five days.

Adelle and Frank dropped Deland off and spent the day exploring Oxford while he signed up for classes, checked out the dorm he'd be living in that fall, and participated in orientation exercises led by a handful of current students. As they split everyone up into smaller groups, he looked around the lawn and suddenly felt painfully self-conscious. At home he'd finally matured into a confident, handsome, successful athlete. In Oxford he was nobody. Were these people really incoming freshmen? They all seemed older. More put-together.

Definitely richer. And all but two kids were white. In Youngstown he was surrounded by Black folks, white folks, Puerto Rican, Greek, Polish, Irish, and every other -ish. He was suddenly very aware of his Blackness.

A sophomore volunteer led his group across the quad to an area under a giant tree and took them through an icebreaker exercise where they had to say their name paired with an adjective starting with the same letter that best described them. At the end each member of the circle would have to try to remember and repeat everyone's names. A smiley brunette started things off: Happy Hillary. A short, stocky guy with a thick neck went next: Soccer Sam. And so it went, around the circle.

Akron Adam. Silly Susan. Funny Freddie. Deland panicked. Who was he?

He'd spent a lifetime asking himself that question. Where did he come from? To whom did he belong? And now he was supposed to sum it all up in two words? He knew it was meant to be a throwaway moment, but it felt heavy for him. Complicated. Maybe for now he'd skip the question and choose another one: Who did he *want* to be? More immediately, who did he want to be here, in college? In a new place where no one knew him. Where no one knew about 270 Jackson or the big orange extension cord. Where no one knew about his job at KFC or his hand-me-down jeans. He could be anyone he wanted here. He'd filled out with football, had a nice, clean high-top fade, and a new mustache. He knew he was fine. He'd let them know it too.

"Debonair Deland," he blurted out.

As soon as it came out, his inner monologue chirped at him: *Debonair? What?!*

He could feel the heat rising and his face getting flushed, but nobody else seemed to notice. The circle kept going. For all those kids knew, he *was* Debonair Deland. Later when the group talked about potential majors, Deland said he wanted to major in finance. He wasn't even done saying the word when that inner voice chimed in again. *Finance? You don't want nothing to do with finance!*

When Adelle and Frank came to pick him up that afternoon for the long drive home, Frank's beat-up Chevy Chevette was another reminder to Deland that he was a fraud. "Finance major Debonair Deland?" What a crock. Who did he think he was trying to fit in with these folks? He was still just Deland McCullough from Youngstown, Ohio. Guy that barely got in, living in the projects, hitching a ride in a junky car from a dude he hated. Deland McCullough: Always doubted, never enough. Why did he think college would be any different? Not with all those rich white kids with their big vocabularies, their privilege, judgment, and prejudices. Deland knew he would stick out like a sore thumb. He slumped in the back seat and scowled at the back of Frank's head the whole way home.

A few weeks later, in June 1991, an incident at Deland's final high school football game triggered those same feelings of anxiety about leaving Youngstown. He was on the Ohio all-star team in the Ohio-Pennsylvania

High School Football All-Star Classic at Stambaugh Stadium on the campus of Youngstown State University. Deland ran for more than 100 yards and scored the touchdown that put the game out of reach to lead Ohio to a win, but the MVP Award went to a white player who didn't have the stats or accomplishments to earn it. Deland wasn't just disappointed, he was shaken. He knew, deep down, that it wasn't right.

Damon was home for the game and that night he and Deland got to talking about it. "Life ain't fair, brother," Damon told him. "You're always going to have to do more. You're always gonna have to go above and beyond. It's always gonna be somethin'."

Since getting to Boston for college, Damon had started to see race in ways he never had back in Youngstown. In the mixed community of Lincoln Knolls, differences were acknowledged only in pursuit of good-natured jokes or cracks at each other's expense. They'd cut on each other and dig in on stereotypes about being Greek or Italian or Black, but everybody was considered part of the neighborhood family. No matter how much melanin you had, nobody was disrespected. When he got to Boston, Damon met a whole lot of folks who seemed to have their minds made up about all Black people. It didn't matter who you were or what you did; all they knew was to be racist. It kept him on edge in a way he'd never experienced back home.

Youngstown had always felt pretty safe to Damon. He knew there were areas and people to avoid, but for the most part his hometown was a mini melting pot in which folks let other folks do their thing. If you stayed out of the drug trade and away from the gangs you could usually stay safe. And Black, brown, or white, you could feel welcome.

That feeling of safety existed for many in Youngstown despite ever-increasing rates of crime. Around the time Deland was readying to leave for college, the city was beginning one of its darkest stretches. Per WKBN News, "In 1991, the city recorded 59 homicides, an all-time high at the time, kicking off a decade in which Youngstown recorded 492 homicides, an average of 49.2 homicides a year." Just as it had been in the years after the steel mills closed, desperation and despair became the city's biggest output. Research done by criminologists points to a rapid fall from wealth to poverty as the prime reason for rising crime and violence in postindustrial cities. According to the *Washington Post*, one 1976 study found that for every 1 percent rise in nationwide unemployment there were 648 more murders per year. In Youngstown, unemployment was high, poverty rates neared 50 percent in some neighborhoods, and crack cocaine use was on the rise. Gang members from other states would visit Youngstown to sell and then stay with the intention of becoming the area's preferred drug lord.

But for all its perils and all its limitations, Youngstown was still the devil they knew. Oxford was a safer place, but Damon knew Deland would face a different set of challenges there. Deland was about to find out that the world would have ideas about him based on his skin color. Damon couldn't change it, couldn't fix it, couldn't protect his little brother. He could only tell him what to expect. And tell him that it was up to him to show them they were wrong. To thrive. To succeed.

Deland was quiet as he listened. *You make the choice*, he thought.

For all the excitement and hope about the opportunities that lay outside Youngstown, both boys felt a deep sense of pride for the city in which they were raised. For all its flaws, there was a community there, one built around resilience. Like soldiers who bonded in times of war, the trauma of deindustrialization and disinvestment brought the people of Youngstown together. The kids who lived through it were raised by the struggle. Youngstown was as much a parent to them as any mother or father. Damon knew it would be tough for Deland to leave that parent behind.

"Remember that Malcom X song we used to listen to?" Damon asked. "'No Sell Out'?" The 1983 Keith LeBlanc–composed single used samples from Malcom X's spoken words over an electro beat. "'White, Black, red, brown, yellow, it doesn't make any difference what color you are, the only thing power respects is power.'"

Deland nodded. "I remember."

"Don't forget it," said Damon. "Your success is your power."

Deland at Miami University

CHAPTER 11

Deland hunched over and leaned the side of his face into his palm like he'd been punched. It felt like he'd been punched. He sat down on the couch and stared at the door Cassie had just slammed on her way out. Her final words kept replaying in his head.

"That's why I don't need to be with your adopted ass."

The two of them had survived plenty of disagreements, plenty of moments where Cassie was accusatory or unreasonable, but Deland couldn't believe she'd turned his most personal confession back on him. Had she always judged him for being adopted? Was she carrying around feelings about it all this time? Was he too different for Cassie—or anyone—to really love?

Telling Cassie about his adoption hadn't been premeditated. Deland hadn't spent weeks building up to the moment, hadn't been waiting for a sign that she was worthy of knowing his truth. That day on the couch, he just suddenly felt like he wanted to tell her. His instincts told him she was safe, and he wanted to bring her even closer to him. Now he didn't trust his instincts.

Steve and Anna were out, so Deland had the spot to himself. *Your adopted ass.* He kept hearing it, over and over. He didn't know whether he wanted to cry or throw something. He knew Cassie probably wasn't "the one," but she was the closest he'd found to it, and now she'd taken the most intimate secret he'd ever shared and weaponized it. After all those years holding things in he'd let a part of himself out, and once again it had come back to bite him. Just like the kids at school. *What you are is different*, he thought. *What you are is something to mock.*

After a few days Cassie came back around full of apologies and tears over what she'd said. She knew that she'd crossed a line. She wasn't even sure why she'd said it, she just wanted to hurt Deland as badly as she could. Now she wanted him back. And despite all the self-doubt and pain he'd suffered that week, Deland still let her back in. Maybe he wasn't confident enough to set boundaries for himself. Maybe the fear of being abandoned or unworthy wouldn't allow him to walk away. Maybe he'd spent too many years watching Adelle and Frank fight and make up, split and get back together. In trauma reenactment, people repeat what's familiar. Even if it feels bad, it still feels comfortable. Sometimes the repetition is done in a subconscious effort to understand the past trauma, sometimes in a subconscious effort to do it again but change the ending. Whatever it was, Deland let Cassie back in. She had some sort of hold on him, and even this betrayal wasn't enough to make him end things. *We crave what we know.* The messaging of family systems and emotional DNA is strong.

Deland had just a few months left in Youngstown before he had to leave for college. He was determined to keep it low-stress—just picking up extra hours at KFC to make money for school, working out to get ready for camp, and hanging out with family and friends. He and Cassie settled back into their normal routine but continued to bicker a lot, both clearly anxious about how Deland's departure would affect their relationship. Some days Deland thought he should just end it and start fresh at Miami, nothing to look back at. But as ready as he was to get out of Youngstown, a part of him was afraid to leave behind the few people he'd gotten comfortable around. Cassie understood him like few others did, and he knew he'd find value and comfort in that when he got to Oxford and had to open up to a whole new group of teammates and friends. Both Cassie and Deland knew they weren't likely to survive the challenges of distance, but they stuck together anyway, against the odds and their better judgment.

It was the fall of 1991. "Motown Philly" by Boyz II Men piped out of the boom box in the locker room, *Terminator 2* and *Boyz n the Hood* were the talk of team dinners, and, whether they were willing to admit it or not, most of the guys knew all about what was happening with Brenda, Dylan, Kelly, and Brandon on *Beverly Hills, 90210*. Deland's anxiety about his "Debonair Deland" introduction to campus had disappeared the moment he stepped on campus for football practice. The rest of the student body at Miami University might have been intimidating, but the football field was his domain and football players were his people.

When he'd first arrived at camp to get his gear from the equipment room, he'd met a tall, lanky white guy with a pronounced southern drawl named Pete. "Who are you?" Pete asked as he scanned his clipboard to cross off Deland's name. "Deland McCullough," he said. "And you're going to know who I am real soon." Pete chuckled. He worked at Miami for years after Deland left, and whenever they saw each other Pete would remind Deland about how he'd walked into the equipment room that day, chest puffed out, announcing he was somebody worth watching. Deland recognized that he was a different guy when it came to football; he hoped one day he could find that same confidence everywhere else too.

Deland's roommate, Randy Hargrave, was a freshman quarterback from Xenia, Ohio. Randy was talkative and outgoing, telling Deland all about his hometown as they moved into their room. Randy warned him that Xenia was only about an hour away, so his high school sweetheart would be visiting a lot. "We should have some sort of system," he said. "A sock on the door or something."

Randy's chatter took some getting used to, but Deland had always liked being more of an observer, so the dynamic suited him fine. He let Randy fill the room with conversation and got to avoid sharing too much about himself. And it didn't hurt that Randy had decked out their room with posters, a bangin' sound system, and an expansive CD collection. Deland had arrived at school with almost nothing—one suitcase, a laundry bag full of clothes, one pair of shoes, and a box fan that he'd gotten as a gift for graduation. He didn't have any posters, picture frames, or personal items—just a poster board on his wall that he'd decorated before leaving for Oxford, pinning up newspaper clippings from his high school football successes and pictures from signing day and his recruiting trip. It was a reminder to him of the success he'd had at Campbell and the work that had gotten him to Miami.

"How come you've only got football stuff and those pictures of your dad?" Randy asked him a few days after they'd moved in. "Got no girl at home? No other family or friends?"

"My dad?" Deland looked over at the corkboard. "Nah, that's me and Coach Smith."

Randy looked closer. Tinted glasses, striped sweater, big grin. It was indeed Coach Smith. "Aha. My bad. I see now. So how come no photos of your mom and dad? How come you don't have any pict—" Randy swiveled back around in his chair, saw Deland, and stopped. Deland had flipped his whole body toward the wall and was reading a magazine. Randy didn't ask about his family or friends back in Youngstown again.

From day one in Oxford, Deland decided he was going to find a way to thrive in the classroom at Miami of Ohio, not just on the football field. Anyone could graduate high school—he'd seen wastoids and drug dealers and total screwups squeeze their way out of Campbell Memorial. Graduating from college meant something, and if it meant something it was worth his focusing and applying himself. That good SAT score he'd gotten and the schoolwork he'd done his senior year helped him see his potential. He was intimidated by the reputation Miami had, but he knew he was smart enough; he just needed to focus and put in the time to succeed. Deland decided that in Oxford his grades would be better, his football success would be bigger, and anyone and everyone who doubted him would finally see what he was made of. *You make the choice*, he told himself.

Deland and Cassie had been talking on the phone nearly every day since he'd arrived, and he told her what campus was like, how practices were going, and how he was fitting in. He shared which teammates he'd hit it off with and which coaches were his favorites. Even though they talked often, Deland rarely shared the feelings of fear and loneliness he had as he tried to fit in and make new friends. He still wasn't good with emotions—talking about them, processing them, or receiving them. Back in Youngstown he'd imagined he would be honest with Cassie as he adjusted to college life, but he was still too scared to be vulnerable, even with her. After eighteen years of keeping things inside, his walls were too high and too thick.

In retrospect, not talking to anyone about his adoption—not Adelle or Damon, not therapists or counselors—taught Deland that by pushing down the reality of his beginnings, he could get by. And if he was able to avoid facing complicated feelings around something as major as his identity, he could avoid facing his feelings about almost anything. Of course, avoidance didn't keep the feelings away—it just prevented him from processing and dealing with them in a healthy way.

When Deland eventually learned about psychological projection, things started to become clearer to him. He better understood why he'd carried feelings of doubt and inferiority for years and why he couldn't get to the root of the trust issues he had. When his birth parents chose not to keep him, he internalized that decision as the ultimate rejection, and instead of reconciling the feelings of self-doubt that resulted, he projected them onto others. By convincing himself that no one believed in him he was unconsciously putting off the pain and discomfort of addressing his own feelings of unworthiness. The shame of past abandonment and fear of future rejection affected every relationship he had; he held on to a powerful fear that showing too much of himself might turn people away. Those unanswered questions remained buried deep inside him: Who will be there for me? Who will stick around? Who do I belong to, and who belongs to me?

Whether his feelings of doubt were his own or something he projected onto others, he would forever feel the need to prove he was worthy.

Eventually, he would grow and mature enough to start to deal with some of his other big emotions, though. And he would eventually meet someone worth breaking down his walls for. Until then, he and Cassie carried on with the classic post–high school relationship, one built on a shaky, immature foundation and further stressed by distance. Deland was content to be half in on Cassie and all in on himself as he tried to get his footing as a student-athlete at Miami.

Deland wore number 20 in high school—Damon's number—but that was taken by an upperclassman at Miami, so Pete had given him the number 25 jersey.

Deland put on that number 25 and committed to bringing a beast mentality to every practice, film session, and scrimmage. He would need it. When Coach Walker had first arrived on campus in the spring of 1990, he'd inherited a winless team that lacked both discipline and talent. In order to make the team competitive, he had installed a grueling strength and conditioning program led by former standout Miami offensive lineman Dan Dalrymple. Walker and Dalrymple's goal was to winnow the team down to all but the toughest and most dedicated players, and they were largely successful. Upperclassmen who had been coasting during the previous regime quit in droves, and by the time Deland arrived in the fall of 1991 the Miami team looked completely different: a wild and boisterous cast of characters with exactly the toughness and discipline Walker was looking for. Deland fit right in. And the demanding nature of the workouts brought the guys together like fraternity brothers surviving pledge week. Deland had an immediate core group of friends who were unusually bonded and went everywhere together around campus.

Before training camp started Coach Walker had decided to move Deland to flanker, a position played by a running back in his Campbell offense, but more of a receiver-type player at Miami. Deland had been a star his senior year, but now he was playing alongside guys who had not only been high school superstars but had already made a mark collegiately. He was happy to play any position and help wherever he could. For three weeks Deland impressed his position coach, Shawn Watson, and the rest of the staff with how quickly he picked up the intricacies of the flanker position. He never got tired, never failed to hit his sprint or drill times, and didn't seem to be fazed by just how grueling camp was for most of the other freshmen. He was on track to get meaningful playing time for the Miami RedHawks as a true freshman, until one memorable scrimmage changed everything.

The RedHawks were a week away from the season opener against Ball State, finalizing plays and sharpening their focus in one final scrimmage of the starting players against the backups who made up the scout team. It was a rainy day, so they spent a lot of time working on defending rushing plays, which meant a lot of carries for a backup running back named Jack Suter. The guy kept getting loose, finding holes, and breaking through against the first-team defense. Deland almost couldn't believe it, but all of a sudden he felt tears coming down his face under his helmet as he watched. *I could do that*, he thought. *I should be doing that.*

Deland had accepted the move to flanker when he got to campus and saw the depth of the running backs room—guys like Terry Carter, a standout from northwest Ohio's Fremont Ross High School (and older brother to future NFL star Charles Woodson), and Kevin Ellerbe, who was only at Miami because of Proposition 48 (his grades kept him from a scholarship at a big program). Those guys were tough. While he still wasn't sure if he could compete with those two, he knew he could do what Jack was doing—and better. And he knew it was worth fighting to play running back. He went to Coach Smith and told him he was willing to do whatever it took to switch to running back—even redshirt his freshman year. Redshirt players are allowed to practice with the team and receive financial aid but can't participate in games. It's a common practice to preserve eligibility but is usually reserved for young players who won't see the field much in their first season anyway.

Coach Smith and Coach Walker were shocked to see a freshman with playing time in his future make such a request, but they respected it. He was 5'11", 160 pounds soaking wet, skinny arms and all, but they respected it. Deland moved into the running back group and immediately turned heads. He was with the backups now on the scout team, so the team's top defenders had to deal with him in practice. Every coach and every player on the team took notice when he started torching those first-string guys during interior drills, seven-on-seven, and full scrimmages.

Backups and redshirts like Deland spent most of their time working with graduate assistants while the position coaches focused on the starters, so he didn't train with Coach Smith much, but he did spend a lot of time with him outside of football. In fact, Coach Smith became the most important sounding board Deland had in Oxford that fall. He had made friends on the team but he kept them all at a bit of a distance, just like he did back in Youngstown. He might have been confident on the field, but he was the same Deland off it—scared to open up, not sure if he belonged. For years guys would crack jokes about how Deland spent all of freshman year with his head down, nodding or replying with one-word answers. They thought he was mysterious and hard-ass; he was just insecure.

There was something different about talking to Sherman, though. Deland asked him about Cassie and listened—really heard—to what he had to say about relationships, maturity, how to treat a woman, and how to be a man. He talked to him about classes he liked and teachers he didn't. He got Sherman's help when he needed orthotics to deal with foot pain. He asked him what kind of work it took to be great at Miami and go on to the pros. Deland had learned from plenty of men over the years, from Hubert, Uncle Yub, and Billy, to a few memorable coaches and teachers, but Sherman had the life experience and football success that inspired Deland to emulate his every move and heed his every word.

Everybody in that football room gravitated toward Coach Smith. He would stand up in front of the group, broad-shouldered, voice booming, with scars all over his knees from his years in the NFL. He didn't ask for attention; he commanded it. He never judged anyone on or off the field; he just gave them sound advice and advocated for them to work hard to be great men as well as great football players. As far as the guys on that team were concerned, Coach Smith was the Man, and all anyone in that room wanted to do was impress him and make him proud.

As one of only two Black coaches on staff, he was a go-to sounding board for many of the Black players especially. But of all the guys who sought out Sherman's counsel, Deland stood out. Sherman didn't mind all the times Deland would keep him at work late talking. He respected how serious Deland was—so much more focused than most of the kids his age. Deland was just the kind of kid Sherman got into coaching for. Not only did he seem like a guy who could use some positive leadership but he was also a guy who had a goal and would do anything to achieve it.

Deland was convinced Coach Smith would be able to help him reach that goal. He knew it was premature to think about the NFL— he hadn't even played a college snap yet—but he would get to dreaming every time Coach showed up at practice in that cherry-apple-red Mercedes. A Mercedes, by the way, that Sherman had bought used a few years earlier from an up-and-coming rapper named Sir Mix-a-Lot. His song "Baby Got Back" would hit the top of the *Billboard* charts the next year and go double platinum.

Growing up with all of Adelle's sayings, Deland loved that Coach Smith also spoke in maxims and aphorisms. "If it's to be, it's up to me," he'd always say, reminding his players that they alone were in control of how hard they worked. *You make the choice*, Deland would respond in his head. Coach just seemed to have a way with words, a way of making 'em stick. He reminded Deland of the coaches he'd seen in movies, ready with inspiring speeches whenever a big game was on the line. He pictured himself as the star of the film, winning it all in the final scene after a rousing call to action from his coach. Deland was particularly fond of something Coach Smith told him during his very first recruiting visit and repeated often: "Sometimes struggles don't just develop character, they reveal character." Whether the struggle was a big one or just a football challenge, Deland felt that phrase deep in his heart. All his life he'd been determined to use his struggles to be better and do better.

It was just that perspective that helped Deland get through his redshirt season. It pained him to sit out every game, but he dedicated himself to getting better every day, putting in work, putting on weight, and learning as much as he could. He knew that once he got the chance he could be a great running back for the RedHawks. Both Ellerbe and Carter earned All-MAC (Mid-American Conference) honorable mentions that season, but Coach Walker could see he had something even more special coming down the pike. Randy pulled Deland aside after the season, looked him dead in the eyes, and said, "You're going to be great."

But whatever Deland was going to do, it wouldn't be under the tutelage of Coach Smith—Sherman had gotten a great offer to coach the tight ends at Illinois and was leaving the program immediately. At first he'd turned the job down, wanting to stay loyal to the guys he recruited. He thought about this group of Miami players and how they'd become family over the course of the season. Now he was going to abandon them? No way. Every year since he'd started coaching, whether it was high school or college, Sherman had made a habit of telling the guys playing for him, "You may not be looking for a father, but I'm going to treat you like my sons." He so valued the influence of his own father that he wanted to pass that down to his players, especially those who didn't have a solid role model in their home. But when he told Coach Walker he was turning down the job, Walker refused to let him stay. Told Sherman he had to keep moving up. That was the business, and it was too great an opportunity to turn down.

Deland was sad to see Sherman go but respected that he'd met with the team to tell them all directly. Most of the men Deland knew back home just up and disappeared. Or worse, kicked down a door on their way out. Sherman handled it like a man. Plus, it wasn't about any coach; Deland knew what he did next would be up to him. The new running backs coach, Don Treadwell, was very familiar with Deland and his game. Tready, as the players called him, had been part of the staff at Youngstown State that had recruited Deland in high school.

When Tready got to campus, Deland started working with him as soon as he could, looking ahead to the next season and a chance to actually play in his first collegiate game. By the time the summer rolled around, he had made his mark in practice and had staked his claim on the starting running back position the next season.

Buoyed by the confidence of a successful first year on campus, Deland didn't want to go back to Youngstown for the summer; he wanted to live with Damon in New York City. Damon's college sweetheart, Laura, had gotten pregnant the previous year, during Damon's junior year at Northeastern. She spent the final months of her pregnancy in Youngstown with Adelle, and after Damon Jr. was born they decided to move to New York to be by Laura's parents. Damon could find work even without a degree, so they decided he should be the one to drop out and take primary responsibility for the baby while she finished her schooling at John Jay College of Criminal Justice and got her degree. Laura's parents told the young couple they would soon be moving out of their Tribeca loft and invited them to live there and take over the place when they were gone. When Deland asked to come stay with them more than a year later, Laura's parents hadn't gone anywhere yet—they were all still living in the apartment together. Damon had a tense relationship with Laura's mother but made it work for the sake of the family.

When Adelle heard Deland was headed out to stay with Damon, she thought it would be a good opportunity for him to learn about the real world—get a job and make some money. She tried to motivate him by telling him that if he didn't get a job, she wasn't paying for his bus ticket back. Of course, Deland's summer was so short, with football camp starting weeks before classes, he didn't have time to find any meaningful work. Friends back in Youngstown often spent summers working for the Parks District, but he would have to leave New York before the summer term was over, so he couldn't commit to a job there.

Damon tried to get him a gig at Tower Records, where he was working, but they scrapped the idea when they realized Deland would be headed back to Ohio before the first paycheck cycle even hit.

So Deland spent his days trying to find ways to make a quick buck and spent the cooler early evenings finding ways to work out despite not having a gym or football facility. He did hill workouts, ran sprints on the unforgiving concrete, and did strength workouts with things like buckets, bricks, and beams. Some real *Rocky* montage type stuff. At night Damon taught him how to haggle with the street vendors for cheap gold jewelry and they'd hit the bars and clubs on Canal Street—"The 'Nal," as Deland called it.

Deland wanted to spend a few weeks in Youngstown before school started, so when it was time to head back to Ohio he just got Cassie to pay the seventy-six bucks for his bus ticket.

Deland suited up for Miami University

CHAPTER 12

BEARCATS ASK: WHO WAS THAT MASKED MAN?

The headline said it all. Redshirt freshman Deland McCullough was introduced to the college football world in Tim Sullivan's piece atop the sports section of the *Cincinnati Enquirer* on September 20, 1992. "His name was nowhere on the depth chart," the column began. "His season had yet to produce a single statistic. He entered the game utterly anonymous, and left it a local hero. His name is Deland McCullough. He is the college football phantom of Miami University."

It was Deland's college football debut. He racked up 118 yards and a touchdown on 25 carries and accounted for a total of 143 yards between rushing and receiving, more than half of Miami's total yards. Adelle was there as the RedHawks grabbed a 17–14 win over the University of Cincinnati Bearcats. She was pressed up against the railing behind the Miami bench all game, screaming Deland's name as he dominated in his first playing time in nearly two years.

Wrote Sullivan of Deland that day, "He was so much a part of Miami's success that you wondered what kind of crime he could have committed to be kept out of the lineup."

Sullivan and the rest of the media never would find out why Deland had been suspended for the first two games of the 1992 season—his redshirt freshman season and second year at Miami. Coach Walker simply told the press that Deland had made a mistake, was contrite, and that the specifics would stay between him and his player.

The truth was, Deland had nearly derailed his college football career before it even began.

During the second semester of Deland's first year on campus, a freshman with a penchant for mischief had tapped him and a few other underclassmen to help with his transgressions. The guy—and everyone else on campus, for that matter—could tell that Deland didn't have much money. "Help me steal a couple bikes using a lock breaker, give them to my older brother to sell, and you'll be helping me out and helping you out," he whispered to Deland one day in the dining hall. "These kids are all rich; they won't even miss 'em," he egged him on. "You've had it rough coming up. Don't you deserve a break for once?"

Deland got that feeling again. Wanting and needing. He wanted to feel like most of his classmates did, not stressing over every dollar they spent at the cafeteria or the school store. He thought about being able to order a pizza after a long practice. Thought about buying a second pair of shoes to wear to class. Thought about being able to afford postage to send letters home to Adelle and Cassie, pens and notebooks, new underwear, a lamp for studying. He might even make enough money to be able to tell Adelle she could stop sending him twenty dollars a month in paper food stamps. He'd love to be able to help her out.

He knew it was wrong. He battled with himself. He keenly felt his lack of resources, his lack of control. He repeated those words in his head: *Don't you deserve a break for once?* He was in.

Come March of that first year in Oxford, one of the other guys involved made the mistake of keeping one of the bikes he stole instead of passing it down the line to be fenced. The bike was spotted in his possession and the jig was up.

Campus officials had been alerted to reports of bikes being stolen and wanted answers. The kid was told he'd get off easier if he told officials who else was involved, so he did. Campus police told Coach Walker about the reported bicycle thefts and that Deland's name was mentioned. When Coach

Walker asked him about it, Deland was honest. It was only a couple of bikes, but Deland was still terrified about what might happen to his football career. Getting caught was also a bit of a relief, though. He knew that if he kept getting away with it, he might always be that guy who gave in to fear when resources started to run dry. Back when he'd nabbed those pairs of jeans in ninth grade he could convince himself he was justified in getting what he needed. As a kid his misbehavior was a means to an end, a flawed but understandable reaction to a problem for which he couldn't find another solution. He was old enough now to know he'd been fooling himself believing he was owed a break. He was old enough now to know anything he wanted in life he'd need to work for. And since scholarship athletes weren't allowed to have jobs during the school year, he would just have to be patient and go awhile longer without some of the material things his classmates took for granted.

A few weeks later Deland was called to testify during the trial for the guy who got caught with the bike. He didn't own a suit so he stood there in black boots, Levi's jeans, and a wrinkled purple-and-black checkered shirt, answering a handful of questions best he could. Deland and the other students recruited to help with the thefts ended up escaping without legal punishment, and while the guy who got caught did face some repercussions, Deland ran into him on campus a few weeks later and he was still in school, on track to finish the year on time. Coach Walker told Deland he was glad he'd escaped legal punishment, but that he would be suspended for the first two games of the next season all the same. That meant Deland had to tell Adelle about it, which felt almost as uncomfortable as speaking in the courtroom that day. When he hung up the phone with his mom the disappointment in her voice stayed with him.

Deland told the *Dayton Daily News* after his impressive first outing that Adelle's advice helped him accept the suspension as a blessing and stay focused on his first game. "She's always been there for me," he said. "And this time she just told me to keep my head up and not get an attitude. She said I'd get through it and do okay."

The close call was also a wake-up call. Deland was going to do things right. School, football, everything. He had another shot to be different from the guys he knew back home. He would never let anyone describe his story as "what could have been." He had entered Miami with big dreams, not just in football but in academics as well, and he'd let himself get distracted—and nearly defeated—just a year in. It was time to get serious. It was time to work. *God gives you an example of what to be and what not to be,* he remembered. *You make the choice.*

Somehow Pete the equipment guy found out about Deland and the bikes—that guy seemed to know everything about everybody. Every once in a while that spring and the next fall when they saw each other, he would give Deland a firm handshake with a fifty-dollar bill in his palm. It felt like a thousand dollars to Deland every time. Pete said he just wanted to help him out. Another guardian angel.

———

The rest of Deland's redshirt freshman season was a blur of Miami RedHawks red. It turned out that that first game against the Bearcats was the beginning of something special. He'd showed up to campus ready to prove Coach Walker right, and boy did he. Deland was the leading freshman runner in the country, rushing for more than 1,000 yards and six touchdowns. He ended the season with a school record seven straight games rushing for more than 100 yards and became the first freshman in Miami University history to top 1,000 yards (a freshman school record of 1,026). He could have put up even better numbers if he hadn't missed those first two games to suspension.

"Deland got more yardage than any back I've ever coached after the initial hit," Coach Walker told Dave Long of the *Dayton Daily News* at the end of the season. "Having him back for three more years is a real nice feeling. Being the best football player he can be is very important to him. He practices like he plays, and he works hard at it in the offseason. Not all of our players do that. And I'm going to challenge all of them to make the commitment in the offseason to become the best players they can be. If we're going to move to the next level and challenge to be champions, all our players have to have the same work ethic and focus as Deland McCullough."

Deland was an honorable mention All-America, First Team All-MAC, and was awarded MAC Freshman of the Year—a first for a Miami player. In addition to leading the MAC in rushing, he was also second in all-purpose yardage per game, eighth in scoring per game, and ninth in total offense. He caught the game-winning touchdown in Miami's thrilling homecoming win over Central Michigan and helped the school to its best conference record in five years.

Success on the football field helped Deland find more confidence in himself. He had ditched the finance thing as soon as he got to campus and had chosen sociology as his major, with a minor in coaching. He wanted to work with at-risk kids who had it tough growing up—kids like him. After a few semesters of classes he realized his interest in sociology wasn't just about helping others, but about learning to better understand himself too. For years he'd let his conscious and unconscious feelings of doubt, otherness, and loss go mostly unaddressed. In his family, the messaging had always been to bury trauma and silence pain. For as long as he could remember, the only solution he had to feeling doubted was to just work harder. He thought all that hard work would prove that he was worthy— of love, of money, of success. Now he was learning that not every child feels he has to earn love. Not every child feels he has to detach or disassociate to feel safe. It was scary to face some of the feelings he'd shoved down, but it was in those moments of honest introspection that he felt lighter.

Whether he was learning about psychological projection, family conflict, or human bonding, Deland started to apply the lessons of his classes to his life, studying how to heal after years of chronic stress, how to recognize triggers and control his reactions to them, how to self-regulate when angry or scared, and how to deprogram some of the damaging messages of the emotional DNA he'd inherited. He was getting better at processing his feelings, but sometimes things buried deep down could still take him by surprise.

One semester his criminology class went to a nearby prison. As they walked past inmates sitting in the cafeteria or passed them in the hall, Deland started mean-mugging them and challenging them. Literally trying to start fights with the prisoners. The guards had to ask him to step outside and wait for the rest of the class to finish the tour. With a bit of time to stew alone outside, he tried to figure out why he'd acted that way and wondered if it was a reaction to visiting Frank at Mansfield all those years earlier. He hadn't had the confidence to stand up to Frank as a kid, so now he'd show these random inmates how tough he was? Ridiculous. He was embarrassed about how he acted but committed to understanding his behavior instead of burying it.

For years it had been enough for Deland to just deal with his anxiety, now he was actually trying to heal it. He began to wonder if he should be talking to someone—a therapist or counselor. He began to wonder if maybe it was okay to look deeper—both at who he truly was and where he came from. He began to wonder if it was actually okay to talk about this sort of thing.

He decided the first step was to come out of hiding. He started to be more open, less scared. He got more comfortable letting people see who he really was without worrying so much that they wouldn't like it. Slowly but surely he was coming into his own and growing in meaningful ways, but he still kept his biggest secrets and insecurities tucked away, worried someone might turn them against him like Cassie had.

Then he met Mya.

Mya was a beautiful biracial girl from Dayton, light-skinned and shapely with dark hair, dimples, and a big smile. She'd been a "Beauty of the Week" in a prominent Black entertainment magazine in the fall of 1991, and when a handful of guys found out she was their classmate it caused quite a stir. Mya kept such a low profile and was so modest that some folks didn't even believe it was her. Deland didn't know about her modeling stint when they first met, though he was certainly drawn to her beauty. He quickly found a much deeper connection when they realized how much they had in common.

Like Deland, Mya came from humble beginnings and sometimes worried she didn't belong at a school full of mostly wealthy white kids. Like Deland, she came from a household marred by violence—in her case, an abusive father. Like Deland, Mya often felt misunderstood, choosing to stay quiet if she didn't feel like she could safely express her feelings. With each other, they began to open up. Deland felt truly seen and understood by Mya. She was the first person besides Damon with whom he felt comfortable fully letting down his guard. She appreciated that he was willing to talk to her about his childhood and she never weaponized the truths he shared with her, even the truth of his adoption.

Deland and Mya had one more thing in common, something that complicated things as they found themselves falling for each other. Just like Deland, Mya had someone back home. Someone who had no idea she was staying up all hours of the night sharing her most intimate secrets with someone new. In the beginning Deland and Mya were both open about the struggles they were having in putting an end to high school relationships that lingered on, but as their feelings grew they just stopped talking about it. Out of sight, out of mind.

When the football season ended, Deland had more time to dote on Mya. He even took her to New York City over Thanksgiving break to meet Damon. Unlike his previous visit, this time he barely ever wanted to go out on Canal Street or explore the city; he just wanted to hang at the apartment with Mya. All day. Damon didn't get it. He thought Deland seemed full of himself around Mya. Arrogant. Damon wasn't privy to the long, deep conversations that Deland and Mya had. He didn't know about the baggage they both brought to the relationship and how it was affecting their dynamic. He didn't know Deland was acting confident and cool in an attempt to win Mya over and convince her to break up with her boyfriend back home. All Damon saw was a good-looking girl whom Deland seemed to want to impress by being cocky.

Like a lot of folks in the infatuation phase of a new relationship, Deland lost himself a bit in Mya. He wasn't sure how to reconcile his feelings for her with the reality of their situations and he still struggled to communicate. For as much as Deland hoped Mya would commit to him, he hadn't yet fully committed to her. Deland was hesitant to end things with Cassie unless Mya ended things with her beau back home first, but neither of them was brave enough to be the first to bring it up. It was easier to live in a sort of euphoric fantasy world than to directly address the elephant in the room.

The summer after Deland's second year at school, he decided to go back to Campbell, where he could use his old high school facilities for training and make some money working too. Adelle had moved out east to be closer to Damon—the two of them had started a maintenance company together (named 3-D in honor of Deland, Damon, and Damon II) so Deland crashed at Uncle Yub's house for the summer. He got a job working for the Street Department with his buddy Brian, cutting grass, removing graffiti around town, and repairing roads. It was tough work and it was hot as hell, but it kept him moving and kept him busy. Some of the guys they worked with couldn't help but rib Deland about his photos and stats in the college football magazines they read. He feigned embarrassment but he loved it. He knew they were proud of a Youngstown boy who had done good—and it made him proud of himself.

While he was back in town he picked back up with Cassie again. He knew they didn't have a real future together, but neither of them was willing to say it. It was so easy to fall back into things and so hard to escape his old patterns. Despite all the work he'd been doing on himself, he still hadn't figured out how to honestly discuss difficult things. Plus, he and Mya had left things open when school ended. Both of them were scared to be exclusive because of how vulnerable it made them. They kept one foot in with their previous relationships so they wouldn't have to talk about how strongly they felt for each other. They knew how much it would hurt if they went all-in and it didn't work out.

When Deland returned to school in the fall of 1993 for his third year on campus (and redshirt sophomore football season), it was immediately clear that any effort he and Mya had made to create distance didn't work. They instantly reconnected and felt closer than ever before. While their feelings were obvious, they still hadn't figured out where those feelings should or could take them. They didn't talk about the terms of their relationship, and the details of their situations back home remained unspoken. They were just content to spend as much time together as possible.

Meanwhile, expectations were high for Deland's redshirt sophomore season. "They might as well paint a big bull's-eye on his chest with a sign that says, 'Here I am, smash me,'" Coach Walker told the *Cincinnati Post*.

Deland would have to adjust to playing for another new running backs coach, Ron Johnson, a graduate assistant who took over the position when Treadwell was moved to wide receivers coach. Coach Johnson was an unassuming white guy with a country accent who had no experience playing or coaching the running back position, but he made up for that lack of experience with a great attitude, a tremendous work ethic, and attention to detail. He got the best out of his guys through love and encouragement, not intimidation. Young and single, he poured every bit of his time and energy into the team and his players. Especially Deland. He worked to figure out what made Deland tick and what motivated him. He bought him groceries, taught him consistency and structure, and offered a perspective on life that made Deland a better, more well-rounded person. Deland quickly came to consider Johnson another one of his guardian angels, and their connection went well beyond football; years later, Deland was even in Johnson's wedding.

Unfortunately, Deland's highly anticipated second season was mostly defined by injury—specifically turf toe. Turf toe is a hyperextension injury to the hallux metatarsophalangeal joint; basically a sprain of the main joint of the big toe. It's a common injury in football—hence the name, inspired by the playing surface—but a tough one to treat.

For half of the season Deland tried to play through the pain, but it rendered him mostly ineffective and he lost his starting gig, with Terry Carter taking over the bulk of the carries. The only way to heal was to rest, so after blowing people away in his first season Deland was now spending more time sitting than playing. Thankfully the time off his feet helped, and he was able to return to full strength for the latter half of the season, rushing for over 100 yards in two games down the stretch. He was once again showing the promise that had excited Coach Walker.

"He's a driven man," Randy told the *Cincinnati Post* that year. "He has the same kind of mentality and intensity as Walter Payton had. Every time I pull him out of the game I have to explain to him right away why I took him out."

Deland never got mad at Coach Walker for favoring Carter after his injury—he knew he was hurt and couldn't be the player he wanted to be. Plus, he really respected the way Coach Walker handled his business: stern, serious, and focused, but never crass or inappropriate. Walker was a straight shooter and told guys what to expect. And he had a little fun when the occasion called for it too. At the end of practice when it was time to assign wind sprints, he would always tent his fingers and wiggle them, à la Montgomery Burns from *The Simpsons*, loudly pondering how many reps the guys were gonna get. "Hmm . . ." he'd say. "Will it be four . . . six . . . ten . . ." with his fingers wiggling and waggling in front of him. "Let's go with eight. Eight wind sprints, guys. Hit it."

One time fullback Skip Tramontana and defensive tackle Mark Staten (a giant of a man nicknamed Ape who later ended up on the New England Patriots) were jawing at each other, pushing and shoving after a play in practice. Two big boys, really getting after it. After they were separated, Coach Walker told them they'd be holding hands for the rest of the practice. "Get to know each other, now," he said. "Get to love each other." The next day when the team watched the practice film, they exploded with laughter—the film crew had inserted a shot of Tramontana and Staten holding hands in between every play.

Coach Walker helped motivate Deland to finish the season strong, and though he ended up with a disappointing 612 yards rushing, Deland still finished number one in the MAC with eight rushing touchdowns. Deland was moved by Walker's belief in him, especially during those stretches in which he was sidelined. When the offseason started he wanted to spend as much time as he could in the weight room and on the track to prove Walker's belief in him was well founded. *Get bigger, get faster, get better,* he thought. *You make the choice.*

Deland and Mya had gotten closer than ever that first semester back but had started to grow apart a little as the year went on, sometimes going weeks without spending quality time together. For as close as they were, Mya was still a bit of a mystery to Deland. Like Deland, she could get quiet at times, withdrawing into herself. He was busy with offseason workouts, determined to recapture the success of his first year, so he accepted the ebbs and flows of their relationship. When they did get to hang out, their relationship felt easy and comfortable, full of fun and passion. When she would pull away and be distant, Deland assumed it was due to unresolved issues with her relationship back home. And of course he had things he was dealing with too. Deland knew it wasn't smart to keep hanging out without addressing the topic of exclusivity, but he also didn't want to bring it up and lose her altogether. He would just have to play it cool and be okay with whatever amount of herself she could give him.

In February of that school year, Cassie decided to come up from Ohio State to surprise Deland in Oxford. It was during one of Deland's lulls with Mya, and he was happy to have the company. The two of them were leaving campus to get something to eat and stopped at a light when Mya and her friends walked right in front of their car. Mya's face dropped when she saw them. Mya's friends looked up and spotted him too, one pointing at him with a look on her face that seemed to say "Caught!" Even though Mya knew they weren't exclusive, she was still embarrassed about her friends seeing him with Cassie. Deland felt a sharp pang of guilt. As weird as things were between them, the last thing he wanted to do was to hurt or embarrass Mya.

The thing he wanted most was to be with Mya exclusively, but he hadn't been brave enough to tell her that. One of those infamous elephants in the room was right there on campus with them—he wondered if this moment might actually force them to address where their relationship was headed.

Later that night things came to a head. When Deland got back to his room after dinner, there was a message from Mya on his machine telling him she'd be coming by to get some clothes she'd left there. It had been a few weeks since they'd last seen each other, so Deland knew the timing of the call wasn't coincidental. Cassie, nosy as ever, demanded to hear the message and grilled Deland about why another girl was keeping things at his place. By the end of the night Cassie was gone—so incensed she cut her trip short—and Mya was gone too. She'd picked up her stuff and made it clear she didn't want to see him.

Deland was surprised at the depths of Mya's anger, considering she had her own situation back home, but he also understood how complicated things could get when strong feelings were involved—especially since they both had deep-seated issues with trust and worthiness. Late that night Deland called Mya to try to work things out, pouring his heart out to her and telling her he was ready to be serious. He finally said all the things he knew he should've said months earlier. He put his feelings out there for the first time in their relationship.

It was too little, too late.

"Deland, I just can't deal with the drama," Mya said. "You know better than anyone how much this kind of uncertainty hurts me."

She was right, he did. They'd spent months telling each other about their deepest fears and insecurities. He knew her trust issues and her triggers. They'd shared how hard it was to open up and had found in each other a safe space to finally do it. Ultimately the things that had brought them together were the very things that drove them apart. They were both still learning how to communicate. How to be vulnerable. How to be open to love by being open to the possibility of heartbreak. Deland didn't know if things would have worked out if he'd been honest earlier or if Mya was always going to keep a little wall up in the form of her relationship back home. Cassie arriving might have just been an easy way out for Mya when things got difficult. Either way, he was devastated. He knew he'd eventually need to learn how to let down his guard.

Deland's progress in football was linear, but his emotional and personal growth saw countless false starts. In football he followed the teachings of his coaches and mentors, folks he knew he could trust when it came to leadership and example. When he heeded their advice and did the work, he knew he'd continue to improve. When it came to decision-making, self-regulation, and emotional maturity, he had less clarity on who to follow and how to grow. Subconsciously he was still hamstrung by the messaging of his family systems, and his questions of identity and origins remained, stirring up feelings around worthiness, trust, and belonging. Escaping the unhealthy patterns and digging deep enough to discover and heal the roots of his struggles would be a lifelong process.

Back at school the next year, Deland was healthy again and motivated to come back strong in his junior redshirt season. All the work in the gym and on the track paid off—he finished with 1,103 rushing yards and eight touchdowns, adding another 181 yards receiving. He was fourth in the MAC in rushing yards, seventh in rushing touchdowns, and tenth in overall touchdowns, making his way back to the All-Conference list, this time Second Team All-MAC. Mya was out of the picture for good and his focus was solely on football and school. He was thriving academically, getting better grades than he did in high school, and he was surpassing even the lofty expectations his coaches had for him when they first recruited him. He stayed on campus that summer to continue training, his sights set on greatness in his final year in Oxford.

Deland put on twenty pounds working construction all summer on campus, weighing in at more than 200 pounds by the start of his senior

year. The NFL had started to feel like a realistic goal after the last season, but he wasn't sure he was good enough until he sat down with the
RedHawks' new offensive coordinator, Sean Payton. Payton had spent
the previous year coaching the running backs at San Diego State, helping his star back Marshall Faulk become the second overall pick in the
1994 NFL draft. When Payton told Deland he had a shot, Deland really believed it. From day one of senior year, Deland's entire focus was
making it to the NFL. If a handful of Miami University school records
got smashed on the way to the pros, that was just a bonus.

The fourth matchup of the season was against Cincinnati, and Damon
would be there—his first time seeing Deland play college ball in person.
Deland made sure it was more than worth the trip. On that September
day Damon and Adelle watched Deland carry the ball 27 times for 116
yards in a 23–16 victory over the Bearcats.

After the game Deland talked to the *Cincinnati Enquirer* about growing up in the shadow of Damon's football excellence and how he'd been
pushed to work harder. He said of Damon's first chance to see him play,
"He told me after the game that all the stuff he had read about me was apparently true. He had only heard about what I was doing or seen a couple
tapes, so it was a great thrill to have him there."

By midseason it was a bit of an inevitability that Deland would finish
his Miami career with his name atop the record books. After the team's
30–2 win over Ohio University in their penultimate game, Deland told
the *Cincinnati Enquirer* about breaking the school record for rushing yards,
"I'm happy to get it over with, so I don't have to hear about it anymore. It
hasn't been my driving force. But people have been asking me about it and
reminding me about it the last several weeks."

In the season finale of his college career, Deland rushed for 185 yards
and two touchdowns to lead the RedHawks to a 65–0 blowout win over
Akron, becoming the all-time career rushing leader for the entire conference (4,368 yards) while breaking four more Miami records: single-season

rushing (1,627 yards), career rushing touchdowns (36), career 100-yard rushing games (24), and single-season 100-yard rushing games (10). Deland also became the first player in Miami history to lead the team in rushing for four straight seasons. He would leave the school as one of the greatest players in Miami University football history.

"Deland is the real deal," Coach Walker told the *Cincinnati Enquirer* that season. "He's one of a handful of guys you get to coach in your lifetime that is really, really special."

With the football season over, Deland focused on finishing his classwork and prepping for the NFL Combine. He knew he wanted to continue his football career as long as possible, but he was also setting himself up for a career in youth counseling. The kid who hadn't really applied himself or believed in his intellect back in Youngstown had not only made it through the so-called Harvard of the Midwest, he had thrived. In fact, he was on track to graduate with more credits than required. The kid who had arrived with just a box fan and a bag of clothes would be leaving Oxford with an NFL contract and a future brighter than anyone ever imagined for him.

Of course, nothing came easy for Deland McCullough. As the Combine got closer and closer, the NFL still hadn't contacted his agent, Steve Luke, a former Ohio State standout and four-year starter for the Green Bay Packers. The two first met after Miami's game against Kent State, and by the end of the season Deland was signed to Steve's roster of current and aspiring NFL players. Steve reminded Deland of Coach Smith—two Ohio natives who had made it to the pros and had a certain presence and swagger to them. Steve instantly became an advisor and mentor as Deland looked ahead to the next part of his football journey. Steve couldn't believe Deland didn't get a Combine invite—he had smashed all the records at Miami and dominated the MAC. *Doubted again*, Deland thought to himself. He would have to prove himself in on-campus workouts, the individual or small-group sessions held for visiting scouts and coaches from pro teams.

Deland worked out for over a dozen teams in the weeks leading up to the draft, sometimes solo and sometimes alongside a teammate or two. He crushed every drill he did, impressing every scout and coach who made the trip to Oxford to see him. He was routinely running 4.4 in the 40-yard dash and getting 28 reps on the 225-pound bench press test. The only less-than-perfect showing was his workout for the Cincinnati Bengals—they had called him midway through a spring break trip with his boys and he'd driven straight back to campus to make it happen. Wasn't his best outing—he had to stop early because of tightness in his hamstring—but he was still more than good enough to make their draft-day short list. Deland's numbers in his workouts were on par, if not better, than the numbers put up by the guys at the Combine. In fact, the National Combine Ratings in the February 2, 1996, issue of the *Detroit Free Press* listed Deland as the fourth-best halfback in the draft. His 4.49 time in the 40-yard dash was the fastest of the twelve players on the list.

As Draft Day approached, Deland knew his life was about to be forever changed.

Deland suited up for the Cincinnatti Bengals

CHAPTER 13

Day one of the 1996 NFL Draft took place on April 20 at Madison Square Garden in New York City. Deland was over at Steve's house in Columbus to watch, though he wasn't expecting to hear his name called until the second day, maybe round 5 or 6. Steve, his wife and kids, and a couple of buddies gathered together with Deland to watch and react as University of Southern California wide receiver Keyshawn Johnson went first overall to the New York Jets and three future Hall of Famers were picked in the first round: offensive tackle Jonathan Ogden, wide receiver Marvin Harrison, and linebacker Ray Lewis. Three running backs heard their names called in the first round, including Ohio State standout Eddie George, who would be playing for Sherman Smith in his new gig as the running backs coach for the Houston Oilers. Every quarterback in the room had to sit, wait, and watch; 1996 remains the last NFL Draft to date without a quarterback selected in the first round.

An hour or two into the first day, Deland's pager lit up. He didn't recognize the number so he went upstairs to take the call privately. It was the Cincinnati Bengals' running backs coach Jim Anderson. "You're smiling, aren't you?" he said to Deland. "You're excited." *No way I'm getting picked this early*, Deland thought. *Especially after that so-so workout. But maybe . . .* "We're not selecting you right now," Anderson said. "We just wanted to let you know we're thinking about you. Talk to you soon, kid." *Thinking about me?* thought Deland. *When is soon? Tonight? Tomorrow?*

He was excited and anxious about when he might hear his name. The next night he settled in with Steve and his family for the later rounds, certain he'd be getting a call from Cincinnati—or maybe another team that would beat 'em to the punch.

The phone never rang.

The draft came and went, with the San Francisco 49ers using the 254th pick on Sam Manuel, a linebacker out of New Mexico State. He was that year's Mr. Irrelevant, a humorous title given to the last player selected. Deland would have killed to be Mr. Irrelevant. He could take a few jokes about going last, but he couldn't take not being selected at all. There was nothing funny about going undrafted. How could these teams not see what he could do? The numbers were all there, both in his seasons at Miami and his workouts. As calls started coming in from teams interested in adding him to their training camp rosters, he got more and more fired up about proving people wrong.

Washington, Dallas, Jacksonville, and Cincinnati all called in the minutes following the conclusion of the draft. Deland and Steve agreed that the best opportunity was with the Bengals, despite the team's basement-dwelling status in the AFC Central for much of the previous five years. Heading into the offseason, Cincinnati's running backs room was led by the first overall pick in the 1995 NFL Draft, former All-American and Rose Bowl MVP out of Penn State Ki-Jana Carter, plus former Colorado All-American Eric Bieniemy, who had finished third in Heisman Trophy voting his senior year. Carter was coming off a rookie season lost to an ACL tear and Bieniemy had accounted for just 398 yards the previous year, his first in Cincinnati and fifth in the league. The team depth chart, which ranks players according to their ability and likely playing time, had Carter and Bieniemy on top but then dropped off precipitously. Deland would be competing for a spot with Wisconsin alum Jason Burns, who had earned just one carry for the team the previous season.

By the end of draft night, Deland had agreed to a standard two-year deal with the Bengals for more than $100,000, complete with a $5,000 signing bonus. He didn't know anybody who made that kind of money. By comparison, No. 1 overall pick Keyshawn Johnson signed a six-year, $15 million contract and received a $6.5 million signing bonus, but Deland didn't care. Even his standard contract felt like life-changing money. He sat in the dining hall at school that week fielding congratulations from teammates and classmates who had seen the write-up in the paper about his big NFL shot. He smiled and meant it, but underneath the relief and happiness the same old fire burned. *I can't wait to get to Cincy and prove I should have been drafted*, he thought. *I can't wait to let these guys know what the deal is. I'm ready.*

The last month or so of school flew by as Deland studied for finals and made arrangements for life in Cincinnati. Coach Smith called to congratulate him on his contract and exchange a little good-natured trash talk since his Oilers were scheduled to play the Bengals in Week 6. Adelle and Damon came back to Ohio for Deland's graduation day, hooting and hollering as he crossed the stage.

Deland gripped his degree and thought about how he'd felt when he first arrived for orientation: Unprepared. Undeserving. He thought about the teacher back in Youngstown who said he'd never make it at Miami. He sure showed her. He showed everybody. He graduated with a higher GPA at Miami University of Ohio than he did at Campbell High School.

"How do you feel?" Adelle asked him after the ceremony, releasing him from a giant hug.

"Proud," said Deland. "I accomplished what I came here to accomplish. I made my impact."

"You sure did," Adelle said, beaming. "Best damn running back in conference history!"

"I proved I belong," said Deland. "I belonged here, Ma."

Deland's concerns about life outside the melting pot that was Youngstown were never realized in Oxford—not in academics, football, or his social life.

Minorities made up just 5 percent of the students at Miami at the time, and he was well aware of the economic and class differences, but he never felt unwelcome. The football team had a mix of different races, and those were his guys—all of his best friends in school were teammates—so it didn't feel all that different from Youngstown. Deland had heard about a small Ku Klux Klan rally that happened on campus just two years before he got there, and a teammate shared a story of a racial epithet being yelled at him from a passing car on campus, but Deland hadn't faced any similar situations himself. By the time he left Oxford he felt empowered by his time there and confident in himself heading to Cincinnati.

Deland went to Bengals minicamp in May and then spent the summer back on campus living with his buddy Ernest, training and working as an umpire for local youth baseball leagues in nearby Reily, Ohio. Deland didn't know much about baseball, but he showed up after workouts with his muscles popping in a tank top under his chest plate, so he didn't get much back talk from the kids or their parents, no matter how bad the calls.

In August it was time to report to Bengals training camp at Wilmington College. Deland walked into camp just like he'd walked into Oxford: chest up, shoulders back, ready to tell anyone who'd listen that he was somebody. That included former No. 1 overall pick Ki-Jana Carter. "I'm not just making this team," he'd say during workouts and drills. "I'm here to take people's jobs." Deland didn't want to make enemies, but he sure wasn't there to make friends. It was all business. He was gonna work like he always did.

By the time the preseason came around, Deland looked primed to beat the odds and earn a spot on the team. Established players often play limited minutes in preseason games, so they're a great chance for backup players or rookies to show off their ability and prove they can contribute. Carter and the rest of the Bengals' starters played sparingly in the team's first preseason game, a 28–25 win over the Indianapolis Colts, leaving plenty of carries for the rest of the running backs. Bienemy and Burns each scored a touchdown, but it was Deland who shined brightest, gaining 67 yards on 16 carries, including an explosive, game-winning touchdown in the fourth quarter, breaking six tackles en route to the end zone. "I thought he had a great run," head coach Dave Shula said after the game. "He ran tough all night. . . . If he keeps progressing he'll do well for himself."

A week later Deland once again led the team in rushes and yards in their 13–10 loss to the Cardinals. Burns carried the ball just twice for 11 yards and was released after the game, upping Deland's odds to make the final fifty-three-man roster. Adelle and Damon were there to see Deland put together another fine effort against Washington (then known as the Redskins) on August 16, amassing 52 yards on 11 carries, just behind Bienemy's 54 yards on 12 touches.

Two days before the Bengals' final preseason game, the Arizona Cardinals cut running back Garrison Hearst despite a breakout 1995 season that saw him put up 1,070 rushing yards. Cincinnati snatched him (and his $2.06 million salary) off waivers and thrust him into action immediately in that weekend's final tune-up against the Lions. Hearst knew only five of the team's plays and ran the ball only six times, but he broke tackles, showed burst, and impressed fans en route to 39 yards. It had just gotten a little tougher for Deland to make the team. The odds were against him as an undrafted player, but he had impressed in practice and in games, showing his new teammates and coaches the same work ethic and focus that had thrilled folks in high school and college. He looked good again against the Lions through three and a half quarters, rushing for 49 yards on 13 carries. It seemed inevitable now. This undrafted kid from Youngstown, Ohio, was about to make the fifty-three-man roster. Just three minutes and one second of meaningless preseason football stood between Deland and his dream.

The Bengals were in the midst of one last drive. Deland caught a pass and turned upfield. His lead blocker missed the angle and blocked Lions linebacker Stephen Boyd low instead of high, sending Boyd flying over him, diving into Deland, his helmet crashing into the side of Deland's right knee. Deland landed in a heap on the Riverfront Stadium turf, writhing in pain and screaming. His anterior cruciate ligament and medial collateral ligament were both torn and he'd suffered a compression fracture to the end of his femur. Deland was carted off the field, done for the season—and potentially his career.

Steve rushed down from the stands to be with him in the training room after the game but there wasn't much to be said. Everyone knew it was bad. Real bad.

"It's tough to see anybody hurt," said Coach Shula after the game. "But it's especially tough with this kid. This kid came in here unheralded and all he did was bust his tail on every snap. He kept a serious face and his focus throughout. This kid is special. He earned my respect and everyone's respect, really." Even Bieniemy, a five-year vet competing for a spot, admitted that Deland had been a leader despite his undrafted status and rookie standing. "He was a guy we kind of all looked up to because of his work ethic," said Bieniemy. "You hate to see something like that happen, especially a guy who worked so hard to get to this point."

The next few days, headlines in every Ohio paper bemoaned the loss of the standout rookie who had thrilled all preseason, leading the team with 201 yards rushing on 50 carries. "I haven't even thought about not coming back," Deland told Alex Marvez of the *Dayton Daily News*. "I'm not going to rush it or anything like that, but I'm optimistic. I won't be tentative when I come back. I'll be hitting holes like always. The way I run will always be the same."

Deland's injury was so severe and the swelling so great that they couldn't perform the surgery for several weeks. The team considered flying him to the newly opened Alabama Sports Medicine and Orthopedic Center, run by highly touted sports surgeon Dr. James Andrews, but Deland elected to have the surgery done locally by a friend of Steve's, Dr. Raymond Tesner. The damage was extensive—ligaments torn, compression fracture, cartilage gone. After the surgery Dr. Tesner delivered Deland the blunt truth about his future.

"I've gotta be honest with you," he said. "We did our best to prime you to come back to play, but you'll probably only have about three or four years before it all comes crashing down." It was as if a clock had started—Deland could almost hear his knee: tick, tick, tick, tick.

Deland lived just across the Ohio River in Fort Thomas, Kentucky, about ten minutes' drive from downtown Cincinnati. Adelle flew out to stay with him after the surgery and stayed for six weeks, making him meals, cleaning up, and running errands. They watched a lot of football—movies too—as he rested and let his leg heal. When the time came to start rehab, it was brutal. Tedious and lonely. Adelle would drive Deland to Spinney Field at 8:00 a.m. five days a week to lift weights alone. It was heartbreaking to watch Carter, Hearst, and Bieniemy handle the running back load without him, and he felt increasingly isolated from the rest of the team.

By the time Week 6 rolled around the Bengals were a dismal 1-4. Sherman and the Oilers came to town, and Deland went out on the field during pregame warm-ups to see his old coach. By then Sherman and his wife, Sharon, had two young kids—Shavonne and Sherman Jr.—and he was thriving in his second year coaching in the NFL. Deland told him that he was struggling. That he was dying to get back and prove himself but the road to recovery felt so long. Instantly it was like they were back in Oxford—Sherman once again telling Deland what he needed to hear. He told Deland he'd come too far to quit now. Reminded him of that tough kid he'd met in Youngstown, hungry to prove everyone wrong.

Reminded him that he'd already beaten the odds in so many ways, this was just another hurdle to get over and past in order to achieve his dreams. Sherman was positive and encouraging, telling Deland to keep working hard and to do everything he could to come back strong. Just like back at Miami, Sherman always knew the right thing to say. Deland felt like they were in a movie again, and this time he was the injured star getting hyped up by his inspiring coach en route to a dramatic comeback. Sherman had gotten him back on track.

Deland had brought a cute young coed from Miami to the game that day, and she was waiting in the tunnel for him as he left the field. He passed by the locker room with the girl on his arm, a little swagger in his step after talking to Sherman. Coach Anderson caught sight of him and pulled him aside. "Hey, starting next week I want you back in meetings, okay?" It was time to remind Deland he was part of the team. Make him feel connected enough to want to forget the girls and get back to the game.

Anderson's plan half-worked. Being around the guys invigorated Deland, despite the team's struggles. Meantime, Deland's evening rehab sessions at the facility often overlapped with practices for the Bengals cheerleading squad. One night he noticed a particularly pretty member of the squad, a gray-eyed gal with a big smile: Jessica. The two started to go out on the sly, as it was strictly forbidden for players and cheerleaders to date.

After a 1-6 start, Coach Shula was fired and offensive coordinator Bruce Coslet was elevated to head coach. The team finished 8-8, closing the year with three straight wins. Deland felt closer to his teammates again and continued to get closer to Jessica too.

By the time minicamp came around in May 1997, Deland was ready to pick up where he'd left off. He blew everyone away with the upper-body strength he'd amassed during rehab, throwing up 225 pounds 32 times on bench press.

The legs were there too. He ran a 4.43 40-yard dash. He was primed and ready to compete in a running back room that still had Carter, who'd had a disappointing season, and Bieniemy, plus newly drafted second-rounder Corey Dillon out of Washington.

Unfortunately, the hands on the clock moved even faster than Dr. Tesner had suggested. When training camp started that July, Deland had a couple great days of practice before his right knee started swelling up. He would practice and then have to get it drained, feel better, practice and then have to get it drained again. Tick, tick, tick. The good days were few and far between, and the days when he could barely bend his knee were far too frequent. When he got into the Bengals' first preseason game against the Colts and faced guys at game speed, he knew immediately: he'd lost a step. He looked at the flow of the game and the way his coaches were slotting in the running backs and realized he had no shot to make the roster.

The very next morning, Deland was cut. The Bengals told him they'd done it right away in the hopes he'd be able to catch on with another team. Deland continued to live with his teammate Rod Jones, an offensive lineman out of Kansas, and waited for another team to call. After a week or so Philadelphia called, and he flew out to Eagles camp to give it a shot, hoping his knee had calmed a bit after some rest. Deland's former offensive coordinator at Miami, Sean Payton, was the quarterbacks coach in Philly at the time and had raved about Deland to head coach Ray Rhodes. Deland started off well, killing the introductory workout, but as soon as he started taking hits in practice, his knee started to swell up again. Tick, tick, tick.

All the grit in the world couldn't strengthen tendons or heal reconstructed ligaments. For the first time in his life, Deland couldn't work his way out of a problem on the field. He had another surgery on his right knee and decided it was time to think about life after football—at least for now. Steve let Deland move in with him and his family in Columbus while he mourned another NFL season that would come and go without him. In early November he got a call from a team in the CFL, the Winnipeg Blue Bombers. Their season had just ended and they wanted to sign Deland to a two-year contract starting with the 1998 season. Deland had nothing to lose. He could go up to Canada in the spring and reestablish himself, hopefully catching the eye of an NFL team again.

In the meantime, Deland had to work. Steve helped him find his own apartment in the suburb of Reynoldsburg and get a job working at the Hannah Neal Center for Children, a residential home for kids in the custody of a county child protection agency. All the kids Deland worked with were sexually reactive boys under the age of thirteen, most of whom had suffered sexual trauma or abuse of their own. Their delinquent behavior, whether it be self-stimulation, hypersexuality, or inappropriate touching, was often the result of extreme neglect or developmental steps missed because of dysfunction in their home. Deland ran one of two pods in the center, making sure the kids took their medications, cleaned their rooms, got washed up, and ate right. He logged their behavior and acted as a mentor for the kids outside of their schoolwork and sessions with clinical therapists. He was stern and strict, but patient and empathetic. They found him kind and relatable and loved to hear about his football escapades, but they knew he was tough too—they didn't dare try him. Deland settled into life in Reynoldsburg, working at the center, going to Cincinnati to hang out with Jessica, and giving his knee a much-needed break.

As CFL camp neared the next spring, Deland received an experimental treatment on his knee, getting liquids injected to help lubricate it. He felt great when he arrived in Winnipeg, but because of roster setup and restrictions he spent most of the early months on the practice squad. University of North Carolina alum Eric Blount was the team's top running back and also excelled as a punt and kickoff returner. Limits on the number of American players per roster meant Blount had the only spot Deland could slot into.

Deland stayed focused in practice but was bored out of his mind in Winnipeg without games to focus on. When he wasn't watching TV in his hotel room he would get into mischief like racing cars with some of his teammates. He worried about how he was spending his time. Without games to look forward to, he could feel himself regressing, struggling to stay focused and self-regulate. "I gotta go home, Coach," he told head coach Jeff Reinebold. "I came here to play." That was all Reinebold needed to hear. "You're starting our game next week," he said. Deland started the next week and for the rest of the season.

It was a terrible year for the Blue Bombers, who finished a dismal 3-15. Their offense stunk—they started six different quarterbacks—and their defense was worse; they gave up more points than any team in the league. Deland's old recruiting host at Miami, Milt Stegall, was a great wide receiver for the team but struggled with injuries that year. The benefit was that Milt's injury allowed the team to move Blount to receiver, opening up the running back spot for Deland. While the team won only one of their last five games, Deland played well once he cracked the starting lineup, and he headed back to Ohio that November with a renewed hope for his future in football.

When Deland got back to Reynoldsburg, things with Jessica felt different. The distance hadn't been good for them, especially since Jessica's ex, a player with the Cincinnati Reds organization, had popped back into the picture. Their normally fun and easy relationship felt strained. Deland was back working at the center during the day, and most nights Jessica was busy in Cincinnati, whether with cheerleading practice or her primary job as a nurse, so date nights were few and far between. Deland wasn't sure they would survive the winter.

Darnell and Deland

CHAPTER 14

"How long you think she got, Deland?" Scott asked, throwing the back of his chubby hand up to his forehead and dramatically feigning a collapse over the back of a chair. "She gonna get the sickness for sure." He collapsed into giggles, his pudgy, prepubescent belly bouncing as he laughed.

"That's enough now," Deland replied, poorly hiding his own laughter.

The kids were always making loose bets on how long the new hires would last. How long till they got "the sickness" and moved on. Working at the Hannah Neal Center was a tough gig, both physically and mentally. Employees had to learn how to restrain kids who acted out and be willing to step in to stop fights on the occasion it was needed. They needed to be tough but have the patience and empathy not to resort to physical force unless necessary. Most importantly, they needed to be emotionally strong enough to help kids process trauma and work toward recovery. What these boys had been through—and what some of them had done to land there—wasn't for the faint of heart.

Darnell Lewis was the latest hire to earn a raised eyebrow from the kids—and Deland too. A tall, beautiful, brown-skinned girl in her early twenties, she looked like she'd walked right off a modeling runway, with a smile that lit up the room. When she first walked in the door in December 1998 they had her pegged for two weeks, tops. On her first day one kid thought she was a news reporter; she had a face for television, not a group home. Darnell had taken the job to get real-life experience for credits at Tiffin University in Tiffin, Ohio, a small town between Cleveland and Columbus. After getting her degree in forensic psychology she was finishing a master's in justice administration with a plan to join the police force.

Darnell was fascinated by crime. She wanted to investigate murders and put together clues in cases involving psychopaths and serial killers. Only problem was, she was still figuring out how to deal with the whole "dead people" part of a murder investigation. She had managed to weasel her way out of the class visit to a morgue so she wouldn't have to attend the viewing of a live autopsy. She didn't want to see any blood and she didn't want to think about the person who died or the devastated family they'd left behind. Darnell might have watched one too many episodes of *Law & Order*, because while the investigating and mystery-solving part sounded great to her, the rest was too much.

Darnell didn't have to reconcile her discordance with forensics on the job at Hannah Neal, but she did have to worry about the way Deland dissected her job performance. He took work just as seriously as he did football and he read her like he read blocks and gaps. He thought she seemed too emotional in staff meetings—taking it too hard when tough issues with the kids would come up.

Plus she seemed too flirtatious with him during shifts—not focused enough on the job at hand. (If you asked her, she'd tell you it was true she was flirting with him—how could she not with those teeth and that butt?) She was still figuring things out while Deland had been around for a while. He didn't have any time to wait on her or any other new employees to catch up.

At a performance review in mid-January, just a couple of weeks into Darnell's employment, Deland suggested to their boss that she wasn't cut out for the job and should probably be let go. Right in front of her! Darnell couldn't believe it. She had a crush on this dude and he was trying to get her fired! She had called in sick the week before—like truly sick, laying up in bed—and he told both her and their supervisors that he thought she was faking. *She's sick all right*—she got *"the sickness,"* he thought.

"She ain't cut out for this," Deland told the room. "Just my opinion. This ain't her thing." It was nothing personal. Deland actually enjoyed the time they spent working together—Darnell had a great sense of humor and kept him laughing in spite of himself—but he took the job as seriously as everything else in his life and didn't think it was the right place for her. Deland could tell that the kids saw Darnell as more of a nurturer than an enforcer, and the Hannah Neal Center required both. He'd seen plenty of new employees—both men and women—fail because they weren't able to find the right combination of gentle touch and firm hand.

Thankfully for Darnell, her boss didn't see things that way and she continued working at the center. One day when they were supervising gym class, Darnell looked over at Deland, stone-faced and alert, monitoring the kids' dodgeball game like it was an Olympic gold medal match. *I guess I shouldn't try to chitchat while we're working,* she thought. *Then again . . . these kids are at gym class. Let 'em go trip each other up. Who cares?*

"What are you up to this weekend?" she asked him. "Got big plans?"

"Going down to Cincinnati," he said, eyes still on the dodgeball. "Got a girlfriend down there."

Girlfriend?

"I know he didn't just tell me he has a girlfriend," Darnell told her friend on the phone that night. "We'll see how long that lasts."

Technically, Deland did still have a girlfriend, but things with Jessica were running on fumes. Deland really liked talking to Darnell and could tell she liked him, but he remembered the way things had ended with Mya and didn't want to create similar drama in his situation with Jessica. He made just a few more trips down to Cincy before he accepted that the relationship had run its course and ended things. Meantime, Darnell hadn't given up on those teeth and that butt. One night at the center she was bragging to Deland about what a great cook she was—mac and cheese, steak, fried chicken, greens. She was a soul food master. "I guess you better have me over and cook for me then," Deland said.

Got him!

Only thing was, well . . . Darnell couldn't cook. At all. Had been the baby of the household her whole life and never learned how. She also didn't have pots and pans at her new apartment in Columbus. In fact, she didn't even have silverware—just coffee cups and plastic forks. When Deland got to her place she told him she'd gotten home late so plans had changed. She couldn't cook for him; they'd have to go out. He saw right through it. *Slick move*, he thought, snickering. *I gotta give it to her.*

They ended up going to a nearby Applebee's and Darnell didn't wait long to admit that she actually couldn't cook a lick. She didn't want to start things off with a lie—even a little one. She wasn't going to lie about watching football either. Deland was wearing his Winnipeg Blue Bombers sweatshirt, and Darnell admitted she'd never heard of them. "You said it's called the CFL, right?" she said. "Is that a flag football league?" She truly believed he spent seven months of the year living in Canada to play flag football. And got paid for it! She also didn't know anything about the Miami RedHawks, the Cincinnati Bengals, or any other football team, college or professional. Instead of turning Deland off, it was kind of refreshing. He was so used to women fawning over him once they heard the letters N-F-L.

Darnell was naturally talkative and led most of the conversation. Even outside the walls of the center Deland was quiet and intense, but the more they talked the more Darnell got to see a bit of softness to him. And he was funny! Not funny like her—she could make a monk sworn to silence giggle in spite of himself—but funny in his own way. He wasn't shooting for volume, he was shooting for percentage. Subtle snark. More than anything, the conversation was comfortable. Both of them felt like they'd known each other for years.

Growing up, Darnell had never fantasized about getting married or settling down. In fact, when friends would daydream about a big wedding or how many kids they wanted she'd always crack jokes. "I don't even know what I'm doing next week!" she'd say. But Darnell felt like her whole world turned upside down when she met Deland. Even though she was fresh out of college and hadn't dated much, she had a feeling he could be something special. Deland was just a few years older, but he was ready to find someone with whom he could eventually start a family. A mature, adult relationship. No more immaturity or games, like with Cassie. No shoulda, woulda, coulda, like with Mya. And no more hoping for the best despite knowing it wasn't a fit, like with Jessica. He wanted something real. And he wanted to be the kind of man who was ready for something real.

That first night, he found himself completely relaxed around Darnell. She wasn't like anyone he'd ever met. She was beautiful—he had noticed that immediately—but he hadn't pursued her for that. Before he'd even thought about going on a date he had gotten to know her, gotten to like her, gotten to see her true character. She brought out the best in him and made him want to make it work. She was different.

This felt different.

Darnell

CHAPTER 15

DARNELL

D arnell Lewis was born in Cincinnati on April 21, 1976, to Donald Lewis and Joyce Simeton. It was a second marriage for both of her parents. Donald had two kids from his first marriage, Donald Jr. and Brenda, who were both already grown by the time Darnell was born. Joyce got pregnant at seventeen and felt compelled to get married, eventually giving birth to three sons with her first husband, Clifton: Clifton Jr., Tony, and a third boy who passed away just a few months after he was born due to a heart defect. Clifton Jr. and Tony were eighteen and nineteen when Joyce and Donald had Darnell, and the two boys instantly became her protectors.

Darnell's mom had several jobs over the years, including selling real estate, working as a notary, as a secretary at Dean Witter Investments, and doing gift-wrapping during the holidays. For all of Darnell's life her father worked on the assembly line making decorative laminates at Formica Group. He didn't miss a day of work in thirty-plus years but was forced to retire a year early because of Bell's palsy.

Joyce and Donald's marriage didn't last long—they separated when Darnell was two, and she spent the next decade living with her mom and Tony in a ranch house in the northern suburbs of Cincinnati. Clifton Jr. lived with Joyce's mother in Avondale, a predominantly Black neighborhood about ten minutes northeast of downtown Cincinnati best known for two major race riots, first in 1967 and again in 1968 after Martin Luther King Jr. was assassinated.

Sometimes Darnell would stay at the house in Avondale on the weekends; other times she would go to her dad's house in Wyoming, Ohio, about twenty minutes northeast of the city. She was too young to remember having lived in her dad's house when her parents were still married so it never really felt like home. She thought it was creepy, and she hated the musty green carpet in the living room. Whenever she was at her father's house, she counted down the hours until she could go back to her mom's.

For most of her formative years, Darnell felt much more connected to her mother than her father, regularly butting heads with Donald. She was hardheaded, he was hot-tempered, and she always felt a sort of loyalty to her mother, like she needed to take a side. Donald worked such long hours at Formica, he wasn't up for much fun at night other than his regular Friday bowling outings.

The baby of the family, and ever protected by her much older brothers and a handful of uncles, Darnell was slow to grow up. She insisted on sleeping in bed with her mother every single night. It felt good not to be alone.

When Darnell was twelve her parents decided to give it another shot and get married again. It was a complete shock to her. The two hadn't mentioned that they were seeing each other romantically again; Donald hadn't even spent any nights over at the house. They just suddenly announced they'd be getting remarried. Darnell wasn't optimistic about their chances of staying together, and she told them as much. Despite Darnell's protestations, she and her mom moved back into her dad's old house with the musty green carpet. Then and only then did she finally start sleeping in her own bed.

When Darnell was a girl, Wyoming was racially split by Springfield Pike, with the Black families living at the bottom, often working for the white families who lived "on the hill" in the bigger, nicer houses.

She went to school with predominantly white, Jewish classmates and enjoyed the privileges of living in a wealthy school district. For her senior prom the school rented out the entire Forest Fair Mall for the after-party so the students could enjoy the movie theaters, rides, and restaurants all to themselves.

Cincinnati long struggled with issues of segregation despite the state of Ohio officially repealing its so-called Black Codes in 1887. In fact, the high school Darnell went to, Wyoming High School, didn't integrate at all until 1965. In 1977, a year after Darnell was born, a full 80 percent of Cincinnati's schools were still failing to meet the integration goals prescribed by the US Commission on Civil Rights. Community-based civil rights activism eventually resulted in court-ordered action to improve issues of racial isolation and reduce segregation in Cincinnati schools.

Joyce had gotten Darnell into modeling as a baby and found her representation with the John Casablancas Agency. Darnell booked local jobs like a funeral home brochure and got a Hallmark contract, posing for a lot of greeting card scenes. She started booking so many gigs her mom made her take a break just before her teens and promised she could start back up at sixteen, if she wanted.

At fourteen Darnell was scouted by a modeling agent at the local water park, Surf Cincinnati, and Joyce relented. As long as she kept her grades up she was allowed to get back into it, working runway shows and weekend events at the mall. Darnell also loved to swim, working as a lifeguard during high school, and she got into organized sports her junior year when she joined the volleyball team.

Darnell was popular and outgoing, always busy with work, school, and the occasional boyfriend. She was a rule follower, and was almost always under the watchful eye of her brothers, but as she got older she rebelled a bit against the conservative ideas of her mother and grandmother. In her senior year of high school she got a nose ring and a dolphin tattoo on her ankle.

"A dolphin? Right there where everybody can see it?" said Joyce. "There goes the modeling jobs!"

Despite Darnell's doubts when they got back together, Joyce and Donald were happy in their marriage the second time around and stayed together until his death at the age of seventy-nine. By then he had become a doting grandfather, attending every Little League game, never missing a holiday or a chance to offer the kind of love he hadn't yet been capable of giving when Darnell was young.

Deland and Damon

CHAPTER 16

"**W**anna come with me to New York City?" Deland asked. "I'm gonna go visit my brother out there."

It was only a few days after that first date at Applebee's and Darnell couldn't believe Deland was proposing that date number two take place in a different state. And she really couldn't believe it when he said he was planning to drive.

"That's like eight hours!" she said, half-expecting him to say he was joking.

But it was no joke. A trip to New York was always worth the drive to Deland. He liked seeing the city and visiting family, plus he really wanted Darnell to meet his brother.

Deland assured her the drive wasn't all that bad, and she'd never been one to turn down an adventure, so that Friday after work she found herself sitting shotgun in Deland's Honda Accord heading east. A few hours into the drive, Deland pulled over into a rest stop and told her he was getting tired and wanted to shut his eyes for a little bit. Her mouth dropped open but he didn't pause long enough to notice. His head leaned back, his eyes closed, and he was out. No chance Darnell was falling asleep in this rest stop! Who knows what kind of folks might be around? So she sat, eagle-eyed, looking for sketchy characters while Deland took a nap. *Never a dull moment with this one,* she thought. They made it to East Harlem a few hours later, pulling up to the brownstone where Damon lived with Laura, Damon Jr., and their youngest child, Kepra.

Damon was thrilled to see that Deland was thoroughly himself around Darnell. No arrogance, no showing off. There was a connection between them that was obvious and natural. And boy, did Damon like Darnell. She was 100 percent an Ohio girl. Funny as all get-out, authentic, and kind. Helpful around the house and good with the kids. "Don't mess this one up, brother," he told Deland with a wink.

That first night in New York as they lay in bed, Darnell turned to Deland. "So . . . you and Damon. Y'all ain't got the same daddy, huh?"

"Is it that obvious?" he asked, chuckling. Deland was a whole head taller than Damon, for starters, and Deland had a deep, commanding voice. Meanwhile, Damon sounded just like Adelle—nasally with that same wheeze when he laughed. You could be convinced that Adelle had birthed both boys and Damon just favored her more, but no chance they shared the same mother and father. They didn't look or sound at all alike.

Deland and Darnell had gotten close very quickly, but he hadn't yet told her the truth about his family. The sting of others' reactions had remained close to the surface for years, and whatever this relationship might be felt too important to lose. He hesitated, then relented.

"Actually, I'm adopted," he said.

Darnell thought he was kidding at first. When she was a kid, joking about being adopted was a go-to for folks in the neighborhood. But Deland didn't laugh.

"What do you mean, your ma really your grandmama or something?" she asked. She'd heard of plenty of families where young moms had given over babies to their own mothers to raise or had cousins or aunts helping out, but she hadn't met a single Black person who was actually adopted.

"No. Really adopted," Deland said. "I got no idea who or where my mom and dad are." He told her a little about Adelle and A.C. adopting him as an infant. Told her about the day he overheard Adelle talking about picking him up in Pittsburgh. Told her how the man whose DNA he shared was a mystery and the man whose name he shared never wanted him. Told her he'd thought about it sometimes and wondered who he was, but . . .

"Well, we had it pretty tough growing up," he said. And left it at that. Everything else—John Comer, Frank Doon, the trips to Mansfield, the orange extension cord—that could all wait.

Darnell sensed that it was hard for him to share, so she didn't push. She had figured out early on that Deland wasn't quick to open up.

Saturday night, Damon took them out to one of his favorite restaurants in the neighborhood and he and Darnell got to know each other even better over several rounds of cocktails. Deland still didn't drink, so he looked on as the two chatterboxes got progressively drunker and louder. "You guys are two peas in a pod," he said, rolling his eyes, but he was thrilled. His two favorite people hitting it off. On the way home, Darnell insisted on an impromptu sidewalk photo shoot, her mittened hands gripping a streetlight as she did some kicks, *Singin' in the Rain*-style, in the January cold.

Back in Columbus, Deland and Darnell spent all their time together, both at the Hannah Neal Center and after work when they'd meet up with friends or pick up dinner and watch TV. They knew they were moving quickly, but it just felt right. They decided it didn't make sense to pay rent on two places if Deland was always crashing at hers, so he packed up his stuff and moved into Darnell's apartment. She still couldn't cook but she was learning, one heated-up jar of spaghetti sauce at a time.

In early April, Darnell kept waking up feeling sick and couldn't kick it, so she went to see her doctor. After running a handful of tests she got the news: "You're pregnant."

"Well, what did you think was gonna happen when you decided you wanted to play house?" her mother told her, shaking her head. "You didn't learn nothing from me getting pregnant before marriage?"

Darnell's mama and grandmama were both conservative Baptist women who had balked at the idea of Deland moving in. It was bad enough that Darnell had gotten that tattoo all those years ago; now she was living in sin? What had they done wrong? Hadn't Joyce told Darnell enough times how tough it had been to be a young mother? And hadn't Grandma Harriet always told Darnell to save herself for marriage?

"Well, you went and got pregnant," Harriet told her. "He ain't got no reason to marry you now. Why buy the cow when you can get the milk for free?"

Darnell was excited but a little scared about the pregnancy. She believed Deland was committed to her, but a baby was something else. This little being would connect them to each other for the rest of their lives. What if things changed when the infatuation stage was over? Deland would be leaving for Winnipeg again in a few months, and they hadn't done the long-distance thing yet. Darnell would have to spend almost the entirety of the pregnancy alone. In fact, if the Blue Bombers had a championship season, she wasn't even sure he'd be back in time for the baby's arrival. *Slow down*, she thought to herself. *Forget nine months from now, let's see what he says today.*

Deland was thrilled. Nervous, but thrilled. He told her he'd take her to every doctor's appointment until he left and send money back from Canada with every paycheck. He was as kind and steady as he'd always been, and she immediately felt at ease. He was gonna stick around. He was gonna do this with her. From the very first date they'd been on, Darnell felt safe if Deland was around. It was the same feeling she'd had with her big brothers growing up. No matter what, if he was next to her, she'd be okay.

Darnell realized how much a baby meant to Deland when he talked to her about being a father. It really hit her when Deland explained that he didn't know a single person who shared his blood. Didn't know anyone who looked or talked or walked like him. For Deland, this little baby would be the start of his lineage. He could put roots in the ground and point to the three of them as the beginning of a family line. While Darnell was still wrapping her head around being pregnant, Deland was already naming all the things he'd never miss—first haircuts, football games, practices, and school pickups. He was ready to embrace a whole new life. He thought about the guardian angels he'd had in the form of teachers, coaches, and uncles. The men who had supported him and believed in him. The men who had shown up when he needed them most and stepped in to set him straight when he needed guidance. Before the baby was even born, Deland decided he would be like those men. He would be the father he never had. This was his chance to change the messages of his family system. Going forward, fathers would choose to be parents. Going forward, fathers would choose to stick around.

When they went to their first doctor's appointment, Deland had to admit that he didn't know anything about his family or his medical history. It was scary for Darnell to wonder about what kind of blood ran through him; what traits, diseases, or genetic issues might come up. As a first-time mom, there was enough to worry about without having to think about the mysteries of his DNA. "All you can control is what's in front of you," the doctor told them. "The information is just going to have to start with him and this baby. You've got his medical chart and now you'll have this child's. That's two people's worth of information and that's how you start this family. Nothing you can let yourself worry about." Darnell relaxed. There weren't answers to be found, so she stopped asking questions.

Darnell hadn't spent any time thinking about being a mother. For as long as she could remember, she felt like her life wouldn't be an average one. None of that husband, house, 2.5 kids, and a white picket fence stuff. But here she was, head over heels for Deland and falling in love with the little baby inside her. She read *What to Expect When You're Expecting* cover to cover several times. ("That book was missing a whole bunch of damn chapters," she'd laugh with Deland months later as they learned on the fly.) She took prenatal classes offered by the hospital and learned about changing diapers, swaddling, breastfeeding, and sleep training. She asked her mother and grandmother for every piece of advice they had. She was excited and scared all at the same time. Sometimes when she looked down at her growing belly she wondered how she could be expected to care for a little human being when she was just figuring out how to care for herself.

Every time she got anxious, she'd imagine Deland rocking a tiny baby in his strong, capable arms and it calmed her down.

Despite everything Deland had been through, Darnell felt certain that he would be an incredible father. She wanted to learn more about how he'd grown up, what he might repeat with his own children, and what he'd do differently. The concept of intergenerational trauma was decades old but wasn't often discussed in mainstream media, nor was the idea that one might need to be intentional about not repeating a cycle of trauma. Darnell knew plenty about both, though. She knew the ways folks passed down patterns of abuse, neglect, or dysfunction, both from her studies and from friends and family.

Deland had cracked the door open by telling her about his adoption, but Darnell could tell it would take some work to pull out more of the past. She found a way in by telling stories about growing up and seeing where they connected with his life and where their paths diverged. She understood about his trips to Mansfield because she'd made her own visits as a child to see a relative at Chillicothe Correctional Facility, a state-run prison a few hours east of Cincinnati. Her parents' divorce meant years of growing up mostly raised by a single mother, so she could relate to Damon and Deland relying on Adelle for guidance. They laughed over her childhood modeling photos and the greeting cards with her face on them and he showed her newspaper clippings from his glory days at Campbell High.

For all the typical childhood experiences they shared, there was much about Deland's life to which Darnell couldn't relate. There were the big things, like questions about where and who he came from. The days spent waiting for a call or a visit from A.C. that didn't come. The weeks without electricity or a phone. And there were little things too, missed experiences that the kids she grew up with got to have. Simple stuff like camping. "We weren't going out staying in no tents by choice," Deland laughed after Darnell told him about being in the Girl Scouts. "We was just doing the basic necessities of life," he said shaking his head and chuckling. Darnell recognized early on that Deland had been through a lot, but he never used it as an excuse, he used it as a motivator.

When Darnell met Deland she never would have guessed he grew up in such turmoil, but the stories he told her helped her understand the push and pull of his childhood. For all the chaos he endured, Adelle's intentions in raising him were clear. It was clear how much she cared for her sons and how important it had been to raise successful, hardworking men. It was clear she was willing to make sacrifices to get the boys to the best schools and to teach them manners, faith, and humility. It was clear that whatever material things the boys were missing had felt less important to them because they always knew they were loved. They were secure in knowing that no matter what else was going on, Adelle was going to be there.

As Darnell got to know Adelle through dinners at their apartment or family get-togethers she also began to understand Deland's tendency to keep things in. Adelle talked a whole lot but avoided sharing the things that might let people get close. Just as she had when Deland was a kid, Adelle still had a lot to say—lots of stories, lots of holding court in the room and demanding attention—and just like back in the day, she kept folks at a certain distance. Darnell felt like even after talking to Adelle all day she wasn't sure she really knew her at all.

Darnell knew one thing about Adelle, though: she didn't want to talk about the tough times. She'd wave off conversations about the adversity they'd been through and their financial struggles. She'd put a stop to any mention of her marriages or the ways she'd been done wrong by men. Adelle continued to carry the messages of those who came before her—don't talk about it, don't get into it, God's got it. And years later, after suffering a stroke, Adelle would tell her sons that God took the bad memories from her. Whether they were talking about John Comer, A.C., or a particularly bad fight with Frank, she'd claim she lost the memory forever.

"God took that memory away from me, you understand?" Adelle told them. "I don't remember them. I don't dwell on them. I moved on. You kids had to go through the hurdle of seeing adults acting stupid, so you know how not to be an adult that acts stupid.

"We all have our moments, okay?" she said, getting defensive. "And we don't dwell on them. Those moments build character, self-respect, dignity, okay? I focus on that."

Adelle felt like she was protecting herself and her sons by never talking about the hard things, but in avoiding the realities of the trauma she suffered, she left that trauma unresolved and passed on unhealthy behaviors. Unable to face the impact of her abuse and recognize future stressors, she'd get triggered and model uncontrolled reactions. That's how you become Ma Barker—shoot first, ask questions later. Adelle clung so tightly to the story she told herself about silence, she couldn't remember the truth anymore. One that wasn't always pretty but that also wasn't all her fault. Adelle was never told that after the truth hurts you, it can heal you. She was never told that you have to talk about this sort of thing.

Darnell understood now where Deland got his secrecy. He had told her very little about those years living with Frank. He'd alluded to some violence. Some darkness. Darnell knew they'd both learned plenty about darkness during their college studies. How it can get to you. How it can change you. Make you bring your own kind of shadows to the next generation. Darnell thought a lot about the boys at the Hannah Neal Center. Innocent little kids who hadn't been able to escape the shadows their adults cast onto them. Deland was private, sure. Guarded, even. And it was clear he needed to spend some time uncovering the effects of all he'd been through. But she marveled at how normal he was. How little he seemed to hang on to what came before. How much he seemed to believe in his ability to decide what would come next.

"I know these patterns," he told her. "We both do. We've seen them at work, we've seen them at home. Look, a lot of people I was around back in the day used those patterns as an excuse. It will never be an excuse for me. Whatever I saw, I'm gonna be the complete opposite."

"If it's being disrespectful to the mother of your kids, I'm not doing it," he said. "If it's being abusive, I'm not doing it. If it's being an absentee father, I'm not doing it. My kids will never wonder if their dad loves them."

They weren't just words. For Deland the ultimate success in life would be to become the man he always believed he could be, not the one the world and his circumstances set him up to be. To prove that you aren't destined to bear the scars of your youth forever, that you always have a choice to heal. To be for his children what he'd never had.

Deland and his mom were such different people, Darnell wondered how much of him came from nature instead of nurture. He certainly took Adelle and Damon's teachings to heart and clearly came up a certain way because of the stories and lessons of his family, but there were parts of him that remained a mystery. She wondered if he often thought about those parts. He didn't talk at all about finding his birth parents. Was he as curious as she was about the stories his body could tell? The family that lived in him? Their relationship was so new, she wondered how much more of himself he'd be willing to show her as time went on.

Darnell's parents lived nearby in Cincinnati, so Deland met them early on, clicking instantly with Darnell's dad. Donald was a huge sports fan and he knew all about the Miami standout turned Cincinnati Bengal that Darnell brought home that first day. He lit up talking to Deland like he never had with Darnell—Donald was a guy's guy, through and through. Darnell wasn't jealous, though. She loved to see their friendship develop, especially when Deland got comfortable enough to call Donald for advice and lean on him as a father figure. Darnell couldn't imagine how it felt not to know your father, and then to lose an adoptive father as well. It really meant something to Deland to have Donald care about him. And for all of Joyce's hand-wringing about the two of them living in sin and getting pregnant so quickly, she couldn't resist Deland's charms. If Darnell was gonna repeat her mistakes, Joyce was glad she'd done so with a man so dependable and kind.

"You're not going to get hurt by us," Darnell told Deland one night as they were tucking into bed after dinner at her parents' place. "My family? We're not gonna let you down." He'd been through so much, she just wanted things to feel calm and safe for him. The urge to protect him had grown stronger as she thought about the baby they were going to raise together. She imagined Deland as a little boy, full of worry and fear. They weren't going to let their child suffer that, and she wasn't going to let Deland's life feel out of control like that ever again.

In May 1999, on the day of her graduation from Tiffin, Darnell shoved her growing belly into a girdle to fit into a dress she'd bought months earlier for the occasion. She'd been suffering from morning sickness and nausea that was made better when she had a little something to nibble on, so she tucked half a Subway sandwich in her bra and grabbed a finger-full of cold cuts every few minutes as she waited for her name to be called. *What a catch I am*, she thought, laughing to herself. She turned back to wave at Deland and her parents, sitting together on folding chairs in the back of the gym. She never could have imagined herself pregnant on her graduation day—or any day for that matter—but she was over the moon with happiness. She wasn't sure if it was emotions from the pregnancy or something deeper than that, but every day her heart swelled a little bigger for Deland. This was love—she didn't care how quickly it had all happened. A house full of little Delands running around suddenly sounded like heaven to her.

Just before Deland left for his second season in Winnipeg, Cincinnati came calling. Of course Darnell didn't know who Mike Brown was, but Deland hopped up quick to take the call when she said he was on the line. The general manager for the Bengals told him they'd seen film from the end of the last Winnipeg season and figured Deland's knee was in good enough shape to give it another go. Deland was still under contract in the CFL, though, and couldn't convince his new coach, Dave Ritchie, to let him out of it. Deland understood. They'd given him a shot up there and he was gonna see it through. Plus, he figured another great year in Canada might make an even stronger case for a return to the NFL.

At the end of May when Deland left for Winnipeg, Darnell decided to move in with her parents in Cincinnati. There was no sense wasting money on rent and she loved having her mother close by to give her advice and calm her nerves. She quit the job at the Hannah Neal Center (no doubt Scott and a few other kids made some cash off the early departure) and found a job closer to her parents' place. If the center was tough, this new gig was worse. She worked at a methadone clinic by the casinos in Indiana, handling and transferring warm urine samples in between bouts of morning sickness. The drive was pretty far—forty-five minutes each way—so she'd be up and out of the house by 5:00 a.m. every day. At 6:00 a.m. folks would start to roll in to get their medicine, many of them coming in straight off nights of stripping, partying, or gambling at the casinos. Folks trying to kick heroin, oxycodone, or other opiates. She'd start her days holding warm cups of urine, trying not to gag, and spend her afternoons taking notes on the samples.

Deland would check in with Darnell regularly, getting updates on doctor's appointments and the baby's size—a peanut, a golf ball, a plum. He was playing well but anxious to get back home. Week 9 against the Saskatchewan Roughriders was the midpoint of the CFL season, and he took a particularly big hit to his left knee. He asked to go back to the training room and have it checked out. The trainers didn't find anything definitive, so he kept playing, but every day after that he thought to himself, *Somethin' ain't right.* He was in pain for the entire second half of the season but trusted their staff and was able to play through it.

Darnell was able to fly up once in the final few months of her pregnancy to watch Deland play, cheer for him as he scored a touchdown, and see a little bit of his life in Winnipeg. After a weekend together talking baby clothes, cribs, and more, she returned to Ohio with the urge to nest. It was time to prepare a space for the baby on the way. Her parents had been wonderfully supportive, but her dad was always knocking about the house when she was trying to nap and she was ready to settle into a place of her own. She quit the job at the methadone clinic and found a little apartment in Mount Healthy, about twenty minutes north of downtown Cincinnati. She got money from Deland to put down the security deposit and first month's rent and crossed every finger and toe that the baby would stay in her belly until he got back.

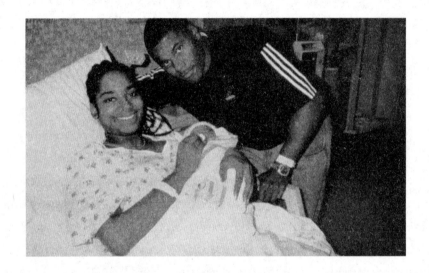

Darnell and Deland with newborn Deland II

CHAPTER 17

"Hold on, lemme trim up my hair quick," Deland said, slipping into the bathroom.

"You're kidding, right?" said Darnell. "Is this a joke?"

Darnell was in labor. Had been for what felt like days. She started dealing with Braxton-Hicks contractions during the day on Saturday and the doctor told her to wait until she had contractions that were two minutes apart. Finally, midday on Sunday, it was time. They had a forty-five-minute drive to the hospital, and Darnell was well past ready to get that baby out—she was already nearly two weeks past her due date. They had scheduled an induction of labor for that Monday and apparently the baby got the memo. *No induction needed—here I come!*

Of course, Deland couldn't become a father without a shape-up first.

"Deland! We got to go!" she yelled over the sound of his trimmer.

A minute or two later Deland came out, relaxed and calm, edged up and ready to go. They got to the hospital, checked in, and by the time Darnell was settled in bed getting an epidural, Deland had already pulled out the cot alongside her and was fast asleep. *Okay then. Make yourself comfortable,* Darnell chuckled to herself. It was just like that rest stop on the way to New York City. The man could sleep. Anywhere, anytime.

Deland woke up when it was go-time and stayed calm and steady for Darnell as she labored. On December 13, 1999, Deland Scott McCullough II was born, weighing in at more than ten pounds. Darnell looked down at the baby boy in her arms and realized the magnitude of her role as mother. *I'm responsible for you,* she thought. *We've got to take care of you.* She was overwhelmed and overjoyed at the same time. As she gazed down at the little boy in her arms, she felt like a switch had flipped inside her. *I won't ever let anything happen to you*, she thought. *If anyone so much as tries to lay a hand on you, I'll . . .* She scared herself with her own thoughts.

She watched Deland hold his son, cradling him in the crook of his arm like a glass football that might shatter into a million pieces if he squeezed too hard. She saw the awe in his eyes. That little baby was the first person Deland had ever met that he was related to by blood. That baby was the beginning of his line. Someone who was tied to him by both blood and choice. And he represented a whole new generation of the McCullough name; a generation that wouldn't suffer from the same absenteeism or abandon as the one before. In Deland's eyes, this new little McCullough wasn't carrying A.C.'s name, he was carrying Deland's. Deland felt an overwhelming desire to protect him. To be there for him and make him feel loved and treasured every single day of his life.

The holidays were a special time for the three of them. They went to Darnell's parents' house for Christmas and family members cooed over the baby and spoiled him with presents. He was the star of every get-together. The best Christmas present they'd ever get. As they settled into life as a family, Darnell and Deland were over the moon getting to know their little boy.

At the end of December, Deland got another call from the Bengals. His Winnipeg team hadn't won a lot, but he'd scored eleven touchdowns and amassed 1,696 all-purpose yards, doing more than enough to keep Cincinnati interested. The Bengals' season ended on Sunday, January 2, and they had him in for a workout the very next day. He looked great, his old teammates were excited to have him back, and the front office was ready to draw up another contract. Finally! Back in the NFL. Back on track to continue his dream.

Just a quick physical first.

The Bengals' trainer spent a lot of time looking at Deland's right knee—the one Deland had gotten surgically repaired while with the team a few years earlier. He administered the Lachman test, a manual test that gauges the firmness of an ACL. Deland's right knee was great. The trainer switched to the left knee—the one Deland injured that season up in Winnipeg—and the ACL on that side gave almost no resistance when the test was administered. The integrity of his left knee was shot. The doctors in Winnipeg had misdiagnosed him; he had been playing on a torn ACL. Deland knew it was over. Everyone in the room knew it was over. He wouldn't be rejoining the Bengals.

In early February the Tampa Bay Buccaneers called to request a workout, and Deland made the trip. Maybe he was hoping for a miracle; maybe he just wanted to prove to himself that he was wanted. That he belonged. He ran a 4.5, crushed the workout, and got an offer to join the team until . . . the physical. The team's medical staff couldn't believe the guy they'd just watched work out was doing it all on a torn ACL. Deland knew a miracle wasn't in the cards. His NFL dream was really over this time.

So that summer Deland went in for surgery number three, this time on the left knee. More resting, more rehabbing, this time just hoping to be healthy enough to play in backyard games of catch and family turkey bowls.

While rehabbing, Deland started working for a nonprofit called We Are The Future that helped at-risk adults learn carpentry, masonry, and plumbing skills to get back into the workplace.

He and Darnell bought their first house, a three-bedroom home with a fenced-in backyard, and got engaged—no fancy proposal, but she didn't mind. They were walking around the mall, pushing little Deland II in a stroller, when Deland steered them into a jewelry store and nonchalantly asked her, "Would you ever want to marry me?" As a little girl she'd never daydreamed about her wedding—not the proposal, the dress, not even the groom—but she realized now that she very much wanted to be married. She wanted to be married to Deland.

She told him so, and a few weeks later he proposed while they were sitting in the car, pulling out the ring he'd circled back to buy that day at the mall.

About a hundred people gathered for the wedding, held on August 19, 2000. Damon and Tony were Deland's groomsmen. Darnell's best friends from high school and college were her bridesmaids. The ceremony was at the church Darnell grew up going to, Lincoln Heights Missionary Baptist Church, and the reception was at the Wyoming Fine Arts Center, about two miles down the road. Darnell wore a simple white satin dress and a two-tiered veil with thick satin trim, had her hair pulled up off her face, and carried a colorful bouquet of red poppies, yellow chrysanthemums, and assorted wildflowers. Deland looked sharp in a black tux, white tie, and pocket square, and a pale pink rose boutonniere. Little Deland II, just eight months old, looked on quietly, big-eyed, wearing a pair of khakis and a sweater vest.

Opening day of the 2000 NFL season came and went without Deland, and he watched the Bengals take the field with mixed emotions. He accepted that his body had told him that the dream of playing was over, but that didn't make him any less sad not to be out there. He and Darnell had moved on and started a life that didn't include planning for seasons spent in Canada or weeks spent preparing for or recovering from surgery. When it came to football, Deland was out of chances. Or so he thought.

A few months later another opportunity came calling—literally. After picking up Darnell from her work at Child Protective Services one day in early December, he got a call from legendary Chicago Bears player Dick Butkus, who was working with the Chicago Enforcers of the fledgling XFL. Set to begin play right after the end of that NFL season, the XFL was a joint venture between NBC and the World Wrestling Federation. Coverage and tone would borrow inspiration from professional wrestling, but with legitimate game play that they promised would be more fun, with looser rules and a rougher style.

"How you feel?" Butkus asked him. "You ready to play some football?"

"Heck yeah, I'm ready," Deland responded. Another chance. He'd take it.

When he got off the phone he could physically feel the look on Darnell's face. "I know you weren't just talking about football," she said from the passenger seat, staring him down.

Deland went down to the Enforcers' training camp in Florida and started out playing well, but the pain in his knees was too great. No more tick, tick, ticking. The clock had stopped. Time had run out, just like Dr. Tesner had predicted.

Deland had a son now, and he wanted to be able to pick him up, run outside with him, teach him the game. He dreaded the thought of another major injury and another major surgery. He had proved all he could, showed up anyone who doubted him, and simply had no answers for the realities of injury. He told Coach Ron Meyer to send him home and finally, painfully, really and truly this time closed the book on his football career.

When he got back up to Cincinnati, Deland got a job at Kelly Youth Services, founded by former Bengals player Joe Kelly. The nonprofit operated rehabilitation homes for at-risk youth ages nine to twenty-one who were referred to them by area agencies. It was a slam-dunk job for a guy with Deland's background and it paid well, but the hours were unbearable. Deland would leave early in the morning, and by the time he got home, Little Deland II was already in bed for the night.

As a house manager for KYS he would take residents to school in the morning and pick them back up later that day. A few of them attended Harmony Community School, a local charter school for troubled junior high and high school kids. Ninety-seven percent of the students at Harmony were Black, compared to the Ohio state average of 17 percent. Most kids had been kicked out of other schools, some kids lived near the poverty line, and some showed up in the same clothes for days in a row. One day during drop-off Deland ran into a former RedHawks teammate who was working as a teacher at Harmony. The guy convinced Deland to consider a position at the school, and the very next day during pickup he interviewed in the parking lot and got offered the job. It was going to be another tough gig, but the hours made more sense and the mission was the same: help kids who grew up like he did.

The next eight years at Harmony were a time of tremendous growth for Deland. He was hired as a communications teacher (an irony not lost on a kid who grew up quiet as a mouse), and because folks knew about his NFL past he was immediately tasked with helping build their brand-new football program too. Deland had no interest in coaching—had even turned down an offer to go back and work as a graduate assistant with his old team at Miami a few years earlier. He wasn't burned-out on the game or anything; he just had his sights set on a different professional path. His focus was on helping kids in rough situations, giving them a sense of purpose, and showing them he believed in them—just what he'd needed as a kid. But when he got thrown into coaching at Harmony, he learned he could do all of that, even more effectively than before, by tapping into the power of the game that had saved him.

When Deland started at Harmony in March 2001, he was the fourth communications teacher his students had that school year. The kids had a way of running folks off. Certain kids in particular. One was Demar Harmon, a big man on campus who, when he did come to class, liked to turn the whole room against the teacher. Demar and a bunch of his friends had reputations as troublemakers and were rumored to be involved in illegal activities. They were unafraid of detention or bad grades and unmoved by their teachers' attempts to assert authority. For a few days Deland dealt with Demar's outbursts by checking him—getting face-to-face and showing Demar he wasn't going to be intimidated by him—but he knew he didn't want to keep that approach.

Deland had had plenty of teachers and coaches who followed the tenet of "If they don't fear me, they won't hear me." He didn't want anything he did to be fear-based. A guy was more likely to work hard if he wanted to make his teacher proud than if he was afraid of him. These kids had enough going on in their lives; they didn't need another adult trying to scare them into submission.

Deland didn't want his relationship with the Harmony students to be a power struggle; he wanted them to know he was just like them, and that he understood them. As he considered the best ways to connect, Deland realized the thing he'd always kept hidden might actually be his secret weapon.

"I'm adopted," Deland told Demar one afternoon, a week or so into the semester. He had asked Demar to stay after class for a few minutes, hoping a one-on-one chat might inspire him to clean up his behavior. "I got no idea who my mom and dad are," Deland continued. "No idea *where* my mom and dad are." Demar finally stopped fiddling with his backpack and looked up at Deland. "I grew up in Youngstown. Single mom, sometimes no heat, no electric, no phone," Deland continued. "Had to deal with crackheads. Had to deal with no one thinking I could do nothing. Had to deal with doubt."

As Deland told his story, he saw Demar's expression change. This wasn't a teacher coming in trying to play savior to some kids with messed-up lives; this guy was one of them. This wasn't some failed NFL star that was out of options; he was a guy who actually wanted to be there. He wanted to help kids because back in the day, he'd needed help too.

Demar felt a connection to Deland he hadn't felt with other teachers. The next day he told his crew to cool it on the disruptions. Word started to spread around school that Deland didn't just talk the talk, he walked the walk. He'd been right where they were and had found a way to be success-ful. The kids felt understood, so they let him in. Slowly but surely Deland was able to take control of the classroom.

Once he won over Demar and his crew, Deland could actually get something done. He could go beyond just teaching the kids and actually motivate them to want more for themselves. And he could use football to convince Demar and the rest of the guys to show up for school every day instead of just a few times a week. He started to think about how powerful sports could be in changing the lives of the students he saw—and not just playing them but using them as an educational tool.

Just four games into the 2001–2 Harmony football season, Deland was bumped up to head coach. Even though he'd only arrived at Harmony seven months earlier, he wasn't scared to make big changes there, and that included filling his staff with guys who believed in his system. No egos, no intimidation, just positive and encouraging words and belief that they could change these kids' lives. He got Miami University and the Bengals to send gear for his players and donate money to the school to get the program going. He made big batches of spaghetti and brought them in for the guys to make sure they got enough to eat before games. It wasn't long before Deland added athletic director to his titles.

Witnessing the impact he could have on his students through sports, Deland started to write down his ideas for a sports curriculum to use as a motivator for education. The second semester of the 2001–2 school year, Harmony implemented a trial run of sixteen students enrolled in what Deland called the "Sports Academy." The Academy started as a Tuesday and Thursday elective that taught students about the various ways to turn a love of sports into a career.

They could learn about becoming a journalist, personal trainer, referee, or agent. By the next year the concept had expanded, with four teachers leading eighty-eight students in their core curriculum, but with sports at the heart of the lessons. In English class the students wrote papers and delivered speeches on sports-related themes. Math class was based on statistics and sports calculations, and science was rooted in the study of an athlete's body or the physics of sport. The students found the material compelling and exciting, and they were still working toward important academic benchmarks at the same time.

"One size fits few." That was the motto of Harmony Community School. Deland set out to understand each student individually and to find a way to motivate, inspire, and transform them. Motivate, Inspire, Transform. Those were the three tenets that drove everything Deland did, whether on the field, in the classroom, or at the administrative level. He knew he could get through to the kids and change them for the better if he tweaked and adjusted things when necessary to meet their needs. He'd watched Demar go from skipping class to rushing for more than 1,000 yards, making the All–Southwestern Ohio team, graduating from Harmony, going to college on a football scholarship, and eventually walking on to the team at Cincinnati. Deland set an example that the students wanted to follow, both as an athlete and as a successful adult.

Harmony's founder and superintendent, David Nordyke, was so impressed with Deland that he named him principal of the school a month before the start of the 2003–4 school year. Just a few months later, in late December 2003, Nordyke died unexpectedly at the age of fifty-one. The board took a few days to deliberate and called Deland to tell him he'd been elevated to executive director. He was running the whole school. It was all very exciting and very overwhelming. While some folks at Harmony were thrilled to see Deland's rapid ascent, some resented his relative lack of experience and still others were angry about alleged promises they'd received from Nordyke before his death.

Because Deland was so green, the board wanted him to get his principal certification and take continuing education classes. His previous work experience qualified him for alternative principal certification, an initial credential that paved the way for full certification via an accelerated master's in education and the passing of a Praxis test for educational leadership. He was determined to prove any doubters wrong with his hard work and stay focused by making student growth and success his guiding principles. He would run the school the same way he ran the football team and the Athletic Department, by ensuring his staff was hardworking, qualified, motivated, and buying into the same ideals he prioritized.

Early on in his tenure, he realized some changes in staffing needed to be made. Most notably, the school's treasurer. The current treasurer was a guy who wasn't specifically qualified or trained for the job. Deland liked him fine but didn't understand why the school hadn't filled the role with someone who had the proper background and experience. Charter schools rely heavily on their treasurers because of the many different factors that contribute to them remaining in good standing with the state. Annual state audits of every school determine things like increases or decreases in funding based on enrollment, checking to ensure students reside in the school's corresponding district, and making certain the school offers the requisite number of hours for learning opportunities as prescribed in their contract. The treasurer directs the school's financial affairs, including accounting and insurance, and is responsible for reporting the progress of the school against its responsibilities, including formulating policies regarding fiscal operations and monitoring the expenditure of funds. Deland wanted everything aboveboard on his watch, so he replaced the treasurer with one of the auditors who had been assigned to Harmony over the years. Deland had worked closely with the guy to get him proper paperwork, connect him with various departments and regularly report on the school's status. Who better to ensure compliance than an auditor?

Darnell wasn't surprised at all by how Deland took to his new role. She saw how different he was. How people were drawn to him.

From his office to the classroom to the football field, Deland's influence could be felt everywhere at Harmony. When a fight broke out during a game against rival Dayton Jefferson, Deland broke things up between parents, players, and staff and got all his players onto the bus and out of danger. A few weeks later, Harmony's opponent called to cancel on the Tuesday before the team's last game. It was senior day, the last chance for the seniors to play in front of home fans. With the field already rented and families planning to attend, it felt right to play some sort of game. Deland recruited male teachers willing to play in a full padded tackle game that Saturday. They practiced on Thursday and started to spread the word, bringing out an even bigger crowd than usual.

This was a big deal: coaches, teachers, and students all facing off in a live tackle football game! Everyone was gunning for Principal McCullough, but they had no idea who they were dealing with. Two touchdowns on offense, five tackles on defense—Deland was back in his element and loving it.

Soon the demands of running Harmony forced Deland to step away from coaching the football team, but he applied the same work ethic and determination in the executive director's office that he had on the field. He whipped the place into shape best he could. That included uniforms for all students and split-gender education to keep the kids more focused in classes—boys downstairs, girls upstairs. He was moved by the book *Why Gender Matters*, by psychologist and family physician Dr. Leonard Sax, a leading proponent of single-sex education. Deland also continued to hone the curriculum of the Sports Academy to keep serving students who found more motivation reading sports biographies for English, using baseball statistics to learn math, and applying physics to football to fall in love with science.

Darnell started working at Harmony, first as a liaison between the school and local social services, then in special education. Deland and Darnell had welcomed their second son, Dasan, in March 2003, and their third son, Daeh, in June 2004, and though Darnell had earned her second degree from Tiffin University—a master's of justice administration—she decided to leave behind her dreams of working in law enforcement and instead continue her path in education. In response to the large number of students at Harmony classified as special needs, the school partnered with Antioch University to hold after-school classes for teachers right on Harmony's campus. Through the program Darnell and others were able to earn their master's degrees in education with an emphasis in special education. It was tough to give up her dream, but Darnell knew it was too difficult to be a mother of three working nights on the streets of Cincinnati investigating crimes. Plus she still hadn't figured out how to deal with that pesky problem of dead bodies.

Working at Harmony was stressful but rewarding for Darnell. She knew how much she and Deland were helping the students and families there. There was a bit of chatter about nepotism at the proverbial water cooler when she was hired, and she laughed thinking about it on the nights she'd stay late cleaning Deland's office and emptying his trash. *No special treatment here*, she'd think. *More like he's e-special-ly tough on me!* They moved three times during Deland's promotions, first to a house near Darnell's parents in Wyoming, then to a bigger home in Liberty Township, and finally a beautiful house in Lockland.

They knew the Lockland house would require some work—it was an old Victorian that had been vacant for five years—but they saw some magic in it. Built in 1890, the five-bedroom stunner had a gorgeous wrap-around porch and more than half an acre of land. They had to update most of the inside, repaint every square inch of the outside, and replace every window, but it was worth it. As Darnell settled into the new neighborhood, she laughed at herself and the way life had surprised her. Husband, house, three kids—might as well put up a white picket fence and finish the stereotype. She imagined the boys growing up there, walking five minutes down the street to the high school, playing football at Roettger Field, just across Mill Creek. She pictured herself weaving greenery and lights on the porch railing for Christmas every year and taking photos documenting the boys' heights next to the tree.

While Darnell was settling in, Deland was getting antsy.

For all the success he was having, Deland missed football. He couldn't let go of the joy he'd felt those few seasons he got to coach the Harmony team.

Discovering the power that sports had to inspire, motivate, and move his students brought him back to his days playing. The pride he took in working hard and seeing results. The lightness he felt on the field; the release of that big backpack of weight and stress. The way sports gave him confidence by evening the playing field. It didn't matter how much money he had, what was going on at home, or if folks doubted him: the box score told the story of who he really was. He wanted to help more kids discover themselves through sports.

Plus the charter school business was messy.

Since its inception, Harmony had been a bit of a lightning rod for controversy as one of the first charter schools in Ohio. Add to that a brash and unapologetic leader in Nordyke, who was one of the coauthors of Ohio's charter school reform movement, not to mention the typical issues that plagued many charter schools—tension between private interests and public funding, racial isolation, and lack of financial transparency. Deland's focus was too often pulled away from the students; he wanted to get back to the hands-on work of helping kids. He wanted back in on the game of football.

In the fall of 2007, Fred Wilson, one of Harmony's top-performing teachers, a program director, and the school's registrar, came to Deland requesting that the school pay for him to get his principal certification. Deland had always liked working with him and had been the one to promote him to his director and registrar roles. He loved his passion for the work and supported his desire to get further certification, but the school already had a principal—him! He couldn't find a reasonable justification for Harmony to pay, so he denied Wilson's request. Wilson felt like Deland had clipped his wings. He was frustrated that the school had paid for Deland's expedited certification but wouldn't cover his and was angry about what he felt were unmet promises made by Nordyke before his death. Wilson decided to pursue the principal certification on his own and continued to work, but he began simultaneously working to undermine Deland and Harmony.

Wilson started using work hours to do his schoolwork, not only neglecting Harmony responsibilities but also using Harmony situations as topics for his assignments, sometimes including sensitive internal information. When someone in the office found one of Wilson's reports in the printer, full of negative commentary about Harmony, she passed it on to Deland. He consulted Harmony's lawyers and they recommended he be fired, soon after sending an associate to the school to inform Wilson of his termination. Furious, he filed an unlawful-termination suit. Unbeknownst to Deland and the rest of his former Harmony colleagues, Wilson also started speaking to a local reporter that had been investigating charter schools and went to the state auditor with allegations about Harmony, triggering an investigation.

The efficacy and legality of the state's charter school program as a whole had become a major focus for local news after several recent scandals. Out in West Toledo, the husband of a former director of a charter school was charged with twenty-nine felony counts in connection to activity at the school. W.E.B. DuBois Academy, another charter school right in Cincinnati, faced an equally dire situation. Two years earlier the school's former superintendent had been indicted on charges of theft, unauthorized use of property, telecommunications fraud, and tampering with records relating to enrollment. He was ultimately sentenced to four years in prison. The potential to catch Harmony on some sort of wrongdoing, even something less severe, would be a big get for the reporter.

Deland was on his way to a school basketball tournament in Erie, Pennsylvania, in early January when the state auditor descended on Harmony's campus with some fifty employees, going through classrooms and offices to seize files, paperwork, and computers. Deland got a panicked call that officials from the auditor's office were searching offices and removing items, so he turned around, rushing back to find Darnell in his office, confused and worried. What, exactly, were they looking for?

Deland was still doing a bit of an audit of his own, vetting and testing employees to make sure they were the best fit. When he took over as executive director, he was forced to put trust in a lot of people to do their jobs without a ton of oversight. Nordyke's sudden death meant there were no notes or instructions left behind about how he had filed things, run things, managed people, and kept the school going. Were there employees Deland should have replaced? Nefarious things going on at the school that he hadn't discovered or properly managed?

Soon Deland would learn the extent of Wilson's accusations: that Harmony was collecting state funds for kids who were no longer actually enrolled at the school and that Deland had used student labor and school funds to get a new deck built at the house in Liberty Township. Deland knew for sure he could prove the deck accusation was a lie. He provided receipts showing that he had an agreement with the school that he would pay for all of the wood and materials, plus the paperwork proving that the school's treasurer, the former state auditor he had hired, had approved the deck project for the school's carpentry class as part of students' required minimum hours of practical learning. As for the state funding, he knew that he had operated in good faith, but worked with each department to try to ensure that the school had fully cooperated with audits, properly tracked student attendance, and kept up to date with any state information requests.

Deland knew this wasn't the first time Harmony had been involved in a case with the state. Nordyke and the school had brought a claim against the Ohio Department of Education years earlier, before Deland was hired. After the school's first year, an audit allegedly showed that enrollment estimates for the second semester didn't match actual enrollment, so the next year the state withheld what they considered an overpayment. Nordyke and Harmony argued that the findings of the state report were inaccurate and won the case. They received the withheld $174,856, with the court finding that the Department of Education had relied on a flawed audit report. Deland hoped Harmony would come out on top again this time.

He spent the next few months awaiting the state's findings and stressing over the case. He exchanged hundreds of emails with the auditor assigned to the case and over time felt confident that the state could see the work he'd put in at the school and the efforts he'd taken to do things right. He yearned more and more for the days he'd spent working directly with students, out on a field or in a classroom. That spring of 2008, Shane Montgomery, the head football coach at Miami University, reached out to him about an opening for a running backs coach. It felt like a lifeline. He was ready for a new challenge and loved the idea of getting back on campus at Oxford, but he also couldn't imagine leaving everyone at Harmony high and dry right in the middle of the investigation. He was torn, but he interviewed for the job. He started to map out all the ways he could blow away the staff and players from day one and jump-start a coaching career. He started to think about how he might tell the teachers and students at Harmony that he'd made the tough decision to leave.

The tough decision never presented itself. He lost out on the job to former NFL third-round pick Jay Graham. Deland tried to tuck away his coaching ambitions and refocus his energy on Harmony, but he wouldn't be at the school much longer.

Bad publicity from the charter school lawsuits and concerns about Harmony's future caused a drop in enrollment for the fall of 2008. Fewer funds because of fewer students, plus hefty legal fees from the case with the state, combined to compromise the school's ability to fund special programs like electrical studies, carpentry, auto shop, theater arts, and, most important to Deland, the Sports Academy. Deland didn't feel like a second-rate Harmony was a Harmony at all. He found himself in long conversations about the school's future with Nordyke's widow, who was still a guidance counselor there and a member of the school board. They both agreed the school no longer matched the vision of its creator, and as the investigation from the state dragged on, they decided to shut down. Harmony Community School officially closed its doors in December 2008. Deland was the one tasked with letting teachers know that they no longer had jobs and telling students and parents that they would need to find a new school for the second semester. He had been so proud of the programs he created and the students he'd seen turn their lives around, but he also felt like he'd let Nordyke down.

During his time at Harmony, Deland had not only elevated the football program, taken over the Athletic Department, invented and implemented the Sports Academy, and become the principal and executive director; he'd also helped more than one hundred of Harmony's basketball and football players get scholarships to go to college. He'd witnessed firsthand guys like Demar find a reason to care, find a passion to pursue, and choose to turn their lives around. He had amended the graduation requirements to include a verified postgraduation plan. He met with every rising senior to help them fill out their college applications and financial aid forms, guiding them through their plans and requiring they document their intentions, whether they be to attend college, trade school, or enter the workforce. He had followed his passion to help underserved kids and had done all the things he'd come there to do—and more—but he'd also been at the helm when things fell apart. That was tough to swallow.

The case against Harmony continued for years, and money is still owed to the Ohio Department of Education after the court ruled in its favor in the amount of more than $2 million. Deland wasn't named or held responsible in the case, but Wilson was. In trying to oust Deland, Wilson, it turned out, had inadvertently implicated himself. Included in the documents and computer files gathered by the auditor were detailed correspondences between him and someone in the school's Finance Department, openly plotting a takedown of Deland and the school. Even worse, as Harmony's registrar, Wilson was the one ultimately responsible for enrollment, scheduling, recording of grades, attendance, and transcript data.

When the school closed down, Deland was drained by everything that had just happened, but nonetheless was determined to try to help his teachers and staff find new jobs, making calls and introducing them to connections in the education industry. He was content to take a little time off himself, but he was a hot free agent in the education world, and so before the start of the second semester, he got a call to teach English at Cincinnati College Preparatory Academy for the remainder of the school year. It was an easy gig compared to running a school, and at least it got him back in the classroom, where he could make a direct impact on students.

He was making a big impact at home too. Starting in preschool, Dasan struggled in class because of how rarely he spoke. Early in the school year a few teachers even thought he was mute. Deland recognized the behavior as similar to his own behavior as a child, but he couldn't reconcile that description of his son with the boy he knew at home, full of things to say. He and Darnell decided to sit in class for a day and were shocked to see their little boy act quiet and closed off. They followed the teacher's suggestion to take him to the hospital for an assessment, where he passed all the tests and showed no signs of physical or mental delays. They sat him down and Dasan finally told them he didn't like the school or the way the teachers spoke to him but that he hadn't been confident enough to vocalize that.

Deland and Darnell pulled him out of class and decided to put him in a different school the next year. As Dasan got older, Deland made a game plan that included improving his confidence and surety in himself. He and Darnell helped him establish good habits and a solid plan for handling his schoolwork, and assured him that teachers and staff at school could be trusted with questions and requests for help understanding things. They helped him come out of his shell and find his voice.

Meantime, Deland II put a lot of pressure on himself as the oldest, taking to heart his role as leader and protector of his brothers. He also had big expectations for himself as a football player, hoping to follow in his father's footsteps. Deland II reminded Deland of himself—a hard worker for whom nothing came easy. Deland II set big goals for himself—sometimes too big to reach—and Deland comforted him in those moments of disappointment. He encouraged him to just keep working hard, telling him that the rewards of hard work were far bigger and more long-lasting than just what happened on the football field.

Then there was Daeh, the most outspoken of the boys. Quick-witted and smart-mouthed, he was as gifted athletically as his brothers but wasn't as naturally hardworking. Deland worked with him to do more listening and less reacting—in sports and in life. He also taught Daeh how to be more intentional as an athlete and have more urgency in his approach to training and games. When Daeh tried to talk his way out of things, Deland reminded him that the McCullough men made their mark with actions and hard work, not words.

Deland told all his boys that he demanded nothing when it came to sports except to always try their very best. He'd support them in athletics and practice with them every day if they wanted, but if they found other passions, he'd support those too. He promised himself he wouldn't be one of those overbearing parents who screams at their kids or berates the officials. He went to games and cheered them on, but he kept his thoughts mostly to himself, especially when it came to other coaches' game plans and decision-making. Except for one time when Deland II was in sixth grade. Deland had volunteered to move the sticks at one of the team's preseason games, an exhibition at Paul Brown Stadium, home of the Bengals. As he worked his way up and down the field along with the game action, moving the pole to mark the line of scrimmage or the distance to a first down, he couldn't help but notice how disjointed Deland II's team looked. The offense looked totally dysfunctional and what he saw in the game didn't look anything like what the team had been working on in practice.

The next day when he and Darnell picked up Deland II from practice, the coaches were handing out the upcoming season schedule. As Deland walked over to grab one he noticed the head coach appeared to be in a mood about something. When he looked up and saw Deland coming, he didn't even let him say a word before launching into a heated tirade.

"Oh man, lemme guess. You comin' up here with a whole bunch to say about yesterday, huh?" the coach said.

It was clear he had been hearing it from a lot of parents about the loss the day before, but Deland didn't care. Who was this guy to come at him like that when he hadn't even said a damn thing? He hated that hostile energy. Hated when people seemed out of control. Deland would try to push it down, but any time a man would get really heated around him he would instantly be back in that living room, watching Frank shove and punch his mom. He would sometimes joke about it triggering his PTSD, but it wasn't a joke. He could feel something in his body shift when he was around that energy, and he sometimes found he couldn't stop himself from matching it.

"Well, yeah, I was gonna ask what the hell you were doing out there," Deland said, now ready for a fight. "Your offense was shit, and the guys looked completely lost."

By the end of their angry back-and-forth, Deland had told the coach he didn't need to worry about Deland II anymore—he would go play for another team and the coach wouldn't have to deal with either one of them. When he got back to the car, Darnell could tell something was up. Deland explained what happened but only remembered the beginning and the end of the dispute. On the rare occasions he became angry like that he'd almost black out, just like he used to do when Frank got violent. Disassociate, then snap out of it and remember almost nothing. "All I know is I told the guy 'Fuck you' and 'We're not coming back,'" he said.

Later that day, the coach called Deland at home and apologized for how he'd come at him. He was overwhelmed by all the criticism he'd gotten after the game and assumed Deland was going to lecture him too. He admitted he was a little intimidated by a parent who was also a coach and a former NFL player. Deland apologized too, saying it was really out of character for him to lose it like that and that he should have reacted differently. He said he hoped Deland II could still be on the team and offered to help out with coaching, only whenever and wherever the guy could use it. By the end of the conversation he'd gone from overbearing parent to volunteer coach in less than twenty-four hours.

In addition to his volunteer duties, Deland had a new job. The summer after his semester teaching at Cincinnati College Prep, Deland had gone to the Charter School Convention in Washington, DC, where he ran into a fellow administrator he knew from the Cincinnati area, Andrea Martinez. She recruited him to come work with her at King Academy, a predominantly Black school in the Over-the-Rhine neighborhood of Cincinnati.

At King, Deland wore a suit to work every day and enjoyed the relative ease of teaching at a strong academic school without the drama he'd dealt with at Harmony. Andrea was preparing for him to take over as principal, so he was studying for his Praxis School Leadership Series test. He was set up for success and on a path to thrive at King Academy, but there was still something missing.

He missed the sports element he'd brought to all his work at Harmony. He tried to convince Andrea to let him start up a basketball program or just some intramurals in the school gym, but it was a no-go—Andrea was all about academics.

By the spring of 2010, Deland had passed his exams and was fully certified to be a K–12 principal, but he was already on his way out of King Academy. Former Notre Dame wide receiver and defensive back Michael Haywood was getting ready for his second season as head coach at Miami University and had been telling folks around the program that he'd like to bring in a prominent alum to add to the staff. Someone to motivate the players, to show them an example of what they could become. Word got to Deland and he called up Michael to throw his hat in the ring. Only problem? The only available job was as a coaching intern.

"Five-hundred-dollars-a-month salary?" said Darnell, her jaw dropping. "Need I remind you we got bills and three kids?"

They did indeed have bills to pay and kids to care for. They had gotten used to Deland's annual $120,000 executive director salary at Harmony and had adjusted just fine to his $70,000-a-year salary at King Academy, but $500 a month was a serious change. They sat down to crunch the numbers. Darnell was bringing in money working at Cincinnati Public Schools, Deland's car was paid off, and they'd bought their house outright, so they had no mortgage to pay.

Between Darnell's car payment, groceries, utilities, expenses for the kids, and such, it would be tight, but they could do it. Deland knew they wouldn't have to make any major sacrifices or lifestyle changes for the next year, but he also knew that if it didn't work out, he'd need to go back to education and the security of a principal's salary.

"We'll make it work," Darnell said. "Look, I ain't gonna be the reason you're talking years from now, sitting up saying, 'If you would have just let me do this or that.' If this is what you wanna do, we're gonna do it."

Deland promised Darnell he wouldn't toil away at entry-level coaching gigs for years. If he was going to make it as a coach he needed this foot in the door, but he intended to move up quickly, just like he'd done at Harmony. Oxford was about forty-five minutes away from the house in Lockland, so Deland would commute back and forth every day, occasionally spending the night at a hotel if he stayed super-late to work. Being back in Oxford was a dream, and coaching college ball felt as natural to him as playing had.

That season he had an outsize impact on the Miami players despite his low status on the coaching totem pole. He was relatable, inspiring, and a great motivator—and it didn't hurt that his pictures and records were all over the facility. The rest of the coaches noticed a special kind of magic he had working with the players. Motivate. Inspire. Transform. Deland remembered the three tenets that had led his work at Harmony and added three simple demands of his players: Be Detailed, Be Dependable, and Be Disciplined. Know what you're supposed to do, do it consistently, and be ready to bring it when it matters most. Deland wanted to prove that change can happen in a positive way. He'd seen so much negativity in life and so much negativity in coaching especially. He refused to scare or threaten guys into succeeding. "I'm gonna get the best out of you by being positive," he told his players.

More than anything, Deland wanted his relationship with his players to be reciprocal. "I don't know everything," he'd often say. "I need you all to help." He'd tell the players the why of what they were doing instead of defaulting to the old "because I said so" model. He made himself available to talk and rejected the idea of authority or hierarchy. They were all going to learn together and make each other great together. "The power of respect is not to disrespect," he would say, letting them know he understood not to abuse his power as a leader and that they in turn had to earn his admiration by not acting disrespectfully. The players felt trusted and believed in, and they responded. Deland was just a coaching intern, but his impact was powerful.

At the end of the 2010 football season, Coach Haywood left for the

University of Pittsburgh. A new coach usually wants to reset the staff and bring in his own guys, so Deland suspected he'd be out at Miami. He called King Academy to confirm there was a job waiting if he couldn't find another gig in football. He started sending out résumés to a bunch of coaches at different schools and called up his old coach Sherman Smith to ask to use him as a reference. They hadn't seen each other in years, but they had talked off and on as Sherman continued a successful career coaching in the pros. Coach Smith was in his first season as running backs coach for the Seattle Seahawks, having spent twelve years with the Oilers (who had become the Tennessee Titans early in his tenure) and a couple of years with the then Washington Redskins. Sherman was thrilled to hear that Deland had gotten into coaching and said he'd be more than happy to talk to anyone interested in hiring him.

The guy Miami University hired to replace Haywood turned out to be a familiar face from Deland's playing days—Don Treadwell. Tready not only wanted Deland to stay, he offered him the job as running backs coach. This was the dream! A chance to lead his old position at his alma mater. Deland never ended up coaching a game in Oxford that season, though. A few weeks after accepting the job working under Tready, Deland got a call from Kevin Wilson, the new head coach at Indiana University. Wilson had been Deland's offensive coordinator at Miami, working above Treadwell back in the day. He said he hated to poach one of Tready's guys but he needed a coach to lead the Indiana running backs. Deland couldn't believe it—a Hoosier? He couldn't say no to the opportunity. Indiana was a Power Five team with a bigger salary, better competition, and higher visibility.

Deland called up Sherman, who had spent three seasons at Illinois, and asked him to share everything he knew about Indiana's football history, coaching in the Big Ten Conference, and how Deland might elevate his game to the next level. Just a year in and Deland's NCAA coaching career was taking off even faster than he could've imagined. He and Darnell began making arrangements to move the family to Bloomington and prepare for life at a Big Ten school. If he hadn't been so busy packing up the house, organizing new schools for the boys, and prepping for recruiting, Deland might have spent a little more time thinking about the phone call he'd gotten from Adelle a few days earlier.

Darnell, Deland (holding baby Diem), Deland II, Daeh, and Dasan

CHAPTER 18

It was near the end of January 2010, and Deland's move to Bloomington was quickly approaching. He was sitting in his office finalizing arrangements when Adelle called from Youngstown with news that the lawyer she worked with on his adoption had passed away. Just idle gossip, no different than when she'd call about somebody in town getting married, divorced, having a baby, or acting stupid. But then:

"I wonder if I could request your files from his office," Adelle said.

"Why?" he asked. "What would be in them?"

"Oh, I don't know. Maybe they'd have information from the home you were at before we adopted you. The orphanage."

"Orphanage?" This was the first Deland had heard about an orphanage. Or even that these files existed.

"Oh, I know I told you this already," Adelle said, wheezing as she laughed. "You were at a maternity home run by the Methodist Church. Out in Pittsburgh. Single mothers went there to have their babies. And it was an orphanage too.

"They called the lady that worked with us on our foster kids to tell her about this little Black baby they had. Baby Jon, the nuns called him. That was you."

"Wait, 'Jon'?" Deland said. "Why'd they call me that?"

"I told you all this before," said Adelle, though she was starting to wonder if she had. "It was nuns; maybe they got the name out of the Bible, I don't know."

When they hung up, Deland's mind was reeling. It wasn't much, but it was something. It was more than the nothing he'd always known. And it was more conversation about his adoption than he'd had with Adelle in more than thirty years. He wasn't mad at her for dumping this new information on him; he was just confused. Why had she mentioned getting his files? Did she think he should go looking for his birth parents? For years and years the line—both in his head and to anyone who asked—had been the same: "I don't know anything and I don't need to know." His adoption simply wasn't discussed. Adelle didn't volunteer information and Deland didn't ask. But now he couldn't fight his growing curiosity. After a lifetime of shooing away every thought that snuck into his head, the questions started coming fast and furious.

What's my mother's name? Is she looking for me? My name is Jon?

J-O-N. A door creaked open with those three letters.

Deland suddenly had an urge to look for his biological mother. He started to poke around on the internet, looking for websites that connected adopted children to their biological parents. He scrolled through a few pages' worth of profiles on one site and downloaded and printed a form to fill out from another, but he didn't even know if it was for the right department, or even the right state. There were so many faces, so many sites. Finding her felt unlikely, but he couldn't quiet the questions that were flooding his brain. There was so much he would ask her. Mostly about the boys. Dasan was shooting up like a weed—did he get all his height from Darnell's side, or did Deland have tall parents too? Daeh didn't look like the other two boys—his face was rounder, his eyes more almond-shaped. Did he favor someone in her family? Of course he also wondered about her. What she was like and why had she decided not to keep him? Had she been looking for him? Did she ever think about him? Had she been the one who named him Jon?

He lost himself in that word again: Jon. Was he Jon, or was he Deland? Was he somehow . . . both?

When Darnell called him in to eat dinner, he tucked the form he'd printed into a moving box, along with his curiosity. It wasn't the time for this—he needed to focus on Indiana. He left for Bloomington a few days later, and Darnell and the boys moved out and joined him after the school year ended.

The next six years in Bloomington were a dream for Deland and Darnell. It wasn't all that different from Oxford; both small towns that revolved around the college. They found their new favorite spots—BuffaLouie's for wings, the Butcher's Block for ribs—and made new friends. The Bloomington housing market was surprisingly expensive, so they lived in rental homes instead of buying. They always made sure to have a yard big enough for the boys and all their activities. They were growing up, getting tall like Darnell, and sporting Indiana crimson and cream every day like their dad.

Deland would request to recruit out in New York so he could spend time with Damon and his family, including his second wife, Valerie, and their daughter, Jazmin. He had a soft spot in his heart for Jazmin and loved surprising her at school every time he was in town. Deland's normal recruiting area included Youngstown, so he got to see more of Adelle too. She had moved back to their old stomping grounds a few years earlier.

Every time Deland went back to Youngstown or neighboring cities, he'd see himself in the boys he recruited. Especially the boys whose families struggled like his had. He'd flash back to sitting in the living room at 270 Jackson, nervously facing impressive men like Sherman Smith or Bob Stoops, hoping they'd see something special in him. Now he was the one sitting in a player's living room and meeting their parents—or a grandma or an aunt who'd taken responsibility for them. He recognized the shame in their eyes when he'd sit on a couch that had holes from cigarette burns or springs popping out. He could feel the boys' longing. It was a familiar longing. A desire to get out, to prove themselves, to be somebody. Deland had wanted so badly to get out of Youngstown, but whenever he went back he felt deep gratitude for the place from which he came. Deep affection for the people who had done their best when he was a kid and the people who were doing their best now with these boys he was recruiting. Deland had gotten out, he had become somebody, but only because of what Adelle had done for him, the ways Damon had mentored him, and the things Youngstown had taught him. Whenever he got home from those recruiting trips, Deland would look around at his house—at the fancy appliances and nice furniture, at Darnell and the boys running around—and take great pride in how far he'd come.

Darnell had believed him all those years ago when he promised to stick around. Had believed him when, just a few months after meeting, he told her she could count on him and that he would be a great father to their children. Now she would watch him with the boys—patient but firm, loving and supportive—and she'd marvel at how he'd become something he'd never seen.

How he could give so much he'd never received. Sometimes he was so perfect it felt like some sort of contest, to get as many Brownie points as possible with the boys. Even if he spent all day at the office and could only make it to see the last snap of one of the boys' football games, he'd pull up for that snap. Any game he couldn't attend Darnell would be in charge of videotaping so he could watch it later and give them pointers. He was there for every skinned knee, twisted ankle, and busted bike chain. He was the father he never had.

When they were little the boys took Deland's constant shows of affection for granted, but as they got older they really listened when he explained why saying "I love you" was so important. "I'm going to tell you I love you as much as I can," he'd say, "'cause Dad didn't have a dad saying that to him. He didn't have a father to give advice or be a role model. No father there when I woke up and when I went to sleep."

Deland knew he had defied the odds by not repeating the trauma with which he'd grown up, but he never chalked it up to chance or luck.

"I'm here because of my choices, not luck," he'd tell Darnell and the boys. "I'm the father I am because I choose to be, every day. God gives you an example of what to be and what not to be; you make the choice."

He never wavered in his commitment to fatherhood. He never let his boys wonder how he felt about them. He was proud of himself. Sometimes he'd get sentimental thinking about what his scared, shy, younger self might think about the man he'd become. He'd pull a Ziploc baggie out of his bedside table to flip through the eight or ten photos he'd taken with him to every stop, from Oxford to Columbus to Cincinnati to Indiana. A shot of him and Damon, bright-eyed and chubby-cheeked, riding bikes in the driveway of Allerton Court. Uncle Billy and his salt-and-pepper goatee. Easter Sunday, Damon and him in matching beige leisure suits and black shirts with big fat collars, Botany 500 trench coats slung over their arms and Adelle behind them looking chic in a long white coat. Coach Smith in his bright red sweater standing next to him at Campbell Memorial as he signed his letter of intent to play at Miami. Coach Smith grinning next to him in the locker room at Miami during his recruiting trip. The support of his family and his successes in football had sent him on quite a journey. He never took any of it for granted.

As for the Indiana team, when Deland arrived, he and the rest of the staff had a big job ahead of them. The Hoosiers had finished in the bottom three in the Big Ten in 2009 and dead last in 2010. Deland was a first-time position coach trying to establish his voice and style, and he was tasked with motivating a group of guys who might not get a single win all season. He made up for the experience he lacked with hard work. Just as he'd done as a player, he was determined to outwork every other guy in the game. Most importantly, because of his degree in sociology, his minor in coaching, and his time at Harmony, he brought with him an incredible ability to connect to and build relationships with the players.

It was clear to Deland that the same skills that earned him the principal job at Harmony would help drive his success as a coach. His heart, his ability to relate and motivate, his desire to go beyond just football to get to the insides of a player—especially the ones who needed a little extra care. Deland still had to learn a lot about the Xs and Os of the job, but he already possessed the most essential qualities of a great coach: love for the game and his players, the capacity to teach and motivate, and the ability to get buy-in. His players would come to practice ready to work and show up to games prepared, passionate, and determined to make him proud. He had also spent so much of his life observing, quietly watching how people acted and reacted. He could read people and situations better than most. Knew when to get loud, when to be soft, when to step up, and when to stand back and let his guys figure it out for themselves.

Deland could also recruit better than anyone, getting commitments from guys like Tevin Coleman, who went on to be a unanimous All-American at Indiana. A three-star recruit getting scholarship offers from programs like Georgia Tech, Nebraska, Oklahoma, and Michigan State, Coleman saw in Deland a guy who was gonna work to make him great. Was gonna help him reach his goals. There was nothing smarmy about Deland when he walked into a house to win over a player and his family. He wasn't a used-car salesman trying to make a deal, he was a human being who understood their excitement, fears, and concerns, and he could honestly assure them he would have their best interests in mind.

"These guys live and die by what you say," Coach Wilson told Deland of the players in his running backs room, shaking his head. "They love you."

Wilson was a tough guy. Pulled no punches. Not with players or his staff.

Sometimes his old-school, in-your-face style conflicted with Deland's more laid-back approach and he'd take subtle jabs at Deland's softer, more supportive style. Deland got frustrated with the digs at his expense but always felt validated when players got sick of Wilson's cursing and insults and came to him to talk things through and cool down. He knew he was doing something right. Not long after he got to Indiana, Deland had called Coach Smith for advice on working with a head coach with a totally different style. He knew he had a lot to learn from Coach Wilson, but he also questioned whether Wilson's aggressive approach got the most out of the guys. Sherman just said to do things his way, don't change his style for anybody.

"I knew from day one that I wanted to be a coach to make a difference," Sherman told him. "And when you know *why* you do what you do, it impacts *how* you do what you do. Just remember your why and continue to do you. It'll all work out."

That first season of Wilson's tenure, 2011, the team finished a dismal 1-11.

They improved to 4-8 the next year, finishing second in the Big Ten with 442 yards of offense per game. They improved again to finish 5-7 with an average of 508.5 yards of offense per game in 2013.

The summer before the 2013 season, Deland was reunited with Sean Payton, doing a monthlong coaching internship with Payton's New Orleans Saints as part of the Bill Walsh Diversity Coaching Fellowship. The program pairs NFL teams with up-and-coming minority coaches with previous NFL playing experience, offering them a chance to watch, learn, and assist during training camp, offseason workouts, and minicamps. While Deland didn't get the chance to participate much, he loved the feeling of being back at an NFL facility. He enjoyed working at Indiana, but he had his sights set on something bigger. At the professional level he could not only help players secure their legacies, he could ensure that he was remembered as one of the best too. A coach who had done the job at the very highest level. He got home from the internship and changed the password to get into his office computer at Indiana to six simple words: "IWillCoachInTheNFL."

As they got older, Deland's boys were falling in love with football too and spent a lot of time around the Hoosiers team, wearing Indiana crimson or their favorite "RUN DMC" T-shirts, a play on their last name. Fourteen-year-old Deland II, nearly taller than his dad already, all gangly arms and legs, would sometimes join the running backs group in the weight room when he was in junior high, pushing through power cleans, pull-ups, and seated presses as players urged him on. He was still hard on himself, but he fed off the encouragement of the older guys. Dasan and Daeh, eleven and ten, joined Deland II once a week for private training sessions with one of the team's strength-and-conditioning coaches.

Dasan had been carrying around a Ray Lewis doll ever since he could walk, telling anybody who would listen that he was headed to the NFL to be just like the legendary Baltimore Ravens linebacker. No longer a shy kid, he had become the most confident of the three boys. Nothing fazed him—he was certain he was going to be the next great NFL star.

When it wasn't football, it was basketball—all three played in local leagues. With all that running, jumping, cutting, and diving, they'd been back and forth to the local spine and joint center for a variety of injuries over the years. Dasan had his first surgery at the tender age of ten after tearing his meniscus playing basketball by himself in the driveway. "I guess bad knees run in the family," Deland said, shaking his head as they drove to the center, thinking about the surgery scars on his legs and hoping for better for the boys.

During car rides to and from games or rehab, Dasan and Daeh loved to steal Darnell's phone and post selfies to her Instagram. "Hacked!" they would caption yet another close-up photo of their own faces. She'd get them back with plenty of sleeping pictures, their heads leaned back against the seat, mouths gaping open, likely dreaming of grabbing another rebound or making a big run. Back at home the boys would pop on their helmets and ride motorized minibikes with their friends up and down the street, the flame decals blurring as they went by.

Sometimes Darnell would spot Deland out there too, knees splayed out to fit on the little bike he'd snatched from one of the boys. He'd go speeding past the house, big smile, head full of memories of rushing to make a shift at KFC or joyriding around town with Tony.

In July 2014, Deland was accepted to another NFL coaching internship, this time with Sherman Smith and the Seattle Seahawks. Being back on a football field with Coach Smith put Deland right back at freshman year in Oxford, eighteen years old and looking to impress the former NFL star. And now Sherman had a big fat ring on his finger too. That February he'd helped lead star running back Marshawn Lynch and the Seahawks to the first Super Bowl win in franchise history. Deland watched everything Sherman did—the drills he ran, the way he talked to the guys, how he commanded the running backs group and kept them focused. He was surprised to see how much of Sherman's coaching style had rubbed off on him despite just one semester together. They were both motivated by a desire to inspire, not intimidate, and they both started by connecting with players as humans, not just athletes. Deland admired that Sherman didn't yell at his players or curse them out. Sherman was respectful, so despite their big paychecks and egos, these pro players respected him too.

Deland was much more involved in the Seahawks practices than he had been in New Orleans. Sherman trusted him to run individual drills every day and watched as the players immediately responded to him. He laughed with the other coaches as Deland jumped in to do some of the drills with the running backs to give them a boost of energy. Of course afterward Deland wouldn't stop talking about his sore knees for the rest of the week! Deland had never felt more confident that he could coach at the NFL level. He wanted to soak up every experience he could and learn as much as possible, so he was never more than a few steps away from his old coach, mirroring his every move. The "me and my shadow" bit earned him a playful ribbing from some of the other coaches and players.

"Did y'all rehearse this?" running back Spencer Ware cracked at practice one day, making fun of Sherman and Deland for using the same motivational phrases and gestures as they worked through a drill. Teammate Robert Turbine snickered and pointed at Sherman. "You can tell he learned from you, Sherm."

"You walk like him, you talk like him, you wanna be him!" assistant coach Pat Ruel would say to Deland, doing a little march with his elbows bowed out, delighting anyone nearby. Ruel and the rest of the staff could tell how much it meant to Deland to impress Sherman and prove he was deserving of an NFL opportunity. At first Deland felt embarrassed, like he was being amateurish or a suck-up. But just like back in his playing days, if he wanted to get far, he knew he had to outwork everybody. *Let 'em laugh*, he thought. *It'll be worth it when I make it big.*

Though they'd talked on the phone on and off over the years, those weeks in Seattle were the first time Deland and Sherman really had time to catch up.

They'd sit in Sherman's office for hours and talk about life, their families, and what it was really like to coach in the NFL. When it was time for Deland to go back to Bloomington, Sherman popped his head into the offices of offensive coordinator Darrell Bevell and defensive coordinator Dan Quinn, pulling Deland behind him. "You get a job anywhere as head coach, you need to hire this guy," Sherman said, pointing to Deland. "This guy is a good coach."

Deland knew he'd done Coach Smith proud and had impressed the Seahawks staff. He knew he could excel at the next level and felt grateful for the chance to show everyone what he could do. As he got on the flight back to Indiana, he set his sights on getting to the NFL as soon as possible. It was time to hire an agent and put the word out to the league; he was ready.

Back at Indiana, Deland's good-cop, bad-cop relationship with Coach Wilson was about to hit its breaking point. It was late September 2014, and Deland was working on returns with the kickoff team ahead of an upcoming game against Maryland. Coach Wilson marched over from the other side of the field, head full of steam, screaming about how he didn't like the way Deland had set up the drill. The man could go from zero to a hundred without warning.

"You know what, man," Wilson said, getting up in Deland's face. "I'm taking you off kick returns. I'm taking over this whole unit."

Deland tried to keep his cool. He was used to Wilson blowing up over little things. He'd been that way ever since their days back at Miami, when Wilson was his offensive coordinator. Deland didn't like it, but he was never surprised by it. He calmly tried to explain why he'd split the guys in half and why he'd set things up that way.

"Stupid shit," said Wilson, getting angrier and angrier. "And you know what, it was a mistake hiring you."

Deland started to feel his face heat up and his teeth clench. He hated being around men who lost their temper. He could feel his nerves kick in, could feel the stress rising. The proverbial foot was on the gas pedal again, ready to send him into fight-or-flight mode. He was back in that room with Frank, too small and too scared to do anything. And this time Wilson had really gone too far by questioning him as a coach. He knew Wilson didn't mean it—Deland had been tremendously successful at Indiana—but he couldn't stand that feeling of being doubted. All those childhood feelings of inferiority came flooding back to him.

Not good enough. Again.

Deland slammed down his clipboard. Everything went black. He started to charge at Wilson, cursing at him, but felt arms pulling him back. Next thing he knew, all the running backs were at his side, pulling him over to the other field, cooling him down. Coleman, D'Angelo Roberts, Tommy Mister, Devine Redding—they were all there. Deland got himself together after a few minutes and started walking back over to practice, heart pounding as he spotted the Indiana athletic director, Fred Glass, standing right on the sidelines. Glass had seen the whole thing.

As Wilson gathered everyone together for the next part of practice, he noticed all the running backs off to the side.

"Come on over, guys," he said. "Let's get back into it."

None of them moved.

"Fuck this, man," Roberts muttered under his breath. "Be talking to my fucking coach like that. Nah. Fuck this shit."

Eventually practice got back underway—running backs too—but when they ended practice for the day no fewer than fifty players lined up to fist-bump Deland on their way inside. "Coach," they said as they nodded at him, bumped fists, and left the field. They appreciated that someone had stood up to Wilson—sometimes that guy needed to get checked. It was a reminder of something Deland already knew—he was more than good enough. His guys knew it and he knew it. Unlike back in Youngstown, he didn't wonder whether the doubters might be right. He knew he belonged, but he'd gotten triggered by Wilson's words all the same. He was frustrated he'd let them land. *Next time, I don't react*, he thought. *I stay in control. You make the choice.*

Deland didn't seek out confrontation, but he was no longer scared of it either. When necessary, he was ready to protect his family or his players, but he knew how to take charge without repeating the violence he'd seen from Frank. He wasn't quite as adept at handling personal attacks, often internalizing his feelings of anger or shame. Most of the time those bottled-up feelings inspired him to work harder to prove himself, but sometimes they resulted in him blowing his top and losing his cool. He wanted to learn how to downregulate his emotions and endure heated moments without flipping back into fight-or-flight mode and losing control. It was time to take that next step in his healing so he could prevent the blackout moments that resulted from previous traumas.

Back in the locker room he got a text from Glass. "You're good, Deland," it read. "Don't worry about today. You're on solid ground here."

That season, Deland's running backs group set a program single-season record with 3,163 rushing yards. Coleman led the way, setting the school record with 2,036 rushing yards and finishing seventh in Heisman Trophy voting. He decided to forgo his senior season and was selected by the Atlanta Falcons in the third round of the 2015 NFL Draft. Deland was voted 2014 Big Ten running backs coach of the year and was a finalist for national running backs coach of the year.

———————————

One night that spring, Adelle was at home watching television and saw a story on the news about adoptees who had fought for the passing of a new bill—Ohio Substitute Senate Bill 23—that would allow adult adoptees in Ohio to request their original birth certificates. As of March 20, adoptees over the age of eighteen could file a request. She called Deland to tell him. There wasn't a guarantee he'd be able to get his, she told him, because birth parents who didn't want their identities revealed had been given one year's time to request that their names be redacted.

Even in those cases, though, birth parents were required to give the state detailed medical histories. Adelle told him not to get his hopes up, but he could try. At the very least he could get some more info on his family's medical background for those three boys of his.

Adelle had felt conflicted ever since Deland told her he'd started looking for his birth parents. She had always tried so hard to control things, but as he got older she'd felt her grip on the situation loosening, especially when he started having kids. She knew he deserved to know more about his history and so did those boys, but the thought of it scared her. She thought about him finding his birth mother and worried about being in competition with her. Worried about losing Deland emotionally. The only tie that bound them was a mutual choice. Would he keep choosing her?

And love, a voice inside of her said. *Choice and love. You have a lifetime of love between you. A lifetime of being his mother.* Adelle tried to remind herself that being a mother doesn't always start with giving birth. She had been Deland's mother his whole life and she would be his mother forever. She told herself he just needed to look. It was okay to look. It was curiosity, he wasn't trying to replace her.

She tried to believe it.

In the end, she thought, *it doesn't really matter what I think. He's an adult now. It's his decision.*

Deland left the next day for a recruiting trip in New Orleans but made sure to stop at a Chase Bank there to get an official cashier's check to send along with the application he'd printed out. Then he waited. And waited. He called the Ohio Department of Health several times but felt like he was getting nowhere every time he spoke to someone. He told Darnell it felt like he was getting the Heisman, but not in a good way—a stiff-arm from the Department of Health.

Darnell was supportive of whatever information Deland wanted to find, but she worried about the kind of heartbreak that might await him. Over the years she had read stories about adoptees looking for their birth parents. People who found out their mother had already died, that their father could've been any number of guys, that their extended birth family was a mess. Someone needed a kidney, someone needed money, everybody resented being reminded that a baby had been given away. In a lot of cases, she read it was something as simple and heartbreaking as finding them, sending a letter, and never hearing back.

"Just don't have any expectations," Darnell told Deland. "You might not find them. Or worse, you might find them and they're just not what you're looking for."

Deland was willing to take the chance.

After weeks of waiting, he finally got a call back in the middle of a spring football meeting. He stepped out into the hall to take it and recognized the voice on the other end as the woman he'd spoken to a few of the times he'd called. She fumbled with her words.

"I'm, uh, sitting here with your records," she said. "But, uh, I . . . I can't give them to you.

"I really shouldn't say anything," she stammered. "But, um . . . you have to get them from where you were adopted," she said.

"Where is that?" Deland asked. "Where was I?"

"I'm, um, I'm really not supposed to say," she said. There was a long pause. Then: "You're going to have to go through Pennsylvania. I wish I could help but I can't tell you anything else." She knew she had the information he wanted, but she also knew she couldn't legally share it.

Deland knew about the maternity home in Pittsburgh, so the Pennsylvania thing made sense, but why couldn't she share the records if she had them? When Deland searched online for an application in Pennsylvania, he realized why she'd sounded so nervous on the phone: Pennsylvania's adoption records were closed. Not only was she not supposed to give him any of the information in his records, she also knew he wouldn't be able to get the papers she'd been holding in her hands.

Now Deland was frustrated. He was *so* close. He couldn't believe that this woman knew more about him than he did! He went back and found the website he'd briefly looked at a few years earlier, with profiles of birth parents and adoptees hoping to find their families. He still didn't make a profile, he just scanned pages and pages of the site, staring into the eyes of the women looking back, hoping to see something familiar. He wasn't really sure what he was looking for. A year and a state was all he had. He hoped he'd just see a face and know. He just wanted to see someone he looked like he belonged to.

The faces scrolled by. Was one of these women looking for Jon? And who would Jon have been if she'd never given him up? Who would *he* have been? Deland's mind started reeling. Just how much control had he had over his own life? He just as easily could have had a different name. A different family. What part of him was his, and what part of him was the result of Adelle's teachings, Damon's guidance, and Youngstown's influence? Would Jon have been a football player? A teacher and coach? Would Jon have been a lifelong bachelor or would Deland have fallen in love with Darnell no matter his name and his upbringing? He slammed the computer shut.

Deland had spent years building up the courage to search for his birth parents and now it felt like even the laws of the state of Pennsylvania were sending him that same old message: it's not okay to look.

———

For the third straight summer Deland was accepted to an NFL coaching internship, this time with the Falcons. Dan Quinn had just taken over as head coach in Atlanta and he'd reached out to Deland about potentially adding him to the coaching staff. For a few years running Deland had been getting calls from NFL teams and doing preliminary interviews, but this time it felt like the leap from college to the pros was really going to happen. Quinn had led the Seahawks defense during their back-to-back Super Bowl runs and he and Deland had hit it off in Seattle. Unfortunately, Deland's chance to get the job ended when the Falcons hired Kyle Shanahan to be the offensive coordinator—Shanahan wanted to hire his own guys. Deland still went down to Atlanta for the internship and tried to learn as much as he could. He knew it was only a matter of time before he'd get his shot.

In the fall of 2015, Deland, Darnell, and the boys—fifteen-year-old Deland II, twelve-year-old Dasan, and eleven-year-old Daeh—were thrown for a loop when Darnell found out she was pregnant again. Ready or not, there was another DMC on the way!

"Dang, this kid's oldest brother gonna be able to drive to the hospital to meet him!" Deland joked with Darnell.

Deland and Darnell were in a different town with a different doctor, but the story was the same the fourth time around—they had to explain that they didn't know anything about Deland's birth parents or his medical history. This time on the way home Deland was honest with Darnell about how all the years of "I don't know" made him feel. He told her about all of the internet searches and websites he'd pored over. And he finally really opened up about his frustration. He didn't want to settle for "I don't know" anymore. He started his search again and found news of a proposed bill that would allow adults adopted as children in the state of Pennsylvania to finally access their birth records. House Bill 162.

Every few weeks he would search for the bill and watch news of its progress, celebrating as he saw stories of it clearing the Pennsylvania House that December. He had fresh hope.

The Hoosiers finished the 2015 season an even 6-6, staying competitive in a tough Big Ten conference. They were invited to play in a bowl game for the first time since 2007—the New Era Pinstripe Bowl on December 26 at Yankee Stadium in the Bronx. They lost to Duke in overtime, 44–41, with Darnell and the boys and Damon and his family in the crowd looking on. A few days before the game, Darnell and some of the other coaches' wives got to meet the hosts of the *Today* show and take photos on set at NBC Studios in Rockefeller Center. Damon and his family took them all out to dinner that night, and

Darnell looked around the table—Deland, her three boys, and another baby on the way. Whew. They'd come a long way from that first road trip to New York in Deland's Honda Accord.

After the season, Deland interviewed to be the running backs coach for the Indianapolis Colts but didn't get the job. He was frustrated, but he knew he was putting together the kind of résumé a pro team eventually wouldn't be able to deny. He was once again nominated for national running backs coach of the year and Indiana's star running back Jordan Howard was selected by the Chicago Bears in the fifth round of the NFL Draft. Every offseason marked another chance for Deland to show his recruiting prowess and add to the growing list of players he had coached up to play in the pros. By that spring he'd have another kid to coach up at home too.

Darnell gave birth to their fourth son, Diem, on May 24, 2016, a month after her fortieth birthday. He was two weeks early but already a big boy— eleven and a half pounds. Deland and Darnell couldn't believe they were starting all over again with the diapers and the late-night feedings. They had doted on their older boys through the toddler years, elementary school, and junior high, and now all three were teens or tweens, going through a whole new set of growing pains. Baby Diem would either be in a rush to get big like the others, or, like Darnell did growing up, want to be a kid forever, protected by older brothers. One thing was certain: he'd be football-crazed just like the rest of the family. Before Diem even left the hospital he was wearing a onesie that read CRAWL DMC. Gotta start somewhere.

After Diem's birth, Deland continued to regularly search for updates on House Bill 162. Even decades after experts began advising that adoptees fared better when given information about their birth parents and identities, legislators in many states still fought (and continue to fight) to keep records sealed. Some believe that opening original birth records violates the rights of birth parents to keep their identities hidden (never mind the right of adoptees to know their own history and identity). Others believe parents won't give up their children for adoption unless they're assured of anonymity, thereby threatening the future of adoptions. Still others believe confidentiality promotes the sanctity of the family unit created by adoption. In the face of their opponents, adoptees all over the country, and in Pennsylvania specifically, were loud and getting louder.

That fall, on October 26, House Bill 162 cleared the Senate in Pennsylvania, and on November 3 Governor Tom Wolf signed the bill into law. Birth parents had one year to issue a redaction of their names, so beginning November 3, 2017, all Pennsylvania-born adoptees eighteen and older would be able to request a copy of their original birth certificate. The countdown was on. Deland had already waited forty-three years and eleven months. What was another 365 days?

He tried to focus on football and his boys, the oldest starting to get college recruiting letters while the youngest wasn't yet crawling. It was an unexpected joy having a baby back in the house, and Darnell and Deland both recognized how different it felt raising a little one in their forties instead of their twenties. They were certainly thankful for the helping hands of Deland II, Dasan, and Daeh.

The Hoosiers, who had lost starting quarterback Nate Sudfeld, star offensive lineman Jason Spriggs, and leading rusher Jordan Howard to graduation and the draft, finished 6-6 that season but were bowl-eligible for the second straight year. Coach Wilson was forced to resign before the bowl game, just one year into a six-year, $15.3 million contract extension. There had been multiple investigations into his mishandling of player injuries. New head coach Tom Allen took charge of the Hoosiers just before their 26–24 loss to the Utah Utes in the Foster Farms Bowl in Santa Clara, California. As usual, Allen would be hiring his own staff, but Indiana's athletic director hadn't been lying to Deland back in 2014—Glass wanted to keep him around no matter the head coach. In fact, Glass wanted him enough to give him a big raise. Deland was the only coach from Wilson's offensive staff to be kept on.

Deland and Diem

CHAPTER 19

Deland took the stage at the February 2017 Glazier Clinic in Cincinnati wearing head-to-toe Indiana Football gear, but he knew his days in Bloomington were numbered. Just minutes after finishing up his presentation on running back drills and coaching techniques, he walked out the front door right into a cab to head to the airport. The West Coast was calling, and he was about to interview for his biggest job yet—running backs coach and run-game coordinator at the University of Southern California. USC was a college football behemoth. With a program dating back to 1888, the Trojans boasted eleven National Championships, thirteen undefeated seasons, more than five hundred NFL Draft picks, and fourteen inductees into the Pro Football Hall of Fame—more than any other university.

Deland nailed the interview and was expected back on campus to start working as soon as possible. He packed up a few weeks' worth of clothes and essentials and boarded a plane back to Los Angeles. Darnell and the kids followed close behind, thrilled to discover that their new home in Redondo Beach, California, was less than five minutes from the ocean.

In just ten months with the Trojans, Deland completely revamped their approach to coaching running backs. He implemented a new daily grading system, set expectations for effort and attitude, and demanded that his players refine and perfect their run reads. His drills were unique and unexpected, causing more than a few raised eyebrows from other position coaches. First there were the water-filled footballs—harder to carry, heavier to run with. When running backs went back to the regular balls, they squeezed them harder, limiting fumbles. Then there was the boxing glove Deland affixed to the end of a three-foot PVC pipe. He would stand alongside drills poking guys with the glove trying to dislodge the ball or disrupt their run. Not everyone was ready for the new guy with the newfangled approach, but it didn't take long for both the players and the coaches to see a difference. No more raised eyebrows—this guy Coach McCullough was good.

Just before the start of the season, a headline on the USC football site predicted big things in Deland's first year with the team: "McCullough's done two years of work in six months." The results on the field proved it true. The Trojans finished the season 11-3, winning the South Division of the Pac-12 and defeating Stanford in the Pac-12 Championship Game. Deland helped running back Ronald Jones rush for a career-high 1,550 yards, the most for a USC player since Reggie Bush in 2005.

It was a breakout season for Deland as a coach, but at home the wins were much, much bigger.

Six months before the start of the season, Deland had filled out and sent away all the required paperwork to receive his original birth certificate. Just like his search in Ohio, there was no timeline given by the Pennsylvania Department of Health, so he had no choice but to call and wait, and call again, and wait some more.

On November 12, Darnell came home to find a thin envelope from the department in the mail. Too thin, she thought. They couldn't find it, she figured. Or maybe his parents hadn't allowed it to be released. *He's going to be so disappointed*, she sighed.

When Deland got home from work she gingerly handed him the letter.

Deland stared at the envelope. He couldn't believe his entire identity could fit in there. He wedged a finger into the back, carefully ripped open the side, and pulled out the letter, half-expecting it to be written on gold leaf or in calligraphy. It wasn't. It was just one page, in black and white, but it was everything.

"This is it," he said to Darnell, almost in disbelief. "It's my birth certificate."

Darnell's jaw dropped. She hadn't exactly pictured how this would go, but she sure didn't imagine such an anticlimactic moment. There were no trumpets signaling its arrival. It hadn't arrived via armored car. There wasn't even a signature required to ensure it was received. This thing—this precious document—had arrived in the mailbox with a Bed, Bath & Beyond coupon and a Ballard Designs catalog.

Here we go, she thought. *For better or for worse, everything is gonna change.*

Deland stared at the document in his hands. It was just an everyday sheet of white paper, containing just forty-two words and eight numbers.

NONCERTIFIED COPY OF ORIGINAL BIRTH RECORD

DATE OF BIRTH: DECEMBER 01, 1972.   STATE FILE NUMBER: 150296-1972

DATE ISSUED: NOVEMBER 7, 2017   DATE FILED: DECEMBER 14, 1972

NAME GIVEN AT BIRTH: JON KENNETH BRIGGS   SEX: MALE

PLACE OF BIRTH: ALLEGHENY COUNTY

PARENT: CAROL DENISE BRIGGS

AGE: 16

PARENT: INFORMATION NOT RECORDED

"My name is Jon Kenneth Briggs," Deland said. "Baby Jon. My mother's name is Carol," he said as he read, almost whispering. "She was sixteen. It doesn't list a father."

Everybody but the baby started googling.

Carol Denise Briggs . . . Carol Briggs Pennsylvania . . . Carol Briggs Allegheny County . . . Carol Briggs Pittsburgh . . . Carol Briggs Philadelphia . . . Carol Briggs 61 . . .

There are a lot of Carol Briggses on the internet.

"Found one!" Deland shouted. He had typed "Carol Briggs Philadelphia" into the search bar on Facebook.

He stared at the picture of the woman in the photo. She didn't look much like him. He tried to find himself in her eyes, her nose, her smile. He couldn't see it. She did look like she was about the right age, though.

Was he looking at his mother?

He went upstairs and lay down next to Darnell in bed, trying to figure out if and what he should message her. His mind was reeling. It took a while, but he finally fell asleep.

On the way to work the next day, he sent the woman a message. He didn't know whether to ask about a baby or start by finding out if she was ever in the Pittsburgh area. Maybe she'd be hesitant to write to a stranger about a child.

"I apologize for reaching out to you," he wrote, "but were you in Pittsburgh in December 1972?"

He could only see six photos on her public account. He cycled through them for nearly an hour, reading the comments and hoping for a clue. One of the pictures was of a group of kids of all ages. Were they her grandchildren? Did he have brothers and sisters? Nieces and nephews? He'd focused so much on his birth parents, he hadn't even thought about all the other relatives that might be out there.

He still hadn't heard anything by that afternoon. He called Darnell. "Maybe she saw my message and had a heart attack," he told her, half-joking. "I mean, this was forty-four years ago."

While eating lunch in his office an hour later, he suddenly felt the urge to search for something different. Just "Carol D. Briggs." No location, no criteria. He scrolled down the Google results and saw a promising link. Without paying for the full profile he could still see her name, including her middle name—Denise—current and previous addresses, related individuals, and more. He switched to Facebook and searched for her there too.

There she was.

She looked like him.

He had never seen anyone other than his kids that looked like him. He looked at the family photo next to his computer and back to Carol's face. My goodness she looked like him. In the eyes, in the nose, in the smile. There were people who spent years looking for their birth parents and still never found them. Could it be this simple? Right there on Facebook? Could this be her?

He felt a little bolder this time.

"Hello, I apologize for reaching out to you like this," he wrote, "but did you have a son in Allegheny County in 1972 that you put up for adoption . . . "

He waited. About an hour later he checked and saw in gray text under his message *Carol added you on Messenger*. She'd seen it. She'd read it. His heartbeat sped up. Another few minutes passed. She hadn't responded. He sent her a question mark under his first message.

"?"

"Yes," she wrote, almost immediately.

He could feel tears coming to eyes. *Hold on*, he told himself. *Just wait.*

"What did u name the Baby . . . " he asked.

"Not Deland," she responded with a smiley-face emoji.

"Clearly . . . " he wrote back. "What first name did you give him."

"Jon," she said.

He froze. It was her. It was really her. He couldn't stop the tears now. He didn't even know what to say.

"Wow." It was all he could come up with.

"?" she responded.

"Can i have ur number please?" he wrote. "Would like to discuss Jon . . . "

He was dying to call her right then and there, but his running backs meeting was about to start. They agreed to talk later that evening, around 6:15 p.m. California time, 9:15 p.m. on the East Coast. While in the meeting, a few of the players noticed Deland looked off. Ronald Jones asked if he was okay. Deland couldn't hold it in. He told the guys everything—the birth certificate, the Google search, and the exchange he'd just had with the woman he believed might be his mother. They were beyond excited for their coach. They all struggled to focus in practice—it felt like it lasted forever. It finally wrapped up, and the guys told Deland good luck. "Almost time, Coach!" and "We're dying to hear what happens, Coach!"

There was a football family dinner with the whole staff and team that night—Darnell and all the boys were already on their way. After practice, Deland told the guys he needed to make the phone call first and pulled out his phone as he started walking from the football facilities over to the dining room. When he started dialing, he realized he hadn't planned at all what he might say. For all the conversations he'd had with Darnell about the law changes, the paperwork, the websites, and searches, they had never talked about what would happen if he actually found his parents.

What if they didn't want to be found? What if they didn't like him? What if they were mean, awful people? What if they were criminals? What if they asked him for money? His heart started racing. He tried to stop catastrophizing, but the thoughts just kept coming. What if he found out about terrible family secrets he could never forget? What if his mom or dad or both were a mess?

What if they weren't a mess at all—what if they just hadn't wanted him? "Whoooohhh." He took a big, deep breath.

Stop, he told himself. *You already know it's worth it. Whatever happens will be worth it. Good or bad.* Deland had seen and been through a lot. No matter what happened with Carol, he'd lived through a lot worse. He was ready for this. He had the tools to deal with whatever came next. He had seen TV shows about people looking for their families. Lost people. People who were broken and beaten down. He wasn't that way. He just wanted to know who he was. He just wanted to find peace. He could honestly say he had no expectations. No way to be disappointed. He just wanted to know.

Deep down, Deland never believed for a second that his story would have an unhappy ending. For his whole life he'd felt blessed. He was grateful in a way many others didn't understand. Adopted, no money, difficult childhood, but all he could see was the love he was given by his family and the guardian angels that helped him stay out of trouble. All he could focus on was the happiness and success he'd found—success beyond his wildest dreams. Kids like him weren't supposed to make it, but here he was. He trusted that if he just kept his heart in the right place, everything would work out.

The phone started to ring.

When Carol Briggs saw Deland's first Facebook message, she wasn't sure whether to respond. She called her cousin and her niece, but neither answered. Her brother picked up.

"Don't get excited," he told her. "You know this might be somebody who got a little information on you. Trying to get money or something. Be calm, be relaxed with the whole thing."

Carol couldn't be calm or relaxed. She'd been looking for her son for years.

She had created profiles on some of the very same websites that Deland had, scanning for hours, looking for a face that matched her own. Every December 1 for the last few years she had even posted "Happy Birthday, Jon" on her Facebook wall. She wasn't sure she believed in sending signs out into the universe, but it couldn't hurt. She had never married and never had any other children. For the longest time Carol had put the idea of finding Jon Kenneth out of her mind, but in the five or six years before her mom died, she would say to Carol every few months, "You know, you ought to try to find that boy." As Carol got older, the desire to find him grew stronger and stronger. She just wanted to know he was okay.

She'd been waiting a lifetime for this. Now here he was. Maybe.

In the hours between the messages and their phone call, Carol scoured the internet to be sure the guy she was emailing was a real person. She found the name Deland McCullough everywhere. Not only was he real but he seemed like a really successful guy. He seemed like somebody.

Most importantly, my gosh did he look like her. In the nose, the eyes, the smile. Her cousin and her niece called her back. They had googled Deland too. He did look like her! He did!

He also looks like his father, Carol thought.

She picked up the phone.

"Hello?"

Carol's voice was nervous but kind. Deland felt his whole body warm up when he heard it, like he was standing in the rays of the brightest, yellowest sun you've ever seen.

"I'm sure you're wondering what's going on," Deland said. He paused, and then: "I'm Jon."

Carol couldn't keep the tears in. It was really him. He told her he'd been looking for her. She told him she'd been looking for him too. Praying to find him. Praying to learn that he was okay.

This was really happening. Deland took a deep breath and let the tears flow.

He had so many questions for his mom.

"Where are you?" he asked.

"Youngstown, Ohio, area," she said.

Deland's jaw dropped.

Carol

CHAPTER 20

CAROL

Carol Denise Briggs was born in Youngstown on September 19, 1956, to Dorothea Gilford and Oliver Briggs. She grew up on the east side of town, at 1313 Berwyck Avenue, less than ten minutes' drive from Lincoln Knolls. If you took a left out of the driveway at 46 Allerton Court, then went west on McCartney and straight up Landsdowne, you could be at Carol's in about eight minutes. Of course it would be another forty or so years before Carol had any reason to think about that house on Allerton Court and who lived there.

Carol was the middle of three children, between Michael, who was two years older, and Gerald, aka Jerry, who was six years younger. When Dorothea called home from the hospital with the news of Jerry's impending arrival, Carol replied without missing a beat, "If you bring him home I'll kill 'im." She thought the family had a perfect arrangement going with two parents and two kids. Michael was a mama's boy and she was daddy's little girl. A third child in the house? No, thank you.

Of course, by the time Dorothea got home with the new baby, Carol had warmed up to the idea. Jerry was too sweet to dislike. Jerry was so sweet and such a quiet baby, in fact, that one day Dorothea, Michael, and Carol were walking down the block to the shopping center when a friend stopped them to ask how the new baby was doing. "The baby!" Dorothea yelped. He was so quiet she'd forgotten to bring him along. They doubled back a block and got him.

Oliver worked as a welder at Youngstown Sheet & Tube, and Dorothea was a stay-at-home mom until the kids got older and she started working in the laundry at Saint Elizabeth Hospital. Carol spent most of her childhood tagging along with Michael and the rest of the boys in the neighborhood, riding bikes, picking berries in the big field down the road, and playing hide-and-seek and kickball. All the girls in the neighborhood were too sissy for her liking, playing with dolls and keeping their clothes clean. She wanted to go on adventures.

When she got older she withdrew a bit. As she approached her teens she left the boys outside and got quieter—her adventures started to take place in the pages of her books.

Dorothea ran a tight ship and expected a lot out of her only daughter. It wasn't until later in life that Carol got to know the woman everyone thought of as fun and easygoing. As a mother of a young girl, Dorothea was anything but fun. She and Oliver made a good pair, though, as he always played the part of good cop, never punishing the kids and letting Carol find herself and her place in the world in whatever time she needed. Oliver and Dorothea almost never fought and seemed as in love as the day they married, even reserving one day a week for a date night.

Every single Friday without fail, Michael and Carol would get dropped off at their grandparents' house for the night to give Oliver and Dorothea some time to themselves. "That's how little Jerry came to be!" her parents used to joke. Carol would lie on the couch at Granddaddy Otis and Grandma Martha's house and read. When she sat at the dining table she'd read whatever she could get her hands on there too. Jelly jars, bread wrappers, cereal boxes. "You're gonna read the words right off that box," Otis would say. The only thing that could pull her nose out of a book was when Granddaddy and Martha—aka Mert—would tell her stories about growing up in the South.

Granddaddy would make popcorn in a giant pot on the stove, put it in a brown grocery bag with lots of salt, and hand it over to her as he talked about working on a farm in Huntsville, Alabama. He told her about the day he realized that if he and Mert didn't hightail it out of town and head north, he might come to blows with the farm's owner and do something he could never take back. He told her about the local man who got the roots put on him and thought he was a frog. Granddaddy explained that root doctors down in the South were healers and conjurers who used roots, herbs, and spells to help or hurt people. This was her favorite story because he'd describe the man hop-hop-hopping around with his eyes bulging out of his head. Carol didn't know if the roots and voodoo were real, but she was enthralled by Otis's tales all the same.

School came naturally to Carol. She was on the honor roll every semester and a member of the National Honor Society. She enjoyed going to Y-Teens, a program for local girls through the YWCA that offered games, events, and discussions about things like racial justice, women's rights, and leadership. It thrilled Oliver to see his little girl fall in love with education. He would always tell the kids, "Me and your mother have everything covered; all you gotta do is go to school and get good grades. That's your only job." Carol wasn't into sports but Oliver loved them, so she'd tag along with her dad and the boys to games all over northeast Ohio. Football, basketball—he kept up with all the local high school and college teams.

Carol was such a bookworm that she was practically invisible at times. She was so shy in junior high that when she joined her older brother at North High School, a handful of his friends learned for the first time that he had a sister. A social butterfly just like his mom, Michael knew everybody from every neighborhood and every side of town. Carol was more like her father—quiet and reserved, happy to spend time alone. She had a couple of girlfriends, but she wasn't close with any of them. In fact, later in life Carol came to understand that she'd been a tough person for classmates to get along with. She was a little too smart for her own good and not particularly drawn to social life. She found her books more interesting, and a quick retort or dismissive comment got folks to leave her to her reading.

North was a small school, only about five hundred students. Everybody knew everybody. Carol was a bit of a mystery, always with her head in a book or held high looking down on everybody. She was cute, though. And she had a dazzling smile. In March 1972, six months after her fifteenth birthday, that smile caught the eye of an upperclassman. She was a sophomore bookworm with no social life. He was tall, handsome, and popular, a star athlete nearing graduation. They would have been an odd couple if they'd ever been a couple. They weren't; he just approached her one day after school and they sort of started hanging out.

Sneaking around to have sex, to be exact. Sometimes at his house, more often at hers, in her lavender bedroom with the pretty wooden bedroom set. They didn't tell anyone; it was their little secret. Months later when Carol realized she was pregnant, he was already off to college. She was overwhelmed and embarrassed by the condition she'd gotten herself into and felt it was her responsibility to handle it. No sense ruining his life. He didn't need to know. Carol did have to tell her parents, however. She was terrified. Their honor roll student, straight-A kid had really screwed up.

She waited. And waited. And waited some more.

Carol couldn't even begin to imagine the response she was going to get from her mother. And if she saw even an ounce of disappointment on her father's face, it might kill her. If her mother didn't kill her first.

About five months into the pregnancy she realized she couldn't wait any longer. She had to tell them. Oliver, always the gentle one, dropped his head and took a beat, then said the decision was hers, he would support her, no matter what she chose to do. Years later Carol's brother Michael told her that Oliver had hidden just how much the news affected him. Carol was his little girl and he never saw a fault or a flaw in her; this lapse in judgment was something he never could have predicted. Carol didn't need to wait to learn that Dorothea was irate.

She was fuming from the moment Carol sat them down and told them. The thought of everyone seeing her little girl with a big pregnant belly made Dorothea sick to her stomach.

"I'm still making your bed and cleaning your room!" she fumed. "You're still a child! Come to find out your fast ass is out there making babies." She stewed for a bit before speaking again.

"You made your bed hard, now lie in it," Dorothea said. She wanted Carol to learn her lesson by keeping the baby and raising it, even though she knew deep down that the responsibility would land on her and Oliver.

At just fifteen years old, Carol couldn't imagine being a mother. It hadn't even been a thought in her mind until now. She couldn't give a child the same wonderful life she had. Her parents were happy and together; she had grandparents on both sides, cousins everywhere, two brothers that she loved dearly. She wanted the baby to have all that and more. She needed to give this baby a chance at a loving home and two parents. Hopefully a couple who dearly wanted and had prayed for a child. She told her parents she'd made up her mind, she'd give the baby up for adoption. Dorothea, secretly relieved, acquiesced. Carol told them she knew who the father was—she wasn't running around with multiple boys—but that she didn't want to tell him. She wasn't going to tell them who he was either, at least not yet. She didn't want Oliver and Dorothea going over to his house and telling his parents off, lecturing them about their son keeping his parts to himself. They all agreed it was best not to involve the father.

It was the early 1970s, and being an unwed, high school–aged mother was socially unacceptable. For several decades psychiatrists had diagnosed unwed mothers as social deviants and victims of psychological neurosis. Some parents threw their pregnant daughters out of the home; some shipped them away to carry and deliver their babies out of sight before surrendering them to an adoption agency. And so it was that in late August, less than a week after telling her parents about the baby, Carol was sent to a private, nonprofit maternity home run by the United Methodist Church.

The Zoar Home for Mothers, Babies, and Convalescents was in Allison Park, Pennsylvania, a suburb of Pittsburgh. Dorothea found the place through one of the nuns she worked with at St. Elizabeth Hospital, then used Catholic Charities to arrange for Carol to get a room there. Carol's cousin and best friend, Robin, was the only person outside her immediate family who knew where she was. When school started that fall, Carol simply wasn't there.

The Zoar Home was a big old Victorian building, originally constructed in 1924. Carol had her own room, a simple space with a twin bed and a dresser. She went to the doctor regularly and took classes, keeping up with school so she could return for the second semester without falling behind. There were twelve or so other girls there from all over, most of them high schoolers like Carol. They were all white except for one other Black girl. She was the oldest there, in her twenties, and from a wealthy family in Pittsburgh. White babies were much more likely to be adopted back then, so more often than not, Black girls who kept a baby would raise it within their family, getting help from aunts, grandmas, and cousins. In fact, Carol was certain that if Oliver's family out in Rockford, Illinois, found out she was giving up a baby for adoption, they would try to convince her to keep the baby in the family.

Youngstown was about an hour away from the Zoar Home but Carol's dad would cut it to forty minutes, resulting in enough speeding tickets to know some of the state patrol officers by name. He would come two or three times a week and take her out to lunch or to explore Pittsburgh. Dorothea would call on the phone and send some of Carol's favorite food with Oliver, but she never once came to visit. "I don't have to see you like that," she told Carol. There would be no further discussion.

Carol cried a lot, missing home, but she got along well with the girls there and cherished her father's visits. She especially loved going out to lunch with him because the food at the home was completely salt-free. Something about retaining water. She didn't care, she wanted salty eggs and potatoes! Besides, she didn't need to avoid salt—she felt like her body really took to being pregnant. She never got sick or fatigued and she marveled at the changes she went through.

She understood that babies were born every day but couldn't believe how quotidian everyone made it seem—she felt like she was part of a miracle. She was amazed by her own body and what it could do.

In September Carol celebrated her sixteenth birthday at the Zoar Home. It wasn't the Sweet Sixteen she'd imagined, but the other girls made her cards and her father took her out to dinner. She was seven months along then and starting to really think about what it would be like to give birth, give up her baby, and to get to go home.

A big snowstorm hit Pittsburgh the last week of November, and on the night of the thirtieth Carol joined some of the other girls outside, dragging big cardboard boxes up the Zoar Home's long, steep driveway. They'd sled to the bottom then climb to the top again, up and down, over and over. Just kids, having fun. She went to sleep that night and woke up shortly before 7:00 a.m., already in labor. She was the furthest along of the girls there so the rest of the house was bustling with excitement as they prepared for a baby. She was in no rush, eating her usual breakfast of unsalted scrambled eggs under their watchful eyes. "How does it feel?" "Are you in pain?" "Are you scared?" She was calm and ready. Someone from the Zoar Home called her parents and they drove out from Youngstown with Michael to meet her at the hospital. The labor was easy—over in less than a half hour once they told her to push.

At 2:32 p.m., Jon Kenneth Briggs was born. Six pounds, thirteen ounces, and seventeen inches long. Jon for the father's dad, Kenneth for the street he lived on. If she wasn't going to tell him about the baby, she could at least honor him and his family with the child's name.

The next morning Carol placed her newborn son on the hospital bed and looked into his big, dark eyes. She tried to find herself in his face—his nose, his eyes, his smile. Not yet. She saw only his father. She took off all his clothes, making a mental note of each of his ten tiny toes, his chubby legs, puffy belly, and two little arms reaching up for her. This little boy was the only person on earth who knew what her heart sounded like from the inside.

This is probably the last time I'll ever see you, Carol thought. She didn't second-guess her decision at all. She knew she was making the best choice for him. But as she looked down at baby Jon, trying to take in every part of him, she wondered how many times she would see his face again in little boys passing by.

Later that day as she signed the paperwork and filled out Jon's name, she wondered for a moment if she should try to call the baby's father and let him know. She decided against it. He was off at college. Why burden him unnecessarily? She decided right then and there that she would never tell anyone who the father was outside of her immediate family and Robin. She finally told Dorothea and Oliver, but swore them to secrecy. She just couldn't bear to have the news get back to the guy some years down the road. This was her responsibility, her burden, her secret. Forever.

Less than thirty-six hours after Jon's birth, Carol gathered her things from the Zoar Home and got into her parents' car to return to life as a sixteen-year-old high school kid and member of the National Honor Society.

When she returned to North High School for second semester, no one in her class even seemed to notice she'd been gone. She'd missed the first four months of school and not a soul asked her where she'd been. *They must've thought I was off at some fancy academic program or something,* Carol thought. And then, in a more honest moment, *They probably didn't think anything. I didn't leave enough people behind who cared where I was.* She decided she would be honest about the pregnancy if anyone asked, but they never did. She realized, strangely, that she hoped someone would. That she wanted to feel more connected to her classmates. Carol recognized that something had changed while she was gone.

She didn't look down on her classmates anymore. Even though she'd managed to make the honor roll again while away from school, she reminded herself that she'd been away because she'd gotten herself pregnant. *I'm the one who got knocked up, not them,* she thought. *Ain't that something. I might not be as smart as I think.* Making a mistake made her feel closer to her peers. Going through the pregnancy alone made her finally feel the need for friends and a community.

Carol was also forever changed physically by the months she spent carrying her baby boy. In a way, she would always carry him. The phenomenon of fetal microchimerism sees small numbers of a baby's cells, including stem cells, migrate through the placenta to the mother's bloodstream, becoming a part of her body and integrating with her cells. In at least one major study these cells were found to have settled in for the remainder of the women's lives. And in one study of female mice, the fetal stem cells found their way into the mother's heart and developed into cardiac tissue and beating heart cells. Carol always felt like Jon had changed her heart; she may have been more right than she ever could have imagined. That baby boy might have become a tiny part of her heartbeat.

Research shows that the structure and components of a woman's brain change during pregnancy and can remain changed for up to two years after the child is born. That change includes a loss of volume in the brain's gray matter, similar to what happens during adolescence. Researchers don't see it as a deficiency, but rather a fine-tuning. Since the areas of a pregnant woman's brain most affected are those that decipher what another person is thinking and feeling, researchers think the mother's brain is preparing to be better attuned to the needs of her child and therefore better able to care for them. In the nine months that she'd carried Jon, Carol's brain had changed to bond with her son and nurture him. After his birth, in his absence, she turned her attention to another child that needed to be nurtured: herself.

She came back to North High School a changed person. No longer shy and stuck-up, no longer buried in her books. That little boy opened up something inside her. She had a light in her now that she let show. It wasn't easy to earn the trust of classmates to whom she'd been nasty. It wasn't a quick fix to convince them she'd lost her attitude. It would take time, but she was ready to let people in. She still wanted to study hard and go to college, still wanted to make her dad proud, but beginning the day Jon was born, she felt different. She had been humbled by his arrival. She didn't want to be alone anymore. She wanted to show care and grace to others, and to herself. She wanted to share that light she had inside.

In early January, Carol and her dad went to juvenile court to finalize the paperwork that made baby Jon available for adoption. A few weeks later her parents got a bill from the Catholic Service League: $83 for baby Jon's boarding, clothes, and medical care for his stay at the Zoar Home from December 7, 1972, to January 5, 1973. Carol's little boy had been adopted.

Carol

CHAPTER 21

"Did you ever go to the Sparkle, over at the shopping center on the East Side?" Carol asked.

She and Deland spoke like old friends, an easy back-and-forth as they shared where life had taken them in the forty-four years since she'd laid him down on that bed and let him go. Carol couldn't remember if she'd heard it from her parents or the adoption caseworker from Catholic Charities, but she'd believed for years that baby Jon went to a doctor and his wife in Columbus, Ohio. To learn he'd been placed just ten minutes away from her was stunning. There were so many moments they might have crossed paths. Carol was certain Adelle and Dorothea must have walked by each other in the aisles getting their groceries at the Sparkle Market every week. No doubt Carol's dad Oliver read about Deland in the papers as he started to make a name for himself on the football field.

Carol wished he and Dorothea were still alive to meet her son.

"Do I have any brothers and sisters?" asked Deland. "Shoot, if you're in Youngstown I might even know them!"

Carol told him she never had any other children. Had never been married.

She told him she was open to it but never met the right person. She'd been engaged once, but didn't go through with it. She said she mothered a lot of people in her life, though, including her nieces and nephews. Both she and Deland had been crying off and on since the moment they started talking, but the tears really came down hard when she learned that Deland had four boys. Four grandchildren! She went from none to four in an instant. Got herself a daughter-in-law too. She couldn't wait to hear about all of them.

"So how come you ended up deciding to give me up?" Deland asked gently.

Carol had spent the last few hours wondering how this question would go. Wondering if Deland had been mad at her all these years for choosing adoption. She explained how young she was, why she felt it was for the best, and how she'd never doubted that she made the right choice for him. He told her he understood. That he held no anger for her, just happiness that they had found each other again. She told him how wonderful her childhood was and how she had wanted him to have everything she did and more, especially two parents in a loving home. Deland swallowed hard and kept silent. He could tell her all about Adelle and A.C. and John and Frank later. Far more important was for her to know he turned out okay. That he was happy and successful. That Adelle had raised him right.

"Wait, I had to get my records through Alleghany County," Deland said. "If you grew up in Youngstown, how come you were in Pennsylvania?"

Carol explained that she and Deland's father weren't the love story he might be hoping for. That they were young, being irresponsible. They were kids trying to act like adults, and Deland was a big surprise. A surprise that turned into a secret.

"Back in those days, girls like me had to be pregnant in private," she explained. "My mom found a place in Pennsylvania. So you were born near there, at a hospital in Pittsburgh, and adopted near there too."

Carol explained that she got to spend some time with him the morning after he was born, but that was it. In less than thirty-six hours she was home. Neither of them could believe he had made his way to Youngstown too. The answers had always felt so far away to Deland, but there they were—right in his own backyard. Youngstown could be like that—sometimes it felt so small, like everybody knew your business, and sometimes it felt like there might as well have been an ocean between you and someone living right across town.

"I noticed my birth certificate didn't list a dad," Deland said. "Who is my father?"

Carol hesitated. In the four decades since baby Jon was born, the Briggs clan had kept their word—not a single soul outside her family had been told who the father was. Once she told Deland his name, Carol was sure he'd try to find him. She wouldn't be able to keep the secret any longer.

"I never told him about you," Carol said. "I don't know if that was fair or not, but I thought I was doing what was best for him. He was off to college on a scholarship, a great athlete, and starting his life. I felt like it was my responsibility to take care of this. Not to burden him with it too. And I didn't tell anyone other than my family and my cousin, because I couldn't bear him finding out through the grapevine years later, walking around wondering if he might run into you. But he's your father, and you deserve to know. It's important that you know."

Carol took a long pause and a deep breath.

"Your father is a man by the name of Sherman Smith."

Sherman (top left in plaid jacket),
with Vincent, John, Lillie, and Darrell

CHAPTER 22

SHERMAN

Sherman Lennel Smith was born in Youngstown on November 1, 1954. His father, John Thomas Smith, was a Korean War veteran and steelworker. His mother, Lillie Beedles Smith, was a county clerk who worked in City Hall.

Sherman was the second of three boys; his brother Vincent was a year older, his brother Darrell seven years younger.

John was a respectable six feet tall but he was dwarfed by two 6'5" brothers, so he had a way of speaking that commanded the room and drew attention his stature couldn't. He often spoke in maxims, choosing his words deliberately and speaking with intention. "If you're going to do something, do it right." "You can't pretend to be a man—you are one or you aren't." "Boys straddle a fence, but it takes a man to make a decision." When John said things, they stuck.

The boys knew to listen when their father talked, and they knew to heed what he said, because, as he reminded them often, they were an example of him and their family. "When you leave the house," John would say, "don't forget your last name. Don't forget who you represent when you're out there in the world."

John and Lillie argued like any other couple did, especially when finances were tight, but after a big fight John would always sit the boys down and talk to them. "Marriage is great, let me start there," he'd say. "But marriage is hard. You're gonna have your problems. No one's going anywhere, though, okay? Your mom and I aren't going anywhere. We're gonna get through this."

That kind of communication was the norm in the Smith house. No one needed to be sheltered or left out of important conversations. "I don't see you boys as acorns," John would say. "You're oak trees. You're ready for the truth and responsible enough to be treated like adults." They were a spiritual family and went to church often, but John and Lillie were keen to instill in the boys a sense of personal responsibility. They wanted their sons to make choices because it's what they wanted and what they thought was right. They wanted them to find their own beliefs and pursue them honestly, not because they were told to.

Spiritual life and practical life weren't two lines running parallel, they were one. Every lesson of the church informed the choices they made on an everyday basis. God wasn't a threat. Goodness wasn't a performance.

As a pair they provided a unified and consistent example of what to do and who to be. When Sherman was in seventh grade, his team lost a Pop Warner football game and he lost his cool. Threw his helmet down on the sidelines, yelled and pouted, drew a lot of attention for being such a sore loser. When he got home he thought his mother might coddle him, put her arms around him, and tell him she understood. She loved football too, and was as competitive as anybody.

There was no coddling.

"I'm going to tell you something," Lillie said, looking right into Sherman's eyes. "If you ever act like that again, that will be the last game you ever play. If you can't learn how to lose, you can't play. I don't care where you're at—I'll come right out on that basketball court or football field and tell you to go home. You respect the game, yourself, and your family, win or lose."

When Vincent wasn't yet ten years old, John pulled him aside. "You're the oldest," he told him. "You'll always be responsible for looking out for your brothers." Vincent never forgot it. One time in ninth grade, Sherman's study hall teacher slapped him right across the face. He never did figure out what set the guy off; he just told Sherman to stop smiling. When

Sherman didn't stop, he walked over and smacked him. John handled it with grace. He went in the next day and told the teacher, "Don't you ever put your hands on my son." Then he turned to Sherman and said, "And you better act right." Vincent wasn't quite as cool. He'd been put in charge of his brother, and he knew there was no reason for that teacher to strike him. It especially bugged him that the teacher was white, slapping a Black student for nothing. After school that day, Sherman had to track Vincent down and physically restrain him from going to find the teacher.

Standing up for family and taking care of each other was a job for everyone in the Smith house. Sherman had a sweet tooth, and one day on his usual candy run he came across some guys messing with Vincent. Without hesitation, he jumped to his brother's aid. "I don't want you to fight," John would say, "but if one of you's fightin', all of you are fightin'."

The Smiths spent the early part of Sherman's childhood living in the projects on the North Side of Youngstown before moving to a house on the East Side, right across from North High School. John struggled to keep his job working on the blast furnace at Republic Steel, so paychecks were sometimes few and far between. He worked hard, but the Youngstown steel business was changing as it neared its collapse and the mills would hire and fire with the ebb and flow of demand.

John recognized the instability of the business and decided he needed to put himself in a position to get steady work. He got active in the union and worked his way up, eventually becoming an assistant to Lynn Williams, international president of the United Steelworkers union. Money was steady then, and when Sherman was a junior in high school the Smith family moved into a house John had built at 1387 Kenneth Street, on the east side of Youngstown. Four bedrooms, one-and-a-half baths—cost them $75,000. Back in 1970 that was a whole lotta house.

Setting himself on a new path gave John perspective, and he pulled Sherman aside and asked him what he wanted to do after high school. Sherman said he had always seen himself doing what most young Black men in Youngstown did: get a job at the steel mill, get a place at the apartments down the road, and maybe one day make enough money to splurge on a cool car. John told him to grab his coat—they were going for a drive. He drove Sherman by the apartment complex down the road—Section 8 public housing—and told him, "Don't buy the lie that this is the only place you can live." John drove him past the steel mill that he'd spent thirty years of his life working in and said, "Don't buy the lie that this is the only place you can work."

"Son, you're better than that," John told Sherman. "Don't buy the lie they're selling young Black men. You can do more. You can *be* more."

Sherman was picked by his teammates as a captain for both football and basketball in his senior year. To realize that his peers saw him as a leader reinforced what his father had told him—there was so much more out there to aspire to. So many bigger dreams to pursue. Sherman started to pay more attention to his behavior. He hadn't been a wild kid, or out of control, but he did start to hold himself to a higher standard. Started to listen more and step into what it meant to be a leader, on and off the field. He had a particularly strong bond with his football coach and teacher, Clifton Knox, and he decided he wanted to lead young men in the classroom and on the field the way Coach Knox did. If his father demanded more from him and his classmates looked to him for guidance, then maybe he was meant for something bigger than Youngstown. If he was going to become a coach, to affirm and uplift young men, he knew he had better start acting like someone worthy of being followed.

He would start by getting a great education. He rescinded a commitment he'd made to Kent State and accepted a full scholarship to academically acclaimed Miami University instead. He started a few games as a freshman, a big deal for a Black quarterback in the early 1970s. In a lot of other places Sherman wouldn't even have gotten recruited, not to mention gotten the chance to start straightaway, but Coach Bill Mallory cared only about playing the best guys they had.

And Sherman Smith was the best. In his last three seasons he led the team to a 33-1 record and won the Mid-American Conference title each of those years. Got drafted in the second round of the 1976 NFL Draft, the first offensive player ever drafted by the expansion Seahawks. Despite being a college quarterback, he was drafted as a wide receiver because of his athleticism but immediately got switched to running back when he got to Seattle. Spent eight good years as a running back with the Seahawks. Then in his first year with the Chargers Sherman blew out his knee—a freak injury during a walk-through in minicamp—and that was the end of his playing career.

The other two Smith boys excelled at football as well. Vincent played at Mount Union College, took a break from the game, and then returned to coach high school ball in Florida. Darrell might have been the most athletic of all three. He shined at Central State University and played in preseason games with the Cowboys and Bengals during consecutive years of training camp, but both years he got cut before the season started. With the Cowboys he brought a girl into the dorms during camp, which was strictly forbidden. With the Bengals his anger got to him. He just couldn't stay focused and disciplined. Darrell never made an NFL roster, but he became a superstar in the CFL, scoring fifty-two touchdowns in seven seasons with the Toronto Argonauts. Darrell died of cancer in 2017 at the age of fifty-five.

That same year, Sherman retired after ten years coaching high school and college and twenty-two years coaching in the pros, including helping the Seahawks to a Super Bowl win in 2013. For as gifted as Sherman was physically, it was his unparalleled work ethic that set him apart, both as a player and a coach. When asked about his successes in life, Sherman always pointed to one thing: "I was always gonna outwork the next guy." He brought the lessons he learned from John and Lillie into his work every day. He got the most out of his guys by building them up instead of tearing them down. He preached communication, hard work, good sportsmanship, be a man, stand up for your brothers. He even spoke in maxims, just like his dad. "You may not be looking for a father," he'd tell every team at the start of the season, "but I'm going to treat you like my sons."

Sherman

CHAPTER 23

Deland suddenly felt like his legs might give out. He slid down the wall of the hallway outside the dining hall and felt his breath catch in his throat, letting out a gasp. Carol heard him take a slow, deep breath and then barely choke out the words:

"I know him. I've known Sherman my whole life."

Deland started flashing back to his memories with Coach Smith. All the times people had joked about him being a carbon copy of his coach. In college, coaching at Miami, during his internship with the Seahawks.

You walk like him, you talk like him, you wanna be him!

In those moments there hadn't been a reason for Deland to even consider connecting any dots between himself and Sherman. For twenty-eight years this man had been a mentor, a father figure, and a chosen influence. And all along he was really his father? It was almost too much to take in. Deland thought about the photo of him and Coach Smith at Memorial High the day he signed his letter of intent to play at Miami University. Thought about the photo of him and Coach Smith in the locker room at Miami, Sherman in the tinted glasses and striped sweater. The same photos that were in the Ziploc bag sitting in the drawer of his bedside table at home in Redondo Beach. Just as they had in Bloomington, Oxford, Cincinnati, and Columbus. The photos that had been pinned up to the poster board in his freshman dorm room.

How come you've only got football stuff and those picture of your dad?

Those pictures of your dad, he thought. *Those pictures of your dad.* He shook his head.

Why had he been carrying those pictures around? Was it always just about football? Had he felt something else, something bigger all along?

It was like he'd been looking through a foggy window for years and all of a sudden the fog cleared. The memories came faster. The first time he saw that cherry-apple-red Mercedes pull up in front of his school. The cinematic feeling of their first meeting, as Sherman turned around to shake his hand. The long talks in Sherman's office at Miami. Dinners with Coach and his wife, Sharon. A lifetime of advice.

Carol was talking again but Deland couldn't hear a word. He was too busy considering how the path he'd taken in life mirrored his dad's. Youngstown, to Miami, to the NFL, to coaching. It was uncanny! He felt a deep sense of pride.

Sherman Smith was his father. His father! If you had asked him who he thought his dad was out of every man he'd ever met, he never would have picked Coach Smith. No way. He didn't feel he was worthy enough to be his son. If you'd asked him who he *wanted* to be his dad, though, Coach Smith would have been at the top of the list. This was the guy. This was his *guy.* Everything Sherman did was worth following, studying, and repeating. Everything he said was worth hearing and heeding. Deland had always wanted to be somebody just like him.

His cheeks were hot from tears. His head bowed in disbelief. Carol was still there, waiting. He picked himself up off the ground—literally. He told her about their bond, about how Sherman had been a role model to him since the age of seventeen, how they'd stayed in touch for nearly thirty years. She almost couldn't believe it.

"He's been in my life for almost all of my life," Deland said.

Carol was thrilled for her son and moved by the joy and pride he was feeling. She was also a little bit relieved. She knew, now, that Sherman would absolutely be contacted, but Deland wouldn't have to go looking for him. She just hoped Sherman wouldn't be too angry with her.

There was so much more to talk about, but Deland had to meet his family and the team for dinner. He and Carol agreed to talk again the next day.

Deland stumbled, almost woozily, into the dining hall to find Darnell. She was never going to believe this.

"Well, I was just talking to Carol," Deland said, sitting down next to Darnell and the boys. They all looked at him expectantly, trying to read his face. How had it gone? Did he look happy? Disappointed?

"It was a great conversation," Deland continued. "We talked about how I found her. She never got married, doesn't have any other kids. She's from Youngstown, if you can believe that!"

"Wow!" said Darnell. "No way!"

"Mmm," said Deland. "And get this. I asked her, 'Do you know who my father is?' And you know who she said? You won't believe who she said."

"Who?" said Darnell, confused. They knew this person? "Who could she possibly say?"

"Sherman Smith," said Deland. "My father is Sherman Smith."

The whole family screamed. Players five tables over turned around to see what the commotion was. Darnell was trying not to make a scene, but this roomful of people had no idea what his family had just been told. No idea the magnitude of what Deland had just revealed. How this news would change his life.

"Deland," Darnell said, tearing up, "this can't be real. Do you remember what you told me after you went to dinner with Coach Smith and his wife at the end of your Seahawks internship?" she asked, her eyes wide. "Y'all were at P.F. Chang's and you told me when Coach got there he had such a serious look on his face. You told me, 'Man, he was so serious I thought he was gonna tell me he's my dad or something!'"

Deland remembered. It was just a joke. A throwaway line. And now it was true. This was wild.

———————

That night Deland texted Coach Smith, asking about some pictures they'd taken together nearly thirty years earlier. It was late near Nashville, Tennessee, where Sherman lived in retirement. Deland didn't hear back.

The next morning, anxious to tell Sherman, Deland texted Carol to ask if he could be the one to tell him. She said, "Of course." Deland tried texting again, 5:30 a.m. California time, 8:30 a.m. Eastern. "Coach i need to talk to u. It's important." He lay in bed and waited. He didn't know Darnell was awake, watching him swipe through pictures of Coach Smith on Google images and examine photos of his half brother and half sister on Facebook. She was worried about Deland. She had no idea how Sherman and his family would respond to the news.

The phone rang.

"Deland, it's Coach. What's up?" said Sherman.

"Hey, Coach," said Deland, nervously. He hadn't quite figured out what to say yet. "Had something to, uh, talk to you about. You remember how I was adopted?"

"Mhmm, yes, I remember."

Deland told Sherman a bit about beginning the search for his original name and birth parents. He told him how he'd spent years wondering about his past, searching websites and trying to find leads through the state of Ohio, only to learn he'd been born in Pennsylvania.

"Well, they just passed this bill in Pennsylvania," Deland continued. "It lets adoptees get all their original information."

"Praise God! I'm happy for you."

"And I was able to get my birth certificate," said Deland.

"Oh man, look at God and what he can do. That's wonderful!"

"I actually found my birth mother!" said Deland.

"My goodness! Praise God!"

"And she's from Youngstown, actually," said Deland.

"Wow, what are the odds? The Lord works in mysterious ways!"

"And, well, my father's name wasn't on the birth certificate I got," Deland continued. "So I asked my birth mom who my father was."

Deland took a breath.

"And she said you."

There was a long pause. Dead silence. Deland couldn't even hear breathing on the other end of the line.

Deland let out a sort of nervous chuckle. Sherman started talking, then stopped. Then started again. And stopped. It was nonsense. No real words were coming out. He went silent again.

"Her name is Carol Briggs," Deland said.

On the other end of the line, Sherman froze.

"I remember Carol. Yeah, I know Carol Briggs," he finally said. The "praise Gods" were conspicuously absent now.

There was another long pause.

"I'm going to have to call you back, Deland," Sherman said. "I just need some time to process."

Deland hung up the phone. He felt like he'd gotten the wind knocked out of him. He had hoped to find in Sherman the same joy he felt. Darnell touched his arm softly. "Give it some time," she said. "This is a crazy thing to find out all these years later."

Deland had that familiar feeling of watching A.C. from across the football stadium, that feeling of knowing he wasn't wanted. Wasn't chosen. He took a deep breath and tried to put himself in Coach Smith's shoes. Deland had spent his whole life wondering about his birth parents. Carol had spent her whole life wondering about the child she gave up. Sherman had gone from zero to a forty-four-year-old son in one phone call; Deland knew he needed time.

Sherman walked into his home office and sat down at the desk.

Carol Briggs. Now that was a name from the past. Sherman was sixty-three years old. He had been married to his college sweetheart for forty-two years and had already raised a grown son and daughter. Sherman thought about his years as a coach, mentor, and churchgoer. He had built his identity around making a difference in young people's lives, talking about responsibility, accountability, and being a man. He'd been honest with his players over the years, admitting to his failures. He was reckless in high school, he told them. He hadn't yet decided to follow Christ. He was cocky back then, so certain he couldn't fail. But that was more than forty years ago! He had long stopped worrying about paying for the mistakes of his youth.

Sherman thought of all the times his father had talked about being a stand-up guy. About one line in particular. "It doesn't take a man to make a baby, but it does take a man to raise one."

Suddenly guilt washed over him. Even though he hadn't been told about the baby, he still couldn't shake the feeling that he had let both Carol and Deland down. He knew how tough Deland had it growing up. He had recruited him. Had been in that living room on Jackson, with the big orange extension cord running out the window. He couldn't help but think that things could have been different for Deland. Sherman so prized his relationship with his own father, he felt terrible that Deland hadn't been able to have the same special connection growing up. Even if it wasn't intentional, he was responsible for that void in Deland's life.

Sherman's own words, said in countless locker rooms over the years, rang in his ears. "Being irresponsible is not neutral. When you're irresponsible, someone else becomes responsible for what you've been irresponsible for."

Sherman loved and respected Deland, had always cared for him and worked to guide him, especially once Deland had gotten into coaching, but this was a shock. He wasn't sure how to feel. He reached out to his brother Vincent, who was always his first call when in need of guidance or advice. Vincent didn't make Sherman feel guilty or judged for his actions with Carol way back when. His first instinct was to comfort and encourage his younger brother, and then to protect him.

"This is nothing but God!" Vincent said. "This is a miracle! You have nothing to be ashamed of, brother. This is wonderful news, as far as I'm concerned."

"I can't help but feel guilty," Sherman said, his voice shaking slightly. "Guilty and sad. I know how Deland grew up. I know what he missed out on, what he didn't have. And I know that I left Carol to handle something that should've been my responsibility too."

"She was a young girl and made the best decision for her and for the baby," Vincent said. "You didn't know. There was nothing for you to do. Now, if you find out that he is, indeed, your son, you have an opportunity to be the father he needed. You have a second chance."

"Oh, if he's mine, I'm not gonna duck it," Sherman said. "That's not even an option. You know I'm gonna choose to be there for him."

"Sherman, you know what I've been through with my own kids," said Vincent. "If you can be in his life, that's the only option. This is a gift, little brother. Nothing but a gift."

Vincent and his ex-girlfriend had three children together, and after her sudden death he endured a prolonged fight with her family to have access to the kids. Sherman knew what Vincent had been through and knew he spoke from a place of pain and knowledge when he said that this opportunity to be a father to Deland was a gift.

"You should get a paternity test, though," Vincent said. "Just to be certain."

At first Sherman balked at the idea, but then he realized it was the right thing to do. As always, Vincent was looking out for him. Sherman knew he couldn't deny the possibility that he was Deland's father, but he wanted proof.

He hung up the phone feeling lighter but still uneasy. That evening he called his wife, Sharon, into the kitchen. He had planned to wait until after the test results came back to say anything, but he knew there was no way he'd be able to keep this from her. "I just got a bomb dropped on me," Sherman said. She could tell by his tone that this was serious. She sat quietly and let him tell her everything, nodding and grabbing his hand when he got emotional. She saw that Sherman was beating himself up and she didn't want to contribute to that, so she kept hidden her own initial concerns and judgments. As she listened, she thought about Deland and what he must be feeling. A young man who had just received life-changing and life-affirming news. Any judgment fell away. This was a blessing, and she would never stand in the way of the two of them being in each other's lives.

"Well, I guess our family just got bigger," Sharon said, a giant grin on her face. She knew Deland to be a good man and a good father; she was more than happy to open up her family to him. Plus, four more grandkids? "Let's go to California and see them!" she said. She didn't need to see a paternity test. She was thrilled.

Sherman wasn't quite there yet. He was worried about what this would say about him as a man. About what it would say about the things he'd done despite the things he'd preached. It would be easier if the test showed he wasn't Deland's father, he thought. If he wasn't the father, he wouldn't have to feel guilty about his absence. If he wasn't the father, he wouldn't have to feel hypocritical about the sermons he'd given about accountability. Wouldn't have to keep thinking about the things Deland grew up without. Wouldn't have to keep thinking about the ways Deland's life was made difficult by the parents who let him go. In quiet moments he found himself hoping the test would show he wasn't Deland's dad. It was a thought that only brought Sherman more guilt. He texted Deland and asked if he could speak to Carol.

———

Carol cried the whole next day waiting for her call with Sherman. This wasn't the icebreaker you'd hope for when reconnecting with an old flame after forty-plus years: *Hi, we have a forty-four-year-old son! And how are you?* It would almost be funny if it weren't so scary. It was one thing convincing herself she'd made the right decision all those years ago; it was another to hear how *he* felt about it. What if he resented her for not telling him? What if, in her desire to protect Sherman and his future, she'd actually done wrong by him? She must have gone through a whole box of tissues trying to keep it together at work. When the time came for the call, her hand was shaking.

"Hey, Carol," Sherman said tenderly. "Long time no talk. How are you doing?"

He always did have a calming way about him. They talked for a good fifteen minutes before Deland even came up. Where they both lived, what they'd been doing with their lives since they last saw each other all those years ago. Carol was put at ease by how kind he was. How earnest he seemed in asking about what she'd made of herself and who she'd become. She told him she knew of much of his success and had cheered on his Seahawks team in the Super Bowl. "A special shout-out to Sherman Smith from your North High School Bulldog family," she had posted to her Facebook in February 2014. "We are so proud of you Sherman. Bulldogs (and Seahawks!) for life." They marveled at how long it had been since those days back at North High.

"Well, you probably know why I'm calling you," Sherman finally said.

He wasn't mad. In fact, he apologized for putting her in a position to make such a difficult decision at a young age. Carol explained why she'd believed it was best not to tell him. She told Sherman she didn't regret her decision—not once, not ever—but over the years she had wondered where baby Jon was. She just wanted to know that he'd grown up okay. Sherman assured her that their son was a good man. Said he'd been through a lot as a kid but had worked hard and made himself into a wonderful father and coach.

"Isn't it wild," Sherman said, as the reality of it all started to hit him, "that I just learned about this child and here I am, forty years later, able to tell you about him. Able to assure you that he's a good man."

It was surreal for both of them. Carol had so many questions about Deland's upbringing in Youngstown, his adoptive family and his life without her, but for now she was just happy that Sherman finally knew their secret. She'd been carrying the knowledge of their little boy for over forty years, and she finally recognized the weight of that burden as it melted away. Carol hung up full of emotions but relieved that Sherman wasn't angry with her. Sherman hung up feeling much more certain that Deland was, in fact, his son.

Sherman called Deland back and apologized for the abrupt way he'd ended their call.

"I spoke to Carol," he said. "I got the story. I heard it now. I want you to know I've been trying to process what it means for me not to have taken this responsibility. Now I know I didn't know about you, but the truth remains I wasn't there. For you or for Carol. I know what you've been through. And I know who you are now, as a man. I want you to know I wouldn't change a thing about who you are. Not a thing."

Deland was relieved to hear from Sherman and to hear a change in the sound of his voice. Less tense, less distant. A little time had helped.

"It wasn't nothing but God what got you here," Sherman continued. "I can't go back and wonder how I would've made things different. Your mama Adelle got you. I couldn't be prouder of who you are."

Deland had heard those words from Sherman before—about football, about coaching, about settling down and becoming a dad. It felt different to hear them now. They talked for a while longer and Deland could feel that Sherman was preparing him for something.

"I don't want you to think I'm rejecting you or anything like that," Sherman said carefully, "but I just need to know for sure. I'm asking you to do something I would've asked Carol to do forty-four years ago too. Before I even knew you I would've asked. I just need to know for sure. I need us to do a paternity test."

Deland understood and agreed. It would take a few weeks to get the results. As Sherman awaited word, he reached out to other trusted family members, including his aunt in Youngstown. She went on the internet and pulled up a couple of pictures of Deland. "Nephew," she said. "I can save you the money on the DNA tests."

Deland had an old article from his days in the CFL saved on his phone and sent it over to Sherman. The profile included stories about Deland's childhood, his recruitment to Miami, and his path to Winnipeg; it was a good summation of his career and made mention of his time playing under Coach Smith. They had stayed in touch over the years, but Deland thought it was a nice way to catch him up on some of his success in Canada.

The article had a much greater impact on Sherman than intended.

When he opened the story and saw the photo accompanying the article, he was confused. *I don't remember taking this picture*, he thought. *I don't remember doing this article.* Then he started reading and realized he was looking at a picture of Deland. At first he'd thought it was him in the photo!

Sherman thought about Deland's coaching internship a few years earlier, how Spencer Ware had been calling Deland "Little Sherm." How Coach Ruel hadn't stopped cracking jokes about him and his protégé acting alike. One day Coach Ruel had even walked into Sherman's office, seen the two of them working next to each other, and said, of all things, "You guys *gotta* be father and son. You're just too similar!" Sherman and Deland had both laughed and told him to scram. They didn't even think about it for a second. But it was true! They did talk alike and walk alike and look alike. He shook his head. It was all too unbelievable, but at the same time it was becoming hard to deny the truth. He was slowly realizing that he didn't want to deny the truth.

The more Sherman thought about it, the more he realized the story wasn't about him and his guilt. It was about Deland and what he had been through. It was about a life lived without a father. It was about the years Deland had spent trying to find his identity, wanting to know where he'd come from. About parents who had chosen to stay, and parents who had chosen to leave. Sherman wasn't given a choice back in high school, but he had a choice now.

"Man, he went through it," Sherman told Sharon. "The fact that he wanted to find his biological parents. He had questions, this hunger to know, this void in his life. And in a way I'm responsible for that. I played a part in it.

"It's been said that humility is not thinking less of yourself, it's thinking of yourself less," Sherman said, dropping his head. "I need to start thinking about Deland."

Sometime in the weeks since that first phone call, Sherman realized that he was hoping he was Deland's father. In fact, he'd be devastated if the test results came back otherwise. He also realized that the words he'd been preaching for years were manifesting in his life in a way far more powerful than problematic. At sixty-three, he was getting news that strengthened the message he'd been telling college kids and NFL players for his entire career. "Being irresponsible is not neutral. When you're irresponsible, someone else becomes responsible for what you've been irresponsible for." Carol had been responsible for his choices. Adelle had been responsible for his choices. The words had always meant something to him; now they meant even more.

Sherman knew he couldn't keep this secret from his kids any longer, but he wanted to tell them in person. His daughter Shavonne lived nearby, so she got the first call. While she waited for Sherman to get to her house, Shavonne's mind cycled through every possible scenario—mostly worried about his health. When she got the news about Deland it was a shock, but also a relief. She instantly turned to compassion for her mother, and once she was assured that Sharon was handling it okay, she asked Sherman how he was doing. He broke down in tears; it was the first time Shavonne had ever seen him cry.

"You don't need to cry," she said. "It's okay. We're all going to be okay."

She looked at some photos of Deland that Sherman showed her and told him she remembered hearing his name back when they lived in Oxford. She told Sherman she didn't blame him for his choices years ago and assured him that Deland would be welcome in the family.

"Wait . . . I'm not the oldest anymore?" Shavonne said, suddenly realizing that her position in the family had changed.

"I'm a middle child!?" She tried to process it. "It actually makes sense, Dad. I never felt like the firstborn stuff fit me anyway."

Sherman's tears had let up, and Shavonne knew it was okay to have some fun with him.

"You got any other kids out there, Daddy?" she joked.

"Not that I know of," said Sherman. "I sure hope not!"

"Well, if the phone rings I'm just gonna hang it up," she cracked.

"That's what I'm gonna do too!" he said, laughing. He was starting to be a little easier on himself.

Thanksgiving week, 2017. Sherman's son Sherman Jr. would be in town with his family. It was time to tell him what was going on too.

Less than an hour after he got to the house, Sharon announced that Sherman had something to talk to him about. Just like Shavonne, Sherman Jr.'s mind first went to some sort of health issue. He braced himself for the worst. Instead, Sherman asked if he remembered hearing about a standout running back he'd coached at Miami named Deland McCullough. Sherman Jr. remembered his dad mentioning Deland—a talented young player who had gone on to great success at the school after Sherman left.

"Well, son, Deland was adopted," Sherman continued. "And you can imagine my shock when he called me up the other day to tell me he'd gotten his birth certificate and found his birth mom. It was someone I knew back in high school, someone I had a little fling with back then. And Deland told me she said I'm his dad."

Sherman went on to explain how he hadn't been told about the pregnancy, how Carol had given birth in secret, and how they were waiting on the DNA test to know for sure. He wasn't sure how Sherman Jr. would respond to the idea of a half brother after years as Sherman's only son. He needn't have worried. Sherman Jr. was understanding and empathetic; he recognized the shock his dad was feeling. He remembered Deland's name but couldn't recall if they'd ever met at a practice or after a game. He was open to having a relationship with Deland and open to the idea of welcoming a new sibling into their family, but he wanted to be sure to get the paternity tests first. He was practical, just like his uncle Vincent.

On Thanksgiving morning the tests hadn't come back yet, but Sherman and Sharon felt certain that he was Deland's dad. They grabbed the kids, cousins, and everyone out of the kitchen to FaceTime Deland, Darnell, and the boys.

"Let's wait a minute, Dad," Sherman Jr. cautioned. "Let's just wait until we know for sure. Then I'll be all in."

It was a good reminder to Coach Smith. Brought him back down to earth.

He and Sharon had gotten so excited about welcoming Deland into the family, they'd forgotten that things might not go as they hoped. They settled for texts and emails, sharing pictures and memories during the day. Sharon called Deland and put to rest any fears about how she might be affected by this surprise—she was overjoyed. The Smiths were acting like family, hoping they had reason to.

At the same time, Carol and all her relatives were over at her cousin's house for Thanksgiving. She FaceTimed Deland out in California and the minute they saw each other for the first time, the waterworks started up again. They had spoken on the phone but this was different. She was looking into his big, dark eyes and could see there was already love there. Darnell sat beside Deland and the boys hovered, peeking over Deland's shoulder every once in a while, surprised to see their dad cry. "Yeah, this the first time they're seeing me like this," Deland said to Carol, laughing through tears. "But actually, I'm a pretty emotional guy. About family stuff, I get pretty emotional." Carol could relate. She was quick to tears as well. A soft heart, both of them. By the end of the call she had started referring to the two of them as the "Boo Hoo Twins" 'cause once they started crying it wouldn't let up.

There were as many smiles as tears, though. Deland couldn't wipe the grin off his face as he was looking at Carol. He got to see her facial expressions, her mannerisms, the way her eyes crinkled when she smiled. He got to see where he came from and find bits of himself in someone else, a wholly new experience for him.

A week later, on the afternoon of Wednesday, November 29, Deland was at his office when the paternity test results came via email. He scanned the page for a clear answer. He was hoping it would say right at the top what was what, but instead it was extremely complicated. At the top it said "Alleged Father: Sherman L. Smith" and "Child: Deland S. McCullough" above a scientific-sounding sentence and a confusing chart full of numbers.

Deoxyribonucleic acid (DNA) isolated from the above specimens were characterized through polymerase chain reaction (PCR) at the following genetic systems:

	CHILD		ALLEGED FATHER		
SYSTEM	ALLELE	ALLELE	ALLELE	ALLELE	RI
D3S1358		16	14	16	1.6281
D1S1656	14	16		14	1.9433
D2S441	9	13.3	11	13.3	86.2069
D10S1248	12	15		15	2.5329
D13S317	11	12	11	12	1.5705
PENTA E	8	9	9	12	10.0000
D16S539	11	12		11	1.6989
D18S51	16	18	17	18	1.9040
D2S1338	18	21	21	23	1.6372
CSF1PO	7	8	7	11	5.8275
PENTA D	10	12	10	11	3.3445
THO1	8	9		8	2.6925
VWA	15	17		17	2.7278
D21S11	29	32	29	30	1.3165
D7S820	8	9	8	11	1.4384
D5S818		11	9	11	1.9150
TPOX	8	11	8	12	0.6786
D8S1179	14	16	14	16	6.3807
D12S391	17	18		17	2.9994
D19S433	11	13	12.2	13	0.8435
FGA		24	22	24	2.6867

CRI = 2.566.242.492.4737
PROBABILITY (W=50%) = 99.9999%

On the next page: "Sherman L. Smith cannot be excluded as the biological father of Deland S. McCullough."

Deland kept reading . . . and then: "The relative chance of paternity is . . . 99.9999%."

99.9999%! There it was! Coach was his dad.

He took a screenshot of it and sent it to Sherman: "Well there it is. 99.9999% chance we are related. Shoot me ur email and I will forward to u."

Over at the Smith house, Sharon jumped up and screamed, hootin' and hollerin' like her team had just won the Super Bowl. She immediately called Deland to welcome him to the family and share just how excited they all were. She was the first of a wave of calls he got all in a row—next his half sister Shavonne, then his half brother Sherman Jr., and finally Coach Smith himself.

"All right, it's on!" Sherman said with a grin so big Deland could practically see it through the phone.

In addition to regular calls with Sherman and Sharon, Deland started talking to Sherman's brother Vincent on the phone once or twice a week, learning more about what his dad had been like as a kid and bonding over football and faith. They talked about their families, their children, and Vincent's role as a MentorCoach for a high school football team. And they spent plenty of time catching up on the years gone by, sharing what they'd missed not knowing each other for four decades. Vincent saw the timing of Deland's discovery as a particular blessing for the Smith brothers.

"Your arrival is almost like God giving us comfort for the loss of our brother," Vincent told Deland, describing the heartbreak they'd felt losing Darrell to cancer just a few months earlier. "Now we have a new nephew and son in our lives. God's mercy and grace coming to us through you. And, Deland, some pictures I see of you, you look just like my brother Darrell."

Deland loved the long phone calls with family, but he really wanted to get the chance to see his birth parents in person. He had recruiting trips in Ohio and Tennessee in the beginning of December, so he didn't have to wait long to see both Carol and Sherman.

Carol was living about fifteen minutes south of Campbell, in a town called Boardman, when Deland first went to visit her. When she answered the door they both gasped; it felt like they were looking in a mirror. They hugged for what felt like a full five minutes, and as they sat down and talked, Deland never let go of Carol's hand. There it was again, that feeling of sunshine—bright, yellow, blazing warmth. They couldn't stop looking at each other's faces, noting every wrinkle, crease, and expression they recognized as their own. Carol's brother, Michael, and his son, Oliver, were there too. Michael wanted to meet Deland and see the moment his little sister had waited decades for. He got emotional right along with Carol and Deland, who had both been tearing up since the moment she opened the door. Michael also wanted to keep an eye on the two of them for a little while, just to be sure Deland seemed like an okay kind of guy.

"You can go, Michael," Carol said after about twenty minutes. "He good. He ain't a psychopath or anything." Carol and Deland laughed, the same laugh. Just like that first phone call, Deland felt like he'd known her his whole life. He didn't put on airs or try to impress her; he was just natural. So was she.

Carol lived alone with her dog, Manly. She was enjoying a successful career as a senior quality assurance analyst for Dick's Sporting Goods, had plenty of friends, and spent a lot of time with Michael and Oliver, who was still quite young—he was born when Michael was sixty years old. She was happy, but the moment Deland arrived she recognized that her life had just gotten bigger and fuller in an instant. A son, a daughter-in-law, four grandsons! "Blessings on blessings," she kept saying, shaking her head in disbelief.

"All I ever wanted was to know you were a decent person," Carol told Deland. "Just that would have been enough. I could've moved on. But all of this? I just couldn't be happier."

That night as they sat and ate dinner in Carol's dining room, Deland realized there was something very important the two of them needed to decide, together.

"What do you want me to call you?" he asked, looking up from his plate. "I'm not going to just call you Carol. That doesn't feel right."

"You can call me whatever you feel comfortable with," Carol said. "You and the boys and Darnell."

Deland had always called Adelle "Ma," so he settled on Momma.

"Momma," he said, as the sunshine pounded down on him right through the night sky. "My Momma."

"I like that," said Carol, her smile as wide as the moon.

Sherman, Deland, and Carol

CHAPTER 24

Deland sat in his car, hands folded on his lap, eyes staring ahead at the steering wheel. He'd been sitting there, parked, for nearly five full minutes, almost incapable of getting out of the car. Why was he so nervous?

Sherman looked out the front window of his home in Franklin, Tennessee, expecting to see Deland pull up any minute. They were seeing each other in person for the first time since they'd learned the news of their biological connection. He scanned the street and noticed a car parked down the hill, at the end of the block. There was Deland, sitting in the driver's seat. Sherman watched for another few minutes as Deland continued to sit there. He didn't move. Sherman chuckled to himself. This cat was nervous.

Eventually Deland managed to get himself out of the car and start the walk up the block to Sherman's house. Meeting Carol had been a bit overwhelming, but he'd always had a mother. Carol was a bonus mom, a welcome and special surplus. This was different. Deland had never had a father. All his life he'd said, "Didn't have one, didn't need one," but when Sherman opened the door, Deland felt the weight of that lie. He had always wanted a father. And if he was honest with himself, for most of his life he had had a father. Just by another name.

Sherman stood there, beaming, his arms open wide.

"My son."

Deland had never heard a man say those words before.

My son.

He couldn't hold back his tears. He stepped into Sherman's arms and let himself be held. The little boy inside him finally exhaled and let go. He was safe. He belonged. He was worthy. He was enough.

Deland remembered the first time he and Sherman met, when Sherman turned around to shake his hand and seemed so imposing, he might as well have been a movie star on a twenty-five-foot screen. He had a kind of energy Deland couldn't describe. Deland felt it again in that moment on the stoop. It was cinematic. There was no other word for it. He couldn't have known, all those years ago, that Sherman was more than just a coach, yet there was that feeling. That energy. That pull. He let go, stepped back, and looked at his father.

My son. He would remember that moment forever.

Those two words mattered to Sherman too. For years he'd greeted Deland with some form of "Hey, man, how you doing?" This time had to be different. For him, to fully recognize the power of their bond, and for Deland, so he would know that Sherman was proud to be his father.

They spent hours talking that day, rehashing the story of Carol and Sherman, laughing about the word salad that had tumbled out of Sherman's mouth when Deland first said "and she told me you were my dad." The next day Sherman's pastor came to the house to talk with them. "Look at you guys," he said, as they sat side by side on the couch. "Man, this is your *son* right here, Sherman." He preached the virtues of God and of the forces that brought them together. He remarked upon the unbelievable circumstances that had allowed Deland to know and learn from his father for nearly thirty years. Both men got emotional. When the pastor left, Deland realized he'd said the words "my dad" more times in that conversation than probably his entire life combined.

"'My dad' has never been followed by something positive," he told Sherman. "It was always 'my dad left' or 'I never knew my dad' or 'I ain't never had a dad.' It's all different now."

Sherman was the same man who had seen something special in Deland when he was just a skinny seventeen-year-old kid living in the projects. Same man who had stayed late in his office to talk to him about relationships, accountability, and integrity. Same man who showed him the ropes in the NFL and helped him advance in his career as a coach. Sherman was the same man he'd always been, yet it was all so different now. Deland realized he had changed too. He saw himself differently now that he knew he was Sherman Smith's son. Now that he knew the source of his dogged work ethic and single-minded focus. He knew that the story he'd told himself about coming from a long line of ambitious and uncompromising workers had been true. Deland had always expected more of himself than anyone else did, but now he had something tangible to live up to: the legacy of Sherman Smith. It was the highest and most impeccable standard he knew.

For his whole life Deland had done right by the name he carried, even though he didn't respect the man he got it from. He would never take Sherman's name, but he was honored to have the opportunity to live up to his example.

Deland and Sherman had lost plenty of years they couldn't get back, but the timing felt right in its own way. Sherman had recently retired and had all the time in the world to devote to getting to know his son, his daughter-in-law, and his grandchildren. If he was still coaching he'd have been at work all day and traveling most weeks. Later Sherman Jr. would remark at how having Deland in the family also allowed their father to stay involved in the game of football, have an outlet for his coaching insights, and keep busy in retirement.

"Can't question God's plan," Sherman remarked that day as they said goodbye to the pastor.

That night Deland got to meet his half sister, Shavonne, and hear all about his cousins, nieces, nephews, and the rest of his family on Sherman's side. He was about to get the chance to meet a whole bunch more family too. Sherman told him that his aunt Debbie hosted a big family reunion in Youngstown almost every summer and that she had insisted Deland bring everyone—kids, wife, Adelle, Carol—to give the family a chance to meet their newest kin.

Deland was excited to have everyone together, but nervous about how Adelle might handle things. Earlier that week when he went to see Carol for the first time, he had gone to Adelle's house first, and it almost felt like she was stalling, trying to keep him there as long as she could. He understood why she might feel insecure or anxious about these new relationships and he tried his best to assure her that their relationship wouldn't change. She was still his mom, he was still her son. Always would be.

Since the moment he'd gotten his birth certificate, he'd kept Adelle and Damon updated with texts and calls about getting to know Carol. When he got home from dinner the night he found out about Sherman, he immediately called Damon. As usual when the two of them were involved, the conversation started with jokes.

"You're not going to believe who my dad is," Deland said.

"Wait, it's someone we know?" said Damon. "What?! Hmm . . . It's gotta be Frank Doon, huh?" Damon continued, deadpan.

"Don't even say that!" said Deland, laughing. "What if it was, like, Uncle Yub?" he said, still cracking up.

After a few more names, each more and more ridiculous, Deland finally stopped laughing and got serious.

"My dad is Sherman Smith," he said, and Damon thought he felt the lid of his head flap open and let in a breeze. Literally mind blown.

Deland called Adelle right after; she was overjoyed by the news. "Just a blessing!" she couldn't stop saying. "A blessing!" She would repeat it whenever she talked to Deland about Sherman. Sometimes to him, sometimes just muttering it to herself. For weeks Adelle cried every time she thought about it. Sherman Smith, Deland's father! And the idea of Carol being right there in Youngstown all that time made her emotional as well. There were tears of joy, but tears of mixed emotion too. Damon and Adelle were thrilled to see Deland so happy and relieved that his birth parents were such wonderful people, but they also knew that things had changed forever. They would always be his family, but he had another family now too. Two other families, really: the Briggses and the Smiths.

Adelle and Damon had done all the heavy lifting; Deland knew that. Through all the difficult times, they stood by him, took care of him, and raised him up right. He owed them everything and loved them as deeply and truly as anyone could. Things hadn't been easy growing up, though, and he understood how this new dynamic might have Adelle feeling defensive. He made sure to tell Carol and Sherman that he didn't hold any of Adelle's decisions against her or resent any of the hardships he'd faced. They had made him who he was. Adelle might have struggled to make her own outcomes match her intentions, but she'd had no trouble making the right choices for Deland. She'd put him on the right path and did everything she could to keep him on it. She'd made the choice to be his mother and had never wavered. Never left, never gave up on him, never let her circumstances change her commitment.

Adelle had long wondered what Deland might find in his search for his birth parents. The last few years she'd always tell him, "You've got parents out there. Don't assume anything negative about them until and unless we find out," but she couldn't help but worry that Deland's birth mother might be a mess—dealing with drug addiction or mental health issues. When she heard about Carol and her wonderful upbringing, tight-knit family, and successful career, it hit her in a way she didn't expect. She knew she raised her boys up right, but wondered if she'd be judged for their struggles. She also felt undeniable, irrepressible tinges of jealousy. She cared for this boy, gave him everything, and had enjoyed more than forty years of loving him and being loved by him, but she could never have the biological tie that Carol did. Every day Adelle was overwhelmed by the joy she felt for Deland's happiness, but every day she dealt with challenging feelings of loss too.

Over the years Adelle had thought about this moment—when and if Deland found his parents—and always thought she'd be able to handle it. Now it was taking some work to confront her fears and envy and push through them so she could focus on her son's happiness. It almost would have been easier if Carol was a mess. Adelle could have just been the savior. The good one. This was more complicated.

It was complicated for Carol and Sherman too. Carol had given up her baby boy so he could have a life as great as hers, with two parents and a safe and loving home. But she also knew if she had kept him, he would have been raised by her parents, not her. Would he have been better off? How would it have affected him to grow up alongside her like a younger brother instead of a child? She could never know. Sherman had seen first-hand how tough Deland had it and felt protective of his son, lamenting the adversity he'd had to face. But he also knew he wouldn't have been the role model Deland needed back when he was eighteen. Sherman knew Carol had made the right decision putting him up for adoption and never felt aggrieved that the decision had been made without him. Both Carol and Sherman agreed that they couldn't have done what Adelle did. Both agreed that Deland grew up to be a wonderful man, clearly molded and made by Adelle's hand. For all the pain they felt thinking about his hardships, they knew he couldn't have turned out better under their care.

"Sometimes the struggles are what make you who you are," Sherman told Carol during one of their early phone calls. "And if you don't go through them, maybe you don't become that type of person that you are. I think his struggles helped him, helped make him better."

Sherman and Carol couldn't have been prouder of Deland. There was so much good in that man; so much strength forged by his fight. They still wished they could take away his pain, though. They still couldn't shake a little bit of resentment. They knew that directing it all at Adelle was unfair; they were mad about the circumstances, some of which were out of her control.

A week or so after Sherman learned the news about Deland, he called Adelle and thanked her. "There's no way I could have given him what you gave him," he told her. "Just from that standpoint of how you were bringing him up, I couldn't have given him that. I didn't have that in me. I didn't have the wisdom that you had at that point. So it's a blessing that you were there because you were teaching him stuff I couldn't have taught him.

"I'd like to think I would have made a difference if I was around," he told her. "But when I look at Deland now and the type of man that he is, the type of father he is, and the husband that he is, I don't know if you can do any better. I look at him and I can't say, 'Man, if you had a stronger man in your life, you'd be this, this, and this.' I look at him now and say, 'You're pretty strong.'"

It took a little longer for Adelle and Carol to connect. This was a tougher conversation. A more sensitive relationship. Carol wasn't sure she was ready to hear all the details of Deland's childhood. She was still sorting through her emotions. She didn't want to be, but she was mad at Adelle for all that Deland went through. But she felt guilty too. She hadn't been able to do it, she'd given him up. How could she judge anyone else? She put off the conversation as long as she could, but when Deland specifically asked her to call Adelle, she wanted to honor his request.

When Adelle picked up the phone, Carol started the conversation by thanking her for all she had done. For the man Deland had become and the lessons she'd taught him. Before she had a chance to explain why she'd made her decision to give Deland up, Adelle got to talking about herself and then didn't stop.

Carol learned about Adelle's determination to get to all of Deland's football games—even the day she had to ride his moped to the stadium— and of all the sacrifices Adelle had made to get Deland a good education. She learned about the very important job Adelle had in Cleveland, about how she started up and ran her company, 3-D, and about her work on the board of New York City–wide Head Start years earlier. About the things Adelle had taught Deland, the ways he took after her, and the special relationship she had with her grandsons.

It was clear Adelle wanted Carol to know that she was Deland's mom, had raised him and reared him and been there every step of the way. It felt like Adelle was explaining herself, justifying herself. Like she wanted to be sure to present herself in a certain way, just in case Deland hadn't. They were on the phone for two hours and Adelle didn't ask about Carol's life at all. Where she grew up, what she did for a living, if she went to college or had other children. She didn't ask about her family, even after Carol mentioned that her parents and some of her aunts had gone to the same high school as Adelle.

Carol understood that Adelle felt threatened and was defensive, but the result was that Carol felt boxed out. Like Adelle wanted to stake her claim over Deland. Carol didn't know if it was Adelle's intention or just her own insecurity, but she was made to feel bad about being in the picture.

He came looking for ME, she thought.

When Carol went to work the next day, she told a few coworkers about the challenges she was facing as Deland connected all the disparate pieces of his life. She understood it was a sticky situation; she just wished everyone could be as happy as she was that a child had found his parents. She told her work friends she was thinking about having a gathering so his people could meet her people and they could eventually be one big, happy family.

"Being happy for Deland isn't the same as being friends with each other," one of her coworkers said. "You have to build a relationship with *him*. You don't have to build a relationship with his family."

Carol considered, for the first time, that they all might have to be okay with less than the perfect family portrait.

That Christmas Deland looked around his living room at the shredded wrapping paper, discarded boxes of freshly opened gifts, and pajama-clad bodies of his sons sprawled on the couch and chairs around him. Over the last month, the boys had started to learn about the family members on their father's side.

They had finally unlocked the mystery of Daeh, who had inherited his rounder face and almond-shaped eyes from Carol's dad. He was the spitting image of Oliver—even wore the same kind of glasses. Dasan, already the tallest in the family by several inches at just fourteen years old, was thrilled when Sherman told him there were relatives as tall as 6'7" in their family. "Could be me!" he told Deland, stretching up as tall as he could and looking down on him. Sherman had FaceTimed Deland II on his birthday and the oldest McCullough boy couldn't believe how much Grandpa talked and sounded like his dad. It was incredible for Deland and his family to be able to make these connections.

Finding Carol and Sherman not only helped Deland know his roots and understand his identity but it also taught him, with certainty, that it was okay to look. That it was *necessary* to look. And that he wanted his sons to learn that they could look too. No more hiding things, no more being ashamed of painful or difficult situations. Loyalty to a family system that perpetuated bad habits wasn't healthy. In his family, they would talk about things. In his family, they would create strong relationships by facing the truth. Deland knew that healing wasn't about being a polished, perfect final product or pretending to be "fixed." Healing was about knowing how to react in difficult situations, understanding how to deal with sensitive family members, and learning how to feel in control of one's emotions and responses. It was a journey he could take both for himself and for others.

Deland realized there was no shame or guilt in unearthing his family's struggles, or in wanting to help Adelle address her pain. He knew his ma hadn't been given the tools to deal with her trauma and that she was just doing her best. He wasn't even angry about the things that he'd been handed. Deland considered it a privilege and a responsibility to start the healing process for his family system. Like the honor he'd given the name McCullough, this was another new beginning he was proud to take on. But he also wasn't willing to leave anyone behind on this journey. He was going to take Adelle, Damon, the boys, and anyone else along with him as he worked through the generational trauma he'd inherited both biologically and emotionally. Deland was no longer a mystery to himself. And he knew now that he wasn't "broken"; he was just the result of his influences. He was a product of the things that happened to him, before him, and around him. By facing it all and bringing the pain to the light, he was changing patterns moving forward and giving Adelle and those who came before him the opportunity to change their patterns too.

Deland felt proud that he'd been brave enough to search for his roots and start the process of mending things. He pulled out his phone and sent Sherman a message:

> Dad, words can't describe how complete I feel that I've been blessed in so many ways throughout my life, even when, on the surface, I may not have deserved it. I'm especially thankful that God allowed me to search for my roots and find you. To find out that my father is a man I have admired, respected, and loved over half my life is something I cannot comprehend, but I'm super thankful for. I salute my new extended family on this great holiday as we continue to build our relationships.

A few minutes later, Sherman responded:

> My son, I am the one that is truly blessed. As I have continued to process what God has revealed this last month or so, I realized just how great God is. They say that Grace is getting what you don't deserve, and mercy is not getting what you do deserve. You are God's grace and mercy in my life. You are an extension of God's grace because he has given me a son and family that I don't deserve. You are God's mercy in my life because God has given me a son and a family that would be an example of what a family is. We both know that this story could have had a much different ending. But once again, God's mercy has been extended to us. I'm so proud of the man that you are and how you demonstrate that by the way you love your wife and the way you love your children. I thank God that in spite of me not being in your life full-time, you have developed into exactly the type of man that I would have hoped for. So this Christmas, for me, is one of the most exciting that I experienced because

this unexpected gift is truly from the hand of God. We will get a chance to talk later.

Please wish everyone a Merry Christmas from us.

"Grace is getting what you don't deserve, and mercy is not getting what you do deserve." Deland reread that part of the message several times. It felt like wisdom that applied to so many of the people in his life, including himself.

At the end of December, Carol went down to Texas to see USC play Ohio State in the Cotton Bowl. She got the chance to meet Darnell and the boys for the first time. A few of Deland's players walked by them in the hotel the day before the game and stopped to ask if that was his momma. The running backs especially were excited to meet her after all they'd heard about her. At dinner that night, Deland fielded several texts and phone calls from NFL teams interested in interviewing him. Despite all the miracles he and his family had experienced in the last two months, he hadn't lost sight of his coaching aspirations, and he felt closer than ever to realizing them.

Just as the McCulloughs were getting used to 80-degree days in winter, they were packing up their house in Redondo Beach and headed back to the Midwest. The first week of 2018 saw Deland's dream become reality; he was hired as running backs coach for the Kansas City Chiefs of the NFL. The whole family went out for one last breakfast at their favorite spot on the beach, the Strand House, and took a walk on the pier to say their goodbyes to the surf and sun. It was a pivotal time for Deland II, who was finishing up his junior year in high school and would now spend his senior year in Overland Park, Kansas. College football offers were coming in for him and, despite being just an eighth grader, Dasan got his first college offer that spring too.

Before he could start working with the Chiefs running backs, Deland had to clean up the lingering effects of his own rushing career. He'd gotten a hip replacement that March just after they moved, and Carol,

Sherman, and Sharon all came out to Kansas to help him recuperate and give Darnell a hand with the boys. That May, Deland posted a photo on Instagram from Carol's visit, the two of them standing outside the Chiefs' stadium, his arm around her.

"Well, well . . . " he wrote. "I wondered who you were my whole life!!! When I found you in November I felt at peace as my biological beginnings came into focus. I'm very happy that you are my mother. The connection was instant and the love is strong—and I couldn't have asked for anything better after 45 yrs!!! So as your only child, on your first official Mother's Day . . . I wish you a Happy Mother's Day!!!"

"You are the best thing I have ever done, Deland," responded Carol. "Love you much."

He also posted a photo standing next to Adelle, writing:

Happy Mother's Day to the woman that laid the foundation for what and who I am today. She raised me with love and discipline. She sacrificed and taught me and my brother lessons that would affect not only us, but those we come in contact with!!! I especially appreciate her support in finding my birth parents which is a testament to the level of person she is. Ma, you did a great job!!! Happy Mother's Day

Slowly, lovingly, and with intention, Deland was figuring out how to make this blended family work.

As he got ready to coach his first offseason camp in the pros, Deland gave himself a moment to reflect on his time in college football and appreciate the work he had done over the last seven years. Just like Sherman had done for him, he had been a role model to his guys, a sounding board, and an example of what you can become, no matter your circumstances. He thought about Demar Harmon, Jordan Howard, Tevin Coleman, Stephen Houston, D'Angelo Roberts, and so many more. The list of young men who learned under Deland and continued to come back to him for advice in life and football was growing with every year that passed. The man who had grown up fatherless had become a father not just to his own sons, but to many others as well.

Author Glennon Doyle has written about how being a mother isn't so much an assignment or an identity, but rather an energy that can be offered or not. That the world would be better off if folks used mothering love "like a floodlight instead of a pointed laser aimed only at the few we've been assigned." The same can be said of fathers, and of Deland. Deland collected all the shadows that filled the spaces a father should have been and turned that darkness into light. A light he was willing to give any young man that needed it.

That June, Deland, Darnell, and the boys were joined by the whole Smith family—Sherman, Sharon, Shavonne, Sherman Jr., and his kids—on the Miami campus in Oxford. They were there to witness and celebrate the verbal commitment of Deland II to the Miami University RedHawks football team. A defensive back, Deland II was following in the footsteps of not just the pair of Hall of Famers—his father and grandfather—but his uncle Sherman Jr., who had played defensive back at Miami as well.

Deland and Sherman Jr. had first met a few months earlier at a coaches' convention in Charlotte, North Carolina. Sherman Jr. had driven the few hours from his home base in Raleigh to see him for dinner. Their phone conversations had been great, but Deland arrived at the restaurant still a little worried that Sherman Jr. might not want to share his father's attention and affection. Deland had nothing to worry about. It was clear Sherman Jr. was raised right.

"Our father is someone everyone wants to be around," Sherman Jr. told Deland. "I would be the last person to have any jealousy or do anything to prevent you from seeing him. He was the best man at my wedding and he's the person that I go to for advice. You'd be foolish not to get as much time around him as you can. Soak it all up. Be around our father. I would never want to get in the way of that. Man, I'm pushing for it. I'm happy for you guys."

Realizing that Sherman Jr. welcomed him and wanted him to have a good relationship with their father was more than a relief. Deland felt instantly connected to his half brother.

It felt great to be on the Miami campus with both Shermans, two guys who knew firsthand what it was like to put on a RedHawks jersey. Deland and his dad talked about what had changed or stayed the same since they were at the school together nearly thirty years earlier. They remarked on the fancy new football facility and posed for photos with the giant photograph of Deland on one wall. They showed the boys their Hall of Fame plaques, walked through the locker room, offices, and down to the field. It was all so surreal for Deland—the place that had brought him together with his father would now be home to his son.

On July 3 Sherman's aunt Debbie welcomed more than fifty members of the family to her house in Youngstown for a supersize reunion. It was a sunny summer day, and the sky was a perfect saltwater blue dotted with a handful of fluffy white clouds. Everywhere he turned, Deland saw new faces—and some of them looked a whole lot like his. It was overwhelming but joyful, almost like another wedding day as he tried to introduce Adelle, Darnell, and the kids to everybody and meet all the aunts, uncles, cousins, nephews, nieces, and neighbors.

Sherman and Carol both told Deland stories about their parents, and their parents' parents. Stories of who and where he came from. Deland learned that Carol's roots traced back to Nigeria, West Africa, Sierra Leone, and Italy. He learned about his great-grandparents, Otis and Martha, and Carol told him she was sure Oliver had followed Deland's football career, all the way from high school to the pros. Carol wished Oliver and her brother Jerry were still alive and sitting next to her, sharing in the pride she felt. They were sports superfans, both of them, and she knew they would have been overjoyed by the football successes of Deland and his sons. Sherman told Deland he wished John and Lillie and his little brother, Darrell, could be there too. He knew Darrell would have loved getting to know his nephew; their shared passion for football would've kept them talking for hours.

Sherman was shocked to learn how worried Carol had been about calling him for the first time. He knew she had sounded a little nervous, but he had no idea she'd been crying all day. They laughed, and cried some more, about how much they'd both wanted to apologize to each other that day, him for not recognizing the potential consequences of their actions, her for making a big decision for them both. Meanwhile, Darnell couldn't stop staring at Sherman, suddenly noticing how much he acted like Deland—from how they talked and their hand gestures to something as silly as the way they chewed on a toothpick. She wasn't the only one—everyone marveled at just how much Deland and Sherman sounded and looked alike.

At one point Sherman's wife, Sharon, spotted Carol waving to two older women standing on the lawn a few houses down, watching from afar. When Sharon heard they were Carol's aunts—her mom's sisters—she insisted on walking down there and bringing them back to the party. Sharon had called Carol a week earlier to break the ice and to make sure Carol wasn't anxious about seeing her and Sherman at the reunion. Told her she was excited to meet her. The two of them got on like a house on fire, and Carol liked her even more now that she saw her in action. Walking over and receiving Carol's family felt like more than a kindness; it was a statement. Sharon was gonna make sure everyone felt like they belonged.

From the day Sharon learned about Sherman and Deland, she had been committed to treating him and his family like they were hers by blood. Try to tell her different and prepare for a fight. She had called not just Carol but Adelle too, offering support as Adelle navigated her feelings.

She called to talk to all of Deland's boys and wanted to learn everything about them. The more time Deland spent with her, the more he realized he was getting a third mother in Sharon. The blessings of the last few months were almost too abundant to process. When he told people about finding his family, some would remark how lucky he'd gotten. He'd tell them it was something much bigger. "This ain't just luck," he'd say. "Luck can run out. This is God's love. I ain't never feel like I'll run out of God's love."

The tears and laughs came easily for everyone at Debbie's that day, and the stories flowed from every piece of Deland's past and present. They all had so many missed years to catch up on, but as Sherman told the group, "We can't turn back the hands of time. All we can do is go forward and build from here."

The next morning, Deland took Sherman, Sharon, and Uncle Vincent on a drive around Youngstown, showing them his schools, favorite spots, and all the houses he'd lived in as a boy. After he dropped them off, he went back to Adelle's and got an earful from her for being later than expected.

"Where you been?" she asked before he'd even made it through the door.

"I was just takin'—" Deland didn't even get through the sentence.

Adelle went off. Going on and on about making her wait. Not prioritizing her. How she felt as though he hadn't put her first at the reunion the day before. This was clearly about so much more than Deland's late arrival, but no matter the motivation, he felt like he didn't deserve it. Deland had done the work over the years to know how to downregulate his emotions, speak from a place of calm, and respond without anger or frustration. He paused and collected himself, and then, for the first time in his life, Deland talked back. Told her where he'd been and what he'd been doing. Told her he was grown. An adult. That she had to stop trying to tell him what to do all the time. Had to stop trying to make everything about her.

"Don't you talk to me like that!" said Adelle.

"Talk to you like what?" he said. "I'm talking to you like an adult. You've been talking to people the way you wanna talk to 'em forever. Come on now."

He paused. Took another deep breath.

"That's where I was. I'm here now. I love you, Ma. Let's move on."

Deland knew it would take some time for everyone in the family to adjust to Sherman and Carol and accept this new normal. He understood that Adelle's anger was a manifestation of fear and love. It was easier to access anger than be vulnerable enough to allow others to see her pain. She was lashing out because she didn't want to lose him. And, frankly, because she didn't know any other way. But it was time to face these things head-on. Deland knew he needed to set a boundary. To advocate for himself and tell Adelle that she needed to make space for him too. He would not participate in the same back-and-forth garbage he fell asleep listening to night after night as a kid. He would not argue with her; he would not exchange cruelties. He knew they both wanted to feel more connected to each other, but bad habits and past behaviors were getting in the way. "Neurons that fire together, wire together." For too long Adelle's feelings of connection and care had been accompanied by feelings of fear and anger. He wanted to help change that wiring.

As an adult Deland had learned how to move past the messaging of his youth to choose healthier, more direct communication. He didn't want to go back to the old ways now. In fact, he wanted to reach back and pull Adelle with him into the future. He knew it wasn't his responsibility to heal her—that he couldn't heal *for* her—but he could be intentional about which family practices to continue and which to let go of. He could be mindful of the language he used and allowed around him; language that he knew would influence reactions and behavior. It's hard work to be the one who changes a family, but it's a gift too. Deland knew it would take time. Healing isn't being fixed; it's having the tools to know how to keep fixing yourself, to keep thinking and behaving differently so your outcomes and experiences are different too. Just like Deland, Adelle was the result of her influences. Being able to see her as a person with her own struggles allowed him to give her grace.

Deland wanted Adelle to see that her legacy lived in his ability to love the way he did. Love hard. Love big. But that love could also look different. More honest, more open, more peaceful. He wasn't going to let Adelle keep setting fires. It was time to start putting them out.

Sherman, Carol, Deland, Adelle, Darnell, and the boys
with extended family at the reunion

CHAPTER 25

The day after the big reunion, Deland went over to Carol's house for her annual Fourth of July party. That year she had invited not just her favorite Youngstown folk but all sorts of family from Rockford, Illinois, and friends from her years living in Chicago. Sherman and Sharon were there, along with Shavonne, Sherman Jr., Darnell, and all the McCullough boys. Carol was overjoyed—all her people were finally getting to meet Deland.

Deland loved learning more about his mother's side of the family. And he loved how proud everyone was of him. They wanted to hear about his football accomplishments, his time with the Bengals, his coaching jobs, and the famous NFL players he considered friends. He'd been loved on by plenty of family growing up, households full at Allerton Court especially, but there was something about his momma's family seeing him all grown up that made him feel especially good. He wasn't that shy, closed-up kid anymore. He was someone anyone would be proud to call their son. And it didn't hurt that he kept overhearing Carol's friends saying, "Dang, Carol, your son is fine!"

When the festivities were all over, Deland, Darnell, and the boys headed back to Kansas City. Over the next few days he got a lot of texts with photos from the reunion, stories about people he'd met and funny moments he might have missed. And, of course, ticket requests from all his new aunties, uncles, and cousins. In the span of a few short months, he'd gone from not knowing a single person other than his sons who shared his DNA to a big ol' family of people who looked and talked like him, shared his history, and gave him back his past.

He had another family system and lineage in which to discover the messaging and lessons that had been embedded deep within him. The parts of him that hadn't lined up with his chosen family found their place in his birth family. He finally had an identity. A beginning to the story he'd started writing in the middle.

For years it had felt like there were two sides to him: Baby Jon and Deland. Jon had always belonged to somewhere else. A place Deland didn't know, full of people he could only imagine. Jon might have had a different life; who knows where he would've ended up if Carol hadn't laid him down on that bed and let him go. Or if someone else had claimed him at that orphanage in Alleghany County. Jon represented all the what-ifs. All the ways it felt like chance had held the reins to a life.

Then there was Deland. The places he knew and the people who had raised him. The choices he had made, the path he had picked, the life he had made for himself.

Deland had been holding on to both identities for as long as he could remember. He didn't want to erase Jon; he just wanted to bring his two halves together. He could do that now. There was peace in that.

There's a traditional African philosophy called Ubuntu that teaches that we are only human through the humanity of others. Not the accepted Western philosophy "I think, therefore I am" but rather "I belong, therefore I am." The *New World Encyclopedia* says a person with Ubuntu "knows his or her place in the universe and is consequently able to interact gracefully with other individuals. . . . At all times, the individual effectively represents the people from among whom he or she comes."

Sometimes *Ubuntu* is literally translated as "I am because we are."

After years of searching for his identity, Deland could look at Carol, Sherman, and Adelle and find in each of them a piece of himself. For the first time in his life, he had all the pieces. He finally felt whole. He was, because they were.

EPILOGUE

They say you don't get to choose your family, but there's no arguing Deland and Sherman chose each other. First in 1990, when they met at Campbell Memorial, then again and again over the three decades of guidance and mentorship they shared.

Carol chose to let Deland go and chose to let him back in.

Adelle chose Deland too, welcoming him as family and loving him as her own. Damon chose to accept him, mentor him, and protect him, with the fierceness of a brother and the strength and influence of a father. Their choices, and Deland's choice to love and embrace them back, were as strong as any bond made by blood.

They all continue to make the choice to be in each other's lives. Carol and Adelle went to Cleveland in early November 2018 to see Deland's Chiefs beat the Browns. (Adelle was wearing head-to-toe Browns gear so everyone would know she was still loyal to her team!) Later that month, Carol, Sherman, and Sharon joined Deland's family at their house in Kansas for Thanksgiving. In the spring of 2019, Sherman joined Deland's family to watch Deland II play in Miami's spring football game. Carol was in the crowd at Hard Rock Stadium in Miami as Deland and the Chiefs won Super Bowl LIV in early 2020. Deland joined the coaching staff at Notre Dame in 2022, and Damon and his family traveled to Ireland the next year to watch him lead the Fighting Irish running backs against Navy.

After helping Notre Dame to its first National Championship appearance since 2013, Deland left to join the staff of the Las Vegas

Raiders in early 2025. He's now working under head coach Pete Carroll, who was the head man for the Seahawks when Sherman coached in Seattle. Deland II is now a recruiting specialist at Notre Dame. After one season at Indiana and two at Oklahoma, Dasan plays linebacker for Nebraska, and after one season at Oklahoma, Daeh plays defensive back at the University of Louisville. Odds are, little Diem's scholarship offers are on the way too.

On plenty of occasions Deland still finds himself moved by the unlikely story of his life. Not just that he found his father—right in front of him, no less—but that he *became* his father. Despite decades spent not knowing their biological connection, despite a lifetime of other influences, despite all the hardships and struggles, Deland's life has mirrored that of the man he would later call Dad.

They are both struck by the similarities to this day:

Sherman and Deland both grew up in Youngstown and played football at Miami University. Both men played running back in the NFL and saw their careers end due to a knee injury. Both went into teaching and coaching at the high school level, then got their first college coaching job at Miami. Both next coached in the Big Ten and both later coached in the pros. Both coached in the NFL under head coach Pete Carroll. Both won a Super Bowl and both lost a Super Bowl (both losses to Tom Brady!). Both men got married and had children, including a son who followed in Dad's footsteps and played football at Miami University.

Strange. Impossible, even. But true.

Ever since that magical few days of discovery in November 2017, holidays, birthdays, big games, and celebrations are always spent with some combination of parents, children, grandchildren, and extended family. It isn't always perfect and it isn't always easy, but isn't that life? And this is as beautiful a life as any Deland could imagine, with a family as real as any family born entirely of blood.

Connected by chance, family by choice.

ACKNOWLEDGMENTS

To my ma, Adelle, and my brother, Damon. Thank you for your openness throughout this process and your unwavering support. You two are the reasons for all the successes I have had. Your guidance and unconditional love have given me the tools and foundation to succeed. Ma, you did good. Real good. At the end of the day, your sacrifices and choices for me and Damon were rooted in love—and we know that and love you for that!

To my wife, Darnell. I am deeply grateful for your support and understanding on this project. You have been my "ride or die," and I love you for that.

To my sons, Deland II, Dasan, Daeh, and Diem. You are my pride, joy, and inspiration. I hope my journey serves as a road map, not just for reaching life's peaks but for navigating and overcoming its valleys. Watching you grow into better versions of me is my greatest joy.

To my dad, Sherman. Thank you for the steadiness and guidance of a father, even when you didn't know you were mine. To my momma, Carol. You have been a breath of fresh air in my life. Your smile and embrace fill a void in my heart. Thank you for being you.

A special thank-you to Sarah Spain, for treating my family story with such care and respect. Your dedication made this process one of trust and authenticity.

Lastly, to the incredible team that helped bring this story to life. Thank you for your hard work and commitment. I am truly grateful.

With appreciation,

—Deland

——————

Thank you to my husband, family, and friends for their support, their patience, and their advice as I navigated this journey as a first-time author. Thank you to the writers who shared their wisdom and tips, especially Kate Fagan, Jeff Pearlman, Tyler Merritt, and Judy Wilkins-Smith. Thank you to Mary Rigdon and the Center for the Philosophy of Freedom at the University of Arizona for the generosity, the kindness, and the gift of time. Thank you to my friend Skip Tramontana for bringing me this story and changing my life. Thank you to Deland and his wonderful family for embracing me, sharing their lives and stories, and trusting me with this project. What an unbelievable honor and gift.

And finally, thank you to my dogs, Fletch and Banks, who were by my side for every word.

—Sarah